The Roman Catholic Church and Economic Development in Sub-Saharan Africa

Voices Yet Unheard in a Listening World

Jozef D. Zalot

University Press of America,® Inc.
Lanham · New York · Oxford

4720 Boston Way
Lanham, Maryland 20706
UPA Acquisitions Department (301) 459-3366

PO Box 317
Oxford
OX2 9RU, UK

Printed in the United States of America
British Library Cataloging in Publication Information Available

ISBN 0-7618-2447-2 (paperback : alk. ppr.)

For Sue and Maria

Contents

Preface

This study is the result of the integration of two of my lifelong interests, economics and theology. While I do not claim to be a trained economist, through my undergraduate and graduate academic programs in business and management I have gained a working knowledge of how economies function and also of the rationales for introducing new economic policies and programs. As a Ph.D. student in theology at Marquette University, the focus of my studies was economic justice, or the role that Christianity (in particular the Roman Catholic Church) can play in helping to construct an economic order that serves all people. Overall, I believe that in order to be authentic one's faith must never remain a purely private affair but must have practical relevance in the world. As such, in this study I demonstrate the important connection between Christian faith and economic justice by focusing on the situation in sub-Saharan Africa.

In terms of what I hope to accomplished in this study, there are two things. First on the theoretical side, I am looking to resurrect discussion concerning a theology of development. From the early 1960s to the mid 1970s (roughly the pontificates of John XXIII and Paul VI), there was a great interest within the Roman Catholic Church in discussing development from a theological perspective, in constructing a theology of development. Concrete examples of this can be seen in the Second Vatican Council's *Pastoral Constitution on the Church in the Modern World*, Paul VI's *On the Development of Peoples*, and through the work of SODEPAX, a joint Roman Catholic/World Council of Churches commission on society, development, and peace. However, from the late 1970s to today, discussion concerning a theology of development has waned. I hope this study may be a first step in sparking renewed attention to this issue.

On the practical side, sub-Saharan Africa is arguably the poorest region on earth and many of the reasons for its poverty can be attributed to Western corporate and government policy. Unfortunately, most people in the Western world do not recognize this nor do they have a clear picture of the present-day African reality. In this sense, I hope my study will help to illuminate what is actually happening in sub-Saharan Africa and demonstrate the role the African Catholic Church has played in past development programs and the role it will hopefully continue to play in the future.

As will become evident through this study, economic development is a vitally important issue facing the sub-Saharan people. If the Roman Catholic Church is to be a relevant force in the lives of Africans, it must not be concerned only with the numbers of people it baptizes or with preparing souls for the next world. Instead, it must draw upon both the principles of Catholic social teaching and the insights of the African people themselves in order to articulate a theology of development that will help to create a more just and equitable society for all. While I do not claim to have all the answers concerning sub-Saharan development, I hope my study will help to demonstrate what the universal Church can offer to the African people and also what the people of Africa can offer to the world-wide Church.

There are many who I would like to thank in helping me to make this project a reality. First I thank Rev. Michael A. Fahey, SJ, for his friendship and support on this project and on various others during my years at Marquette University. I thank the faculty of the Marquette University Department of Theology and all my colleagues and friends for their help and guidance in all of my theological studies. I also thank the Archdiocese of Milwaukee and the Jesuit Fathers of Marquette University for their assistance in allowing me to attend the World Council of Church's "Theology and Economy" conference in Geneva, Switzerland during the summer of 1998. I thank my parents, Joseph and Barbara Zalot, for both their prayers and financial assistance that allowed me to participate in the Maryknoll Institute for African Studies in Nairobi, Kenya during the summer of 2000. Finally and especially, I thank my wife Sue for her love, encouragement, and patience throughout all of my academic endeavors.

Introduction

One of the fastest growing areas of Roman Catholicism today is sub-Saharan Africa. Over the past twenty years the number of African Catholics has more than doubled, seminaries are at or near capacity, religious orders are steadily gaining new members, and Catholics represent significant percentages of national populations. Thus, even in light of a significant Islamic presence, the Church is becoming increasingly more influential in the region as a whole. However, at the same time sub-Saharan Africa is arguably the poorest region on earth. A significant percentage of its population subsists at or below the level of absolute poverty, most countries owe massive and unpayable debts to foreign financial institutions, and ever-increasing numbers of its people are afflicted by AIDS, famine, ethnic division, and seemingly unending political turmoil. In light of these many problems, one may ask, "What is the Catholic Church doing?" Based on the mandate of its own social teachings, what is the Church doing in sub-Saharan Africa not only to counter the effects of poverty, but also to assist in the integral development of the poor and to help move them toward economic self-sufficiency?

The issue of human development, and in particular economic development, has been an important challenge in Catholic social teaching in the post-Vatican II period. The Council's *Gaudium et Spes*, Pope Paul VI's *Populorum Progressio*, along with John Paul II's *Laborem Exercens*, *Sollicitudo Rei Socialis*, and *Centesimus Annus* each in varying degrees speak of the Church's role in critiquing economic policy and suggesting those principles which must underlie a just, participatory, and human-serving economy. In sub-Saharan Africa, similar theologically based writings on economic development exist as well. Along with African liberationist theologians who speak of the necessity for a greater Church commitment to economic development, various African Catholic bishops' conferences on the national, regional, and continental levels have claimed that Christian evangelization must be linked with "human promotion" and have also spoken out against the economic policies imposed on Africa by the West. Specifically, these liberation theologians and bishops' conferences employ ethical arguments to critique the policies of European colonialism (policies whose effects are still being felt today) as well as the present-day debt reduction and structural adjustment programs of the World Bank and International Monetary Fund. However, in addition to offering these critiques, they also propose foundational principles upon which they believe African economic structures should be based. Particularly for African liberation theologians, these principles are based primarily on biblical teachings and include liberation from oppression, faith in community, and fundamental option for the poor. For the bishops, these principles are based primarily on the social teachings of the universal Church and include common good, universal destination of goods, and participation. Notwithstanding their different starting points and methodologies, the final goal of both the theologians and the bishops is the same: contributing a specifically Catholic perspective to the articulation of an African theology of development.

Before continuing, I should note that the role of the Catholic Church in economic development is only one of a number of important issues facing the Church in sub-Saharan Africa. During the 1994 Synod for Africa (to be discussed in greater detail in Chapter Four), topics for study and discussion by the African bishops were divided into five general categories: evangelization, inculturation, dialogue, justice and peace, and social communication. While each of these categories is of vital concern to the sub-Saharan Church, in this study I focus on only one of these general categories, justice and peace, and more specifically on one aspect within this general category, namely economic development. Nevertheless, while my focus is on economic development, I do not neglect other aspects of justice and peace, nor the other general categories. In the Church's role in African society, there is an interrelationship among the five general categories, an interrelationship that is so deeply intertwined that it would be very difficult to discuss issues within one category without including issues from another. For example, it is difficult to speak of evangelization without speaking of inculturation, or dialogue, or social communication because true evangelization incorporates each of these three. Similarly, the theme of justice and peace is also intimately related to each of the other four general categories because true evangelization cannot occur if the Church does not work for justice and peace within society; true justice must inculturate the traditional cultural, political, and religious practices of the indigenous people; true peace cannot exist in the absence of dialogue with secular leaders as well as with people of other religious traditions; and any work the Church does accomplish in this area will not bear fruit if it is not adequately communicated to the people. Thus, although the specific focus of this study is economic development, I ask that the reader keep in mind development's intimate relationship to both justice and peace and to the broader issues facing the sub-Saharan Catholic Church.

With this understanding, the specific question my study addresses is this: what contribution can the African Catholic Church make toward the articulation of a truly African theology of development, a contribution that takes into consideration both the realities of present-day African life as well as the social teachings of the universal Church? Can the theological contributions of specific Catholic theologians and bishops' conferences concerning economic development be integrated into a single voice that speaks to both Africans and the world as a whole? Or do their theological starting points and methodologies render this mutual collaboration impossible? In his *A Listening Church: Autonomy and Communion in African Churches* (1996),[1] Nigerian theologian Elochukwo Uzukwu, C.S.Sp., argued that, in order for the African Catholic Church to move toward both autonomy and maturity, its clergy must follow the African tradition of having "large ears" so it can truly hear and understand the voices of those they shepherd. According to Uzukwu, having "large ears" is crucial for true leadership because it is only through listening that leaders can comprehend the actual, concrete situations faced by the people they lead. Here I embrace and re-appropriate Uzukwu's metaphor and demonstrate that if they are to succeed in contributing to the articulation of an African theology of development, both the Roman Catholic bishops and theologians in sub-Saharan Africa have two separate but closely related mandates. First, they must faithfully listen to Catholic social teaching, to the voices of the African people, and to each other in order to determine how the Church as a whole can better empower the faithful to assume greater responsibility for their own economic well-being. In doing so, each will come to a better understanding of how the Church has participated in bringing about both dependency and development, and also those actions the Church as a whole must take to rectify economic inequality in the future. Second, both the African Catholic bishops and theologians must forcefully speak out to the international community concerning what is in the best economic interests of the African people. They must speak both to those who for too long have viewed sub-Saharan Africa simply in terms of economic dependency, political oppression, and cultural inferiority, and to those in the West who have waited impatiently for

---

[1] Elochukwu Uzukwu, *A Listening Church: Autonomy and Communion in African Churches* (Maryknoll, NY: Orbis Books, 1996), 141-143.

the emergence of a truly African voice. Because of the Catholic Church's increasingly influential position in the region and because there do not appear to be many other institutions worthy of the task, it is the duty of both the African Catholic bishops and theologians to challenge the world concerning the reality which is present-day sub-Saharan Africa.

The problem as presented, constructing a particularly Catholic contribution to the articulation of an African theology of development, one that takes into consideration the contributions of both the African Catholic hierarchy and theologians, is an issue that has not been previously studied. The great challenge and opportunity of the study is that very little secondary literature exists which specifically addresses this issue. While a limited number of studies (e.g. Berthouzoz et. al., Cheza et. al., McGoldrick, and Munono Muyembe) deal with the various themes of the African bishops' statements, these works are primarily descriptive and do not offer much in the way of critical or methodological analysis. Other studies (e.g. Geffré & Luneau, Ike, and McGarry) concern specific challenges facing the African church and how the Church's universal social teachings might be applied in specific parts of Africa, however no one has written a comprehensive critique of the bishops' contributions to economic development, especially in the period following the 1994 Synod for Africa. Similarly, although a number of the African liberation theologians I focus upon have been mentioned in studies concerning related issues, to my knowledge no one has synthesized their works in terms of how they both challenge present-day Western economic policy and contribute to an African theology of development. Theologians Engelbert Mveng, Jean Marc Éla, and Laurenti Magesa have written extensively on the need to liberate the African people from various forms of oppression and a critical synthesis of their work will help to identify both the commonalties and differences among them and hopefully offer their statements some added weight in their challenge to the world.

Because economic development is such a large topic and because the African sub-continent has so many diverse voices, in this study there are certain parameters to which I must adhere and certain clarifications I must make. In terms of parameters, the time period I focus upon begins with the First General Assembly of the Symposium of Episcopal Conferences of Africa and Madagascar (SECAM) in 1969 and ends with the 1994 Synod for Africa in Rome. The reason I limit myself to this time period is that although there is a long history of

Roman Catholic involvement in sub-Saharan Africa, I am most concerned with those theological statements that speak to the economic challenges facing the African people in the post-independence period. Second, with only a very limited number of exceptions, I deal almost exclusively with the Roman Catholic Church's involvement in sub-Saharan economic development and not with the contributions of other Christian denominations. In stating this I recognize there are many non-Catholic Christian theologians on the sub-continent who have their own methods for dealing with the issue of economic development. However in the interests of time and space their contributions must be left for future study. Third, although it has had a profound effect on certain aspects of African theology, I will not deal with the issue of apartheid in South Africa for the simple reason that once again it is too broad an issue for the subject matter at hand.

In terms of clarifications, the theological sources I employ in this study are primarily African, understood as those who are native to Africa but also including a number of Western theologians and missionaries who have lived, worked, and taught for significant periods of time on the sub-continent. Once more, although there is a myriad of scholarly work concerning the social teachings of the Church by authors of numerous nationalities, religions, and ethnic backgrounds, I restrict myself to "African" contributors in order to discover a distinctly African viewpoint as to the Catholic Church's role in the development of the sub-continent. Second, although this study focuses on the Church's role in sub-Saharan economic development, I do not rely solely on theological statements to advance my arguments. Both in identifying and analyzing the reasons why present-day sub-Saharan Africa faces such grave economic challenges and also in presenting critiques of Western imposed reform programs, I draw upon the work of both African and Western social scientists in the fields of economics and political science. This is not to say that I intend to bring theology and the social sciences into detailed dialogue. Instead, I employ contributions from various economists and political scientists to establish a context within which the theological arguments take shape. Third, I also fully recognize that this study has limitations simply by reason of my own ethnic and national origin. I am a white, middle-class, North American male who, although having studied in Africa, cannot write as an African. Nevertheless, by enlightening North Americans to the economic realities of the present-day sub-continent, I hope to be of service to the African Catholic Church and the people of sub-Saharan Africa.

Finally, I must also clarify that it is not my intention (or claim) within this study to articulate a *comprehensive* theology of economic development for sub-Saharan Africa. A truly comprehensive theology of development would have to take into consideration the various economic practices of traditional African societies (each within its own local context), African cultural values and beliefs, as well as the theological contributions of other non-Catholic traditions especially the indigenous African religions. For obvious reasons the scope of a project this large exceeds both the length and content limits of this study. Instead, the purpose of this study is to demonstrate the particular contribution the African Catholic Church can make toward the articulation of a truly African theology of development, a contribution whose success or failure depends in large measure on how the African Catholic bishops and theologians can communicate, cooperate, and thus provide a unified voice for those they are mandated to serve.

List of Abbreviations

ACEAC	Association of Episcopal Conferences of Central Africa
ACERAC	Association des Conférence Episcopale Régionale de l'Afrique Centrale
AECAWA	Association of Episcopal Conferences of Anglophone Africa
AHCE	Catholic Hierarchy of Egypt
AMECEA	Association of Member Episcopal Conferences in Eastern Africa
CEM	Conférence Episcopale de Madagascar
CERAO	Conférence Episcopale Régionale de l'Afrique de l'Ouest
CERNA	Conférence Episcopale Régionale du Nord d'Afrique
CIDSE	International Cooperation for Development and Solidarity
EATWOT	Ecumenical Association of Third World Theologians
GNP	Gross National Product
IMBISA	Inter Regional Meeting of Bishops of Southern Africa
IMF	International Monetary Fund
NGO	Non-Governmental Organization
OPEC	Organization of Petroleum Exporting Countries
SECAM	Symposium of Episcopal Conferences of Africa and Madagascar
SEDOS	Servizio di Documenatzione et Studi

Chapter One

The Present Day Economic Crisis in Sub-Saharan Africa

In order to discuss the African Catholic bishops' and theologians' contributions to a theology of economic development, one must first gain an understanding of the present-day economic situation on the African sub-continent, how it got that way, and what is being suggested to address the many problems faced by the various nations.[1] According to figures published by the United Nations Development Programme in its 2000 *Human Development Report*, sub-Saharan Africa is without question the poorest region on earth. Based on the Programme's own Human Development Index, of the thirty-five nations in the world classified as "low human development," twenty-six are located in Sub-Saharan Africa. Of the forty-three countries on the Programme's list of "least developed nations," twenty-nine are in sub-Saharan Africa, and of the fifty-nine world nations classified as "low income" (defined as per capita income below US$760), thirty-four are located on the sub-continent. Average Gross Domestic Product per capita of US$1,607 is the lowest of any region on earth and from 1990 to 1998 the annual growth rate in the region's per capita Gross National Product actually declined by four-tenths of one percent per year. In addition, from 1995-2000 average life expectancy in sub-Saharan nations was the lowest in the world at 48.9 years while the infant mortality rate of 10.6 percent and the under-five mortality rate of 17.2 percent were the highest of any region on earth.[2]

Reasons for poverty and a lack of economic development on the sub-continent are many. General structural problems of African economies include that they are externally dependent as a result of European colonialism, they are primarily rural, and they also lack the capital and technical know-how to increase productivity and produce a variety of export goods.[3] Further reasons include the imposition of state-controlled price structures that do not provide adequate incentives for agriculture and exports, unfavorable exchange rate and trade policies, a bloated bureaucracy that wastes both time and resources, government officials who direct scarce resources and materials to extravagant but unnecessary projects, unfavorable economic and political relationships with the outside world (especially the West), unfavorable weather, and political unrest.[4]

In the mid-1990s the World Bank commissioned a task force to study the situation in Africa and determined that the causes for the continent's poverty lie in a series of varied but interrelated causes and effects. While citing many of the reasons mentioned above, the task force also claimed that as a result of "geographic isolation" the poor have inadequate access to employment opportunities which in turn causes low savings rates, a lack of domestic investment, and an economy which does not grow enough to provide an adequate number of jobs. In addition, the African poor have limited access to credit, to assistance programs, and to formal markets where they can sell their goods and services. Furthermore, the task force also found there is a "low endowment" of human capital as a result of a lack of access to education, health, sanitation, and water supplies; inadequate participation of the poor in designing development programs; and a general failure to take into consideration the actual needs of the poor in donor/recipient discussions.[5] Further exacerbating the problem is the fact that the continent is made up of thousands of ethnic groups, a multiplicity of languages and dialects, and fifty-five different countries with diverse social, economic, and political realities.[6] Finally, Africa has one of the highest infection rates for HIV/AIDS of any region on earth, a reality that poses profound social, political, and economic challenges for its national governments. Thus, for both the present and the foreseeable future, many African nations face continued economic crisis with no real end in sight.

Simply through presenting these statistics and identifying the various and interrelated problems they face, one recognizes very quickly both the scope and complexity of the issues that confront the present-day sub-Saharan economies. However, the question must be asked how the situation got to where it is today? Why is the African sub-continent the poorest region on earth and can the present-day situation be blamed on the African people themselves or is it the fault of institutions exterior to the continent itself? In this first chapter, I aim to shed some light on these questions by first offering an overview of sub-Saharan economic history starting from the colonial period, moving through the period of independence, and ending with the present-day. It should be noted that the material in this overview is drawn primarily from the works of various economists, historians, and political scientists. The reason for this is that I wish to present, as thoroughly as possible, an accurate understanding of the economic problems facing the sub-Saharan nations through the eyesof those who study them most closely. Following this overview, I draw upon theological sources to introduce the concept "theology of development," an introduction that includes a theological justification for participation in development-related activities, the identification of the various limitations within any development theology, and also a working definition of what development actually entails. It is only from this foundation drawn from both social science and theological sources that one can truly appreciate both the magnitude and importance of the task that lies ahead.

The Colonial Legacy

To understand the reasons for the present-day economic difficulties in sub-Saharan Africa, one must begin with the period of European colonization from the late 1800s to the mid-1960s.[7] In short, in the economic realm the intention of the European colonizers was not to help the native populations develop into self-sufficient, thriving communities. Instead the European colonizers exploited the African people and their land to extract resources for their own personal wealth and the wealth of their mother nations. While many books have been written on the subject and hundreds of examples could be given, I will highlight just a few tangible effects of specific colonial policies in sub-Saharan Africa and demonstrate how these effects continue to mitigate against economic development in the region today.

First, colonization was a labor intensive enterprise in that it required a great deal of physical labor to extract natural resources from the land, transport them to the nearest port, and load them on ships for the mother country. Because so much manual labor was required for the system to operate efficiently, the colonial powers realized very early that they needed to secure a reliable work force and that the native

African populations provided them with exactly what they needed. In general, the colonial powers employed two methods to secure an adequate number of manual workers. First, they would seize the most valuable tracts of land for themselves and force those inhabiting them to either relocate to inferior land or turn to manual labor in order to provide the necessary material goods for their families. By forcing people off their ancestral lands, the Europeans created conditions where the native Africans had no choice but to work in manual labor jobs and in fact become dependent upon these jobs for their very survival. Thus, the seizure of their land deprived many Africans of their means to self-sufficiency and their ability to control their own destinies.[8] One recognizes the effect of this today in the fact that, to varying degrees, every nation in the sub-continent is dependent upon Western economic systems and Western aid in order to maintain any semblance of economic viability. While in the pre-colonial days the native populations were able to support themselves through traditional familial and clan structures, today the economic survival of sub-Saharan nations is so intertwined with global economy that the very survival of the people is dependent upon the decisions of the Western economic powers. As will be demonstrated further on in this chapter, the problem with this relationship is that many of the economic policies imposed on sub-Saharan nations by the West are policies that do not take into consideration the interests of these nations and thus act as a detriment to their economic development.

In addition to helping create a climate of economic dependence, the colonial seizure of land has caused political nightmares for the post-independence African states. By forcibly moving the native populations off their ancestral lands, the colonial powers caused a mass displacement of people, a sharp increase in the number of squatters, and an increase in ethnic tensions among varying groups vying to inhabit whatever land was still available. So long as the colonial powers maintained political and military control the consequences of these situations could be held in check. However, in the years following the independence of many sub-Saharan nations (from the late 1950s to the mid 1960s), this would not be the case. In Kenya, for example, the question of what to do with the "public" lands that had been held by the British crown underlay the foundation of its two original political parties. KANU (Kenya African National Union) favored maintaining private property and the forced seizure of land in order to form a more unified country while its opposition KADU (Kenya African Democratic Union) favored the creation of regional assemblies whose function would be to distribute the newly acquired land on a more equitable basis. In the end, KANU emerged victorious and adopted a constitution that upheld the right of private property regardless of how that property was gained. As a result, large tracts of land were maintained in the hands of a relatively small group of people while the masses were left to migrate to the cities, live nomadic existences, or fight with other ethnic groups for whatever land they could find. Thus, instead of redistributing the land in ways that would benefit the nation as a whole, post-independence government policies further underscored class inequality and also instilled a greater sense of social and economic domination in those who possessed land over those who did not. Today in Kenya, and no doubt in other nations as well, the land issue is one which retains vital importance both economically and politically. Private ownership of large tracts of land by a small number of individuals has helped to maintain a permanent underclass in Kenyan society and has also forced the land-less to resort to either squatting on land that is "owned" by others or continuing to move to the cities in order to survive.[9]

A second means the colonial powers used to maintain a viable number of manual laborers was a dual program of low wages and heavy taxation. Those who were forced off their land had no choice but to work within the manual labor system. However, because wages were so low and the price of material goods so high, African workers had little hope of saving enough money to escape the necessity of working for the colonial powers. Those Africans who were able to maintain their homes, livestock, or land were then so heavily taxed that they also had to participate in the labor system simply in order to earn the money to pay their taxes.[10] In addition to further relegating the native populations to a state of dependency, the colonial policies of low wages and high taxation also caused the erosion of the "social security" systems which had been built into the traditional African organization of family and community. These colonial policies destroyed both the traditional "modes of subsistence" and "insurance mechanisms" in

African society because as the family, clan, or community became too impoverished to be of any real assistance, one could no longer rely on the traditional family structure in times of crisis. In short, the effect of these low pay, high taxation policies was to destroy both the structures and value systems upon which the people's social security needs were based without offering any viable options in return, a reality that can still be readily seen in post-independence Africa today. Because the colonial powers reserved the social services primarily for the white settlers and because they maintained an attitude of indifference toward the developmental and social needs of the native populations, when they left the sub-continent in the 1950s and 1960s they did not leave behind any viable social systems to provide for the needs of the people. As a result, the new African governments were not prepared to address these needs and to this day they have to rely on foreign donors to maintain any semblance of welfare or social service programs.[11]

A third effect of colonization concerns the drawing of arbitrary and artificial boundaries to differentiate between the European nations' "rightful" colonial territories. In 1884-1885, the European colonizing nations including France, England, Belgium, Spain, Portugal, the Netherlands, and Germany met in Berlin to discuss disputes concerning territorial limits and ultimately forged an agreement as to where the colonial boundaries would be located. Unfortunately, in drawing up these boundaries the Europeans did not take into consideration natural frontiers such as rivers or mountain ranges, but instead drew them around their own economic and political interests, oftentimes with devastating effects to the native populations. The creation of these artificial borders forcibly separated families and ethnic clans because if people from the same family or clan were on opposite sides of a border when it was closed they were not allowed to be reunited. Perhaps even worse, the creation of these borders also forcibly joined rival families and ethnic clans because if these groups happened to be on the same side of a border when it was closed by the Europeans they were "caught" and forced to live together. As a result, while people of similar languages, cultures, and political/economic systems were oftentimes forcibly separated, those with different languages, cultures, and political/economic systems were forced to live together in the same colony. Thus, the sub-continent was partitioned by European officials who had never actually seen Africa, who never took into consideration the traditional familial, ethnic, and cultural ties that bound the people together, and whose only concerns were the maximization of profits and the avoidance of war.[12]

As with seizing land and imposing systems of low wages and high taxation, the effects of drawing artificial boundaries also can be seen in sub-Saharan Africa today. Although it was the Europeans who partitioned the sub-continent into arbitrary geographic regions, in the early post-independence period the newly formed African nations really had no choice but to inherit the borders established by their former colonial masters. Yet because the colonial powers did not take into consideration the ethnic, cultural, or political sensibilities of the native people in forming their colonies nor offer them any viable models of self-government, many of the independent states that came into existence in the 1950s and 1960s could not be seen as functional states in the true sense of the word. These newly-formed states lacked the ethnic and cultural ties that would have greatly aided their development, and also lacked the ability to collect taxes, build roads, provide health care and education, and enforce laws to protect their citizens. In short, most of these African states continue to exist today simply because the international community says they should, even though the colonial powers that created them never envisioned (or intended) that they would become independent nations.[13]

One final way the colonial enterprise had a direct negative impact on present-day sub-Saharan Africa was in the creation of "mono-culture" or single crop economies. A mono-culture economy is one where a colony focuses on producing a single product or "cash crop" for export to the mother country, and thus its economy is dependent upon the fortunes of this single product. While these mono-culture or cash-crop economies were established during the colonial period to produce goods that could not be produced in Europe, they remained in place in the years following independence and in many nations remain even to this day. According to prevailing economic theory, the rationale for present-day cash crop economies is that by focusing on a particular product or cash crop the African nation can specialize, gain a competitive advantage in the international markets, and thus earn a greater profit. As a result, many African nations today are still pressured to focus on a single product as the primary means of moving them toward prosperity and self-sufficiency.[14]

However, maintaining a mono-culture economy is problematic for a number of reasons. First, there is an inherent vulnerability in focusing on a single crop because if there is a drought, disease, or other natural disaster and the crop is ruined, there is no income generated for that season. This is a particularly difficult problem on the African sub-continent today because nations that suffer from natural disasters have no "mother country" they can immediately turn to (as was the case during the colonial period) and as a result they become almost completely dependent upon foreign humanitarian assistance for the very survival of their people. Second, by focusing so heavily on producing specific products or cash crops (products demanded by the West), many African economies fail to produce the variety of goods their own people need to survive. The result of this non-production of necessary goods is that the African people are forced to purchase products such as oil, machinery, and medicine on the international markets, a situation that renders self-sufficiency next to impossible and also creates further dependence upon the West. Third, although Africans produce the various cash crops and other products for export, the prices paid for these goods are determined by the buyers in the international markets. In other words, because of the structures of the international markets, African producers have no power to set prices for their goods but are almost always at the mercy of what the market will bear. So long as the prices for exports remain relatively high and the prices for imports remain relatively low, these mono-culture economies can remain economically viable. However, when the prices for exports fall and the prices for imports rise, a situation occurring with ever-increasing frequency, the consequences for a mono-culture economy can be devastating.[15]

Historian Walter Rodney offers an excellent assessment of the colonial legacy by claiming that although the colonial enterprise in sub-Saharan African lasted just over seventy years, the "decisiveness" of the period resulted from the simple fact that Africa "lost its power" to the European colonizers. For Rodney, power is the "ultimate determinant" in society because it is basic to the fundamental relationships both within and amongst groups, it implies the ability to defend one's own interests and impose one's will, it determines the extent to which one group respects the interests of another, and it also ultimately determines the extent to which a people survive as both a physical and cultural entity. When any society is forced to relinquish power to another, this is in itself a form of underdevelopment.[16] Rodney's words are squarely on mark because by seizing land, paying low wages, imposing unpayable taxes, determining artificial boundaries, and creating mono-culture economies, the colonial powers usurped power from the African peoples and left them in a state of economic dependence that continues to the present day. In fact, because of its twin legacies of economic dependency and underdevelopment, it is claimed that European colonialism precipitated the creation of the so-called Third World in sub-Saharan Africa.[17]

Before concluding this brief overview of the present-day effects of European colonialism, I must also note the effect the slave trade had on the development of indigenous African economies. In addition to being unjust, inhumane, and immoral, the slave trade had a negative effect on sub-Saharan economic development primarily because it caused a mass reduction in the native populations. While no one knows for sure exactly how many people were taken from the continent, it is known that in order to develop economically, a nation, region, or even village must make maximum use of both its labor and natural resources. The slave trade prevented this from happening because not only did it deprive the local African communities of their strongest and healthiest members, but because population growth is essential for economic development in that it generates a larger labor pool, bigger markets, and the necessary "social pressure" which leads to further advancement, the slave trade also deprived local African economies of their primary means to both grow and prosper.[18] I should note, however, that there is an opposing point of view that claims the slave trade, notwithstanding its injustice and immorality, actually benefited some African economies because when the European traders arrived in the African ports their presence acted as a stimulus to local economic activity. As examples, the European slave traders created a demand for locally produced products such as food and salt, imported iron and other materials to be finished by local artisans, and supplied currency which functioned to expand exchange. Because of these activities, the slave trade actually increased both production and consumption in local African economies, two elements that are necessary for economic development to occur.[19] Although it is beyond the scope of this study to ascertain what particular effects the slave trade had on indigenous African economic development, suffice it to say that it did have an effect but to what degree we will probably never know.

Post-Independence Sub-Saharan Africa

When examining the post-independence economic history of sub-Saharan Africa, three dominant development strategies emerge. First, in the 1950s and 1960s, modernization theory held that the difficulties faced by sub-Saharan nations were due in large measure to the fact that their economies were not modern. Peter Lewis, an assistant professor of political science at the American University School of International Service, argues that this theory is based on what he terms the "dichotomy" it maintains between the traditional and modern structures of society. In this theory's view, traditional society is based on agricultural production, has little or no change in either its economic or social structures, and has hierarchical forms of government. Modern society, on the other hand, is industrialized, has social and economic structures based on specialization and interdependence, maintains high levels of technical development, and governs democratically through the promotion of both human rights and popular participation in politics. The theory claimed that economic development would not be possible until a nation advanced from the traditional to the modern understanding of society.[20]

Unfortunately, modernization theory was never able to fulfill its promise of true economic development. From the late 1960s through the 1970s, modernization theory was challenged by dependency theory, one that proposed the reason for the lack of development in Africa (and in the Third World in general) was the ongoing, unequal struggle between the nations of the North and those of the South. Dependency theory maintained that nations of the North gained wealth through exploiting the markets, labor, and resources of the South, and thus underdevelopment could be attributed to the structures of the international markets. In addition, many in the South even distrusted the word "development" claiming it was a Western term that implied individualism and competitiveness, values alien to their own cultures.[21] In response, dependency theory maintained that in order for nations of the South to develop, they had to radically change their relationships with the other nations in the international economic system. Internally they had to minimize the exploitation of the North while externally they had to work to correct the structures of the system as a whole.[22]

However, as with modernization theory, dependency theory was not sufficient to effect lasting change. By the 1980s, dependency theory was being challenged in part on the premise that the problems faced by sub-Saharan economies were not going to be solved by simply focusing on external market structures. Instead, many researchers began to believe that African nations themselves needed to assume greater responsibility for moving toward real, sustained development. Thus, a new theory emerged which claimed that African governments and public institutions had a central role to play in managing their nations' domestic and foreign affairs. This state-centric theory held that a strong central authority was necessary to provide vital societal "goods" such as national security, enforcement of law, construction of infrastructure, and the creation of new market institutions. In addition, it was argued that a centralized state could better secure social relations, establish property rights, and mediate differences between social groups. Although recognizing the challenges posed by both modernization and dependency theory, state centric theory held that a strong centralized government would be best equipped to deal with the challenges facing many African nations, and it led to a concentration of power into the hands of the state.[23]

However, as with the previous two, state-centric development theory failed to bring about sustained economic growth and in the minds of many its effect is one of the root causes for sub-Saharan Africa's present-day economic crisis. By the early to mid-1980s, many economists and political scientists were realizing that political power had been given to the wrong people, that those most responsible for the poverty and lack of development in sub-Saharan Africa were the corrupt leaders and élites. In fact, in its 1989 *From Crisis to Sustainable Growth*, the World Bank concluded that Africa's economic woes could be directly attributable to a lack of accountability, transparency, predictability, openness, and rule of law within many of its nations' political systems. The World Bank judged that economic growth was directly proportional to good governance, which in the Bank's view entailed less government interference in the economy. As a result, it began imposing structural adjustment programs that sought to limit the role of government in African economic affairs.[24] While structural adjustment will be more fully explained later in this chapter, it is with the principles and limitations of modernization, dependency, and state-centric development theory in mind that I now turn to the concrete factors that underlie the continued lack of economic development in sub-Saharan Africa today.

1. Internal Factors

Probably the single most important internal factor preventing development in the post-independence period concerns government. According to Leonardo A. Villalón, an associate professor of political science at the University of Kansas, the post-colonial African state can be defined by the following five characteristics. First, it is a client state in that from the 1960s to 1990 the "major sustaining force" for many African nations was a major Cold War superpower. However, when the Cold War ended so also did this "client" support and as a result over the last decade these nations' political, economic, and social systems have rapidly deteriorated. Second, the African state is personalized in that it is administered by a paternalistic form of government influenced primarily by a single political figure. Third, because the personalized state must maintain a large number of people within its "apparatus" to support its policies, the African state can be characterized as both overdeveloped in that there are too many people employed in the public sector, and centralized in that the power to allocate resources is concentrated within a small number of government institutions. Fourth, most African nations can be characterized as prebendal or rentier states in that the political leaders allocate public resources to a select group of individuals who actively support the state and who thus enjoy "preferential access" to it. Finally, the African state may be characterized as extractive in that it serves as the primary instrument of obtaining resources for the exclusive benefit of those who control it. Villalón's overall point is that although the extent to which these five characteristics are practiced varies from nation to nation, in reality virtually every African state exhibits some combination of them and thus poor governance is endemic across the continent as a whole.[25]

One of the reasons for poor governance in present-day sub-Saharan Africa can be traced once again to the colonial legacy. Because colonial governments did not model any form of democracy or offer any viable examples of self rule, when they departed in the 1950s and 1960s the newly-forming African nations adopted the only form of government they had ever known: one that was based on authoritarianism and complete control in the hands of the ruling élite.[26] In addition, in many cases independence came to African nations as a result of the colonial powers negotiating with a small group of nationalist leaders who had been hand-picked and educated by the colonial powers themselves. Because they had already been "trained" in how to lead their new nations, these hand-picked officials did not encourage popular participation in decision-making processes but maintained all power for themselves.[27]

In perhaps the most scathing critique of the African political situation, George B. N. Ayittey, an associate professor of economics at American University,[28] claims the main factor which keeps Africa mired in poverty today is the inability of its people to either rid themselves of "predatory" governments or to force those already in power to adopt policies that benefit their nation as a whole. According to Ayittey, any serious examination of the continent's numerous and seemingly unending political crises reveals that they all share a common root cause. Each crisis begins when a so-called educated person from either civilian life or the military assumes political power through an election or coup d'etat. Upon entering office, he solidifies his power by "surreptitiously debauching" the major government institutions including the military, civil service, judiciary, and banking system. With power solidified in his hands, he transforms the state into his own personal property by plundering the treasury for his own benefit and the benefit of his political allies and ethnic tribe. The masses who do not belong to this privileged group are then left to suffer the consequences of these actions, resulting in what Ayittey terms the "politics of exclusion."[29]

Ayittey continues by claiming that these government officials have no sense of morality, justice, or even patriotism and in fact they are only faithful to their foreign bank accounts. They would resort to violence and even destroy their own countries to protect their fortunes because, as "functional illiterates," they are incapable of employing the knowledge and skills they were taught in school to gain wealth on their own in the private sector. Helping the poor to become self-sufficient, improving the people's standard of living, and promoting economic growth are not the priorities of these ruling élites. Instead, they "hijack" the state, monopolize political and economic power to advance their own personal interests, and in effect transform their nations into "vampire states." According to Ayittey, the "simple rule of thumb" for African development is that the economic prosperity of any nation is inversely proportional to the length of time a military official has held political power, "the longer [the official] stays in power, the greater the economic devastation."[30]

In terms of economic development, the devastation to which Ayittey refers can be best seen through the various methods employed by African political leaders to remain in power. One of the primary methods is through a system commonly referred to as clientelism. In a clientelist system which a national leader protects the interests of a select group within society and in return the select group provides the leader with unqualified political, economic, and military support. The basis of this relationship lies in the fact that the leader is in absolute control of the nation and is under no political obligation to distribute public goods and services to the population in an equitable manner. He can offer jobs, favorable terms of trade, and even military protection to whomever he chooses and in fact does so for those who are his most ardent supporters. As already noted, the result of this relationship is the creation of a very small but privileged class of people who control virtually every aspect of public life, a class that also reaps personal benefit at the expense of the masses.[31]

In addition to being illegal, immoral, and simply unfair, clientelistic relationships also cause greater government intervention in the operations of African economies, interventions that have profoundly negative effects on efforts to move toward sustained economic development. According to Jeffrey Herbst, an associate professor of politics at Princeton University, because of the weak tax bases in many African nations, political leaders cannot simply funnel money to their supporters in the form of cash payments or "pork" spending projects. Instead, through direct intervention, they rig markets to benefit those whom they choose. One of the ways this is done is through state-owned corporations or "parastatals" that arose in Africa shortly after the period of independence. Parastatals function as excellent sources of patronage because they employ large numbers of political and ethnic supporters, facilitate the diversion of public resources to favored geographical regions, and, because they are classified as "private" enterprises (hence the term "parastatal"), they can operate without the degree of external scrutiny that a publicly-owned corporation might face. However, while acting as a source for government patronage and intervention in the economy, these parastatals have been chronically poor performers and in most cases have actually cost more money than they have earned. Citing the 1981 World Bank report "Accelerated Development in Sub-Saharan Economies," Herbst claims these parastatals are constantly pressured to provide preferred groups with key goods and services at low prices, increase employment even when they are notmaking money, and shape investment decisions with "other than economic and financial returns in mind."[32]

A second area where Herbst claims government intervention has negatively effected sub-Saharan economic development concerns imports. Using a system of tariffs and quotas, African governments are able to selectively reward import licenses and thus protect specific industries or favored clients. The problem with this practice is that controlling imports in this way almost always leads to overvalued exchange rates because by relying on tariffs and quotas the governments do not adjust exchange rates to counter inflation. On one hand, overvalued exchange rates can favor importers because with overvalued rates it is less expensive to import goods and thus the importers earn greater profits. However, on the other hand, overvalued exchange rates also make exports more expensive and thus make it more difficult for exporters to remain competitive in world markets. This is especially a problem for nations with cash-crop economies because in order for their economies to remain viable the goods they produce must be sold on foreign markets. If exchange rates are overvalued, the goods these nations produce either are not sold or their prices are reduced. Either way, the nation as a whole earns less in foreign income.[33]

A third example of negative government intervention can be seen in the agricultural sector. In order to keep retail prices low for their urban political supporters, Herbst claims that some African governments will purchase crops from rural farmers at lower than market value and then pass this "savings" on to their supporters. The obvious problem with this practice is that peasant farmers lose valuable income and as a result are not able to invest in better equipment or technology to increase future production. These peasant farmers are all but powerless in getting prices raised because their governments control the marketing and distribution systems for their products and also have the ability to crush any potential protests either through paying bribes or by military force. As a result of earning less for their crops in one season, the rural farmers are not able to produce as much in the next and thus further exacerbate the food shortages common in sub-Saharan Africa.[34]

One further social effect of clientelism is that it has also led to an increase in ethnic tensions or "tribalism." As previously mentioned, African political leaders tend to favor their own ethnic groups by preferentially allocating state resources to them, a means by which they both build and maintain loyal constituencies. In the economic sense, tribalism can be understood as different ethnic groups competing with each other to ensure their "fair share" of state-controlled goods and services.[35] An excellent example of this can be seen in post-independence Kenya. When Jomo Kenyatta came to power in 1963, he came under great pressure from his own Kikuyu people to allocate them a greater portion of the "goods" that had come under the control of the newly-independent Kenyan government. The Kikuyus reasoned that since they had borne the brunt of the struggle for independence they had a greater claim to the nation's wealth. Eventually Kenyatta bowed to this pressure and the Kikuyus were given the most important political positions, allocated the best public lands, appointed to both civil service and parastatal positions "in a disproportionate majority," and were able to secure government loans more easily than could those from other ethnic communities. Naturally these clientelistic policies alienated the other ethnic groups in Kenya but when these groups raised objections to the government's policies their people began to suffer violence, oppression, and even the assassination of their leaders.[36] While many more examples of this practice could be offered, suffice it to say that clientelistic relationships further undermine economic development because they foster ethnic tensions and result in greater political instability, factors that are obviously detrimental to true economic development.

Closely related to the negative effects caused by clientelism are the impacts on economic development that occur as a result of government corruption.[37] There is no dispute that in most sub-Saharan nations today corruption is rampant at almost every level of government. In the former Zaïre (now the Democratic Republic of Congo), it is estimated that the late President Mobuto Sese Seko and his supporters were able to divert upwards of eight *billion* dollars (US) into foreign bank accounts, private business ventures, and personal real estate holdings. In Zimbabwe, at least five percent of the nation's total economic output (approximately US$300 million) is lost each year to corruption, and in Nigeria, which has been named the most corrupt nation on earth, government corruption drains between two and three billion dollars (US) per year from the national economy.[38] When speaking of corruption in relation to foreign aid the numbers are even more alarming. In Kenya for example, from 1990-1995 an average of 25.5 billion Kenyan shillings (US$344 million) or one-sixth of the entire national budget was lost every year due to corruption. In other words, 12.5 billion shillings was lost during every six month period from 1990-1995, roughly the same amount of money the nation is seeking to receive through the World Bank and International Monetary Fund.[39]

There are many reasons for the rampant corruption in sub-Saharan Africa. First, because in many African nations the ruling élites exercise absolute control over state resources, no distinction is made between their public and private interests. As a result, these leaders openly loot the public treasuries with no fear that they will ever be held accountable for their actions. Second, because governments have assumed control of virtually every aspect of economic life, a new level of bureaucracy has evolved in many African states, one whose "discretionary power" has been used as a "conduit for graft" by unscrupulous government officials. As one needs permission from the government to obtain a driver's license, have telephone service, start a business, or even sell crops, and also because there is no mechanism to stop it, bribery is simply viewed as a normal part of doing business. Third, because many low-level government officials receive little pay and are the ones hardest hit in times of economic restructuring, they must pursue corrupt practices in order to maintain a reasonable standard of living for themselves and their families. In this sense, corruption becomes a necessity because even those who do not wish to engage in it face the choice of either lowering their ethical standards and surviving, or maintaining these standards and dying.[40]

Along with the many causes for corruption in sub-Saharan nations, there are also many consequences. In the economic realm, corruption costs money because bribes and kickbacks ultimately have to be absorbed into the prices paid for both government programs and consumer goods. In fact, it is claimed that in some cases African leaders approve projects not on the basis of their cost efficiency or because they are in the best interests of the nation as a whole, but simply because a specific project presents a greater opportunity to generate a bribe or kickback. In addition, corruption results in increased capital flight, the practice of diverting state funds into foreign bank accounts for the private use of an individual person. For developing nations, capital flight is a very serious problem because it destabilizes both interest and exchange rates, contributes to the erosion of the domestic tax base, reduces domestic investment, and necessitates greater foreign borrowing. Furthermore, corruption also reduces the amount of money available for development-related activities, drives away potential foreign investment, and breeds both economic inefficiency and waste because the size of the bribe being offered is more important than the quality of the work being done.[41]

One final internal factor contributing to the lack of economic development in many sub-Saharan nations concerns governmental economic policies that have both created and aggravated balance-of-trade deficits.[42] In the late 1960s, inflation began to increase in many African economies. However, instead of lowering their exchange rates (even when major European governments were depreciating their currencies) or enacting other measures to counteract the effects of rising inflation, many African governments did nothing. The result of this inaction was that while the prices of foreign imports remained relatively inexpensive, the prices of African exports became very expensive on the international markets. In turn, many African nations stopped producing those products which were cheaper to buy on the international markets and thus began to import increasing amounts of foreign goods. However, because African exports were becoming ever more expensive on the world markets, many foreign nations stopped buying African goods causing a marked drop in the African export revenues. Coupled with the rapid increase in imports, this dramatic decrease in exports caused an alarming balance-of-payments deficit for many sub-Saharan economies, a situation that necessitated increased foreign borrowing and thus foreign debt.[43]

Further aggravating the balance-of-trade deficit was the African mentality that "foreign is better." During the colonial period, the Europeans imported so much of their food, clothing, and other material necessities from their mother countries that Africans came to believe these imported goods were of higher quality than similar goods produced on the African continent. Even after independence this mentality remained. Many of the élites in the post-independence period claimed they needed to have the best food, clothing, cars, homes, etc., and since they believed the highest quality products came from foreign countries they began importing heavily from their former colonial masters. When the masses saw the élites consuming these foreign products they desired to do the same and as a result many African nations not only fell further into debt, but also became even more dependent on products that they themselves could not produce.[44]

2. External Factors

In addition to the internal factors that work against efforts at economic development, most sub-Saharan economies face challenges from external factors as well. One of the major external obstacles facing sub-Saharan nations is that although they participate in foreign trade, both the composition of their own economies and the structures of the international markets actually work against them. As previously discussed, because many nations retain cash-crop or mono-culture economies their economic fortunes are tied to the prices they receive for their goods on the international markets. This is problematic because by being focused on a single product these nations are vulnerable to fluctuations in the world commodity markets, fluctuations that can result from natural disasters such as flood and drought or from human actions including speculation and the varying of production levels to meet specific needs. In addition, because the prices for African goods are set by either multinational corporations (to the benefit their own interests) or by the mechanisms of the international markets, African producers are left to the mercy of what the markets will bear. This situation is problematic because since they cannot set the prices for their own goods, African producers become ever-more dependent upon the preferences of buyers in the international markets. Further compounding these trade problems is the fact that Western corporations purchase African raw materials at a price which they (the corporations) set, bring the materials to their own manufacturing plants to produce finished goods, and then sell these finished goods back to African consumers at a much higher price.[45] As a result of each of these realities, in recent years the sub-Saharan nations as a whole have been losing in the game of international trade and have become increasingly poorer because of it.

Other external factors working against sub-Saharan economic development include the declining level of foreign investment and the unintended effects of foreign aid. Due in large measure to the "donor fatigue" felt by so many foreign investors, in the 1980s net foreign investment in Africa fell by over fifty percent from (US)$1.22 billion to $498 million. In addition, between 1989 and 1994 over half the British manufacturing companies with subsidiaries in Africa divested, and in 1994 alone the United States Agency for International Development closed eight of its thirty-five offices in Africa. If these figures were not damaging enough, in 1995 the World Bank reported that approximately $231 billion in foreign investment flowed into the so-called Third World, yet as a whole Africa's share of these funds amounted to less than one percent.[46] Obviously a decline in foreign investment is detrimental to sub-Saharan economic development because with less money coming into the continent there is less money available for building infrastructure, creating jobs, and providing necessary social services.

In addition to the effects caused by decreases in direct foreign investment, there are also negative effects on African economies as a result of foreign aid. Although since the 1960s the amount of foreign aid to sub-Saharan Africa has remained relatively steady,[47] this aid has failed to bring meaningful development for a number of reasons. First, as previously discussed, the potential benefits of aid packages are oftentimes eclipsed by the clientelism, corruption, and faulty policies of African political leaders. Second, aid is often given by foreign nations or private donors (especially non-governmental organizations or NGOs) for projects that are not relevant for the receiving nation. In other words, as a precondition for offering aid, donor organizations will dictate to the recipient country exactly how the money is to be used and because most African nations are so desperate for aid they willingly agree. However, by ceding to the donor organizations the responsibility for identifying, designing, and implementing aid-based programs, the receiving nation loses its sense of ownership and thus many aid-based programs are doomed to failure before they even begin. Third, in many cases there are also ulterior motives behind the donation of aid. Because donor agencies have their own agendas and have to answer to their own constituencies, they frequently place "conditionalities" upon the offering of aid packages. For example, donors will tie aid packages to a variety of non-economic objectives including the containment of communism, the spread of democracy, and the promotion of human rights. If an African nation cannot meet one or more of these conditionalities it runs the risk of losing the aid. Lastly, aid programs are oftentimes ineffective because the packages received from various sources are not coordinated into a single development strategy. The sheer number of governmental and NGO stand-alone projects demonstrates this problem. Non-coordination of aid leads directly to inconsistencies in policy, to the overlapping or duplication of projects, and in the end to outright waste.[48]

Although foreign trade, investment and aid are important factors in and of themselves, perhaps the two most important external factors that militate against sub-Saharan economic development are the forced repayment of foreign debt and the imposition of structural adjustment. I emphasize these two factors because not only do they generate the most controversy and pose poignant ethical questions for society as a whole, but they are also issues that will arise numerous times throughout the remainder of this study.

3. Foreign Debt

To understand the scope and magnitude of the African debt crisis, one must go back to the 1960s and the attempts of the newly independent governments to modernize their economies. In effect, these governments were practicing modernization theory which, as previously stated, maintained that if African nations could modernize they would develop faster and more quickly begin to participate in the world economy. However, in the absence of any real private sector that could provide the capital necessary to facilitate this transformation, the impetus for modernization fell on government. As a result, African political leaders increasingly assumed greater responsibility for planning and directing economic activity (state-centric theory). Unfortunately, as has also been demonstrated, African governments as a whole were not effective guardians of economic development. Because government leaders redirected agricultural earnings away from private farmers and into state-owned industries (parastatals), introduced protective trade measures and price controls, maintained artificially high exchange rates, and limited both foreign credit and foreign exchange to "priority" clients, many African nations began to experience a balance-of-trade deficits. To address this situation, the various governments had the choice of either adopting stringent financial strategies to narrow these deficits or borrowing money on the international financial markets to finance their continued deficit spending. Many chose the latter and as a result between 1972 and 1977 Africa's total external debt tripled from US$9 billion to $27 billion.[49]

A second source of foreign debt concerns the "development loans" made to many African nations during the 1970s, the so-called "second development decade." Following the OPEC (Organization of Petroleum Exporting Countries) oil price increases in 1973, oil-producing Arab nations had deposited millions of dollars into Western commercial bank accounts. Looking for ways to invest these petrodollars, the banks offered loans to nations around the world ostensibly to be used for development-related projects. These loans were originally issued with low but variable rates of interest that would increase or decrease according to the prevailing rates in the international financial markets. For the first few years after the loans were made interest rates remained relatively stable so although debt principal continued to increase, most nations were able to keep up with their interest payments. However, by the late 1970s and early 1980s this situation would change dramatically. In 1979, OPEC once again increased the price of oil while at the same time the United States adopted monetary policies to reduce its domestic inflation, policies that ultimately led to a world-wide recession. As a result of this recession, the prices for African raw materials and other cash crops decreased dramatically on the world markets leading to decreased revenues for African producers. This reduction in revenue coupled with an increase in the price of oil forced African governments to borrow even more money on the international financial markets, and thus from 1978 to 1982 the total African external debt increased from US$27 billion to $72 billion.[50]

Further compounding the problem, at the same time the world economy was moving into recession the interest rates in the international financial markets were beginning to rise. Interestingly, this increase was fueled in large measure by the Reagan administration's massive borrowing in the international financial markets to finance both its domestic tax cuts and its increased military spending. The reason these policies had such an effect on international interest rates is a function of supply and demand. As the United States increasingly borrowed money on the international markets, the amount of money available for other nations steadily decreased. According to the law of supply and demand, as the supply of any product decreases the price one pays for it (in this case the rate of interest) increases. Thus, as a direct result of US borrowing, global interest rates began to increase dramatically. These increases were especially harmful for sub-Saharan nations because as global interest rates began to rise so also did the rates on their outstanding loans. To illustrate, a one-percent increase in the interest rate on a one-billion dollar loan would force an African nation to pay an additional ten million dollars per year on top of its already existing payments. In reality, the actual outstanding balances totaled well over one billion dollars and interest rates as much as doubled and tripled.[51] Because they could not produce the revenue to meet their new debt obligations, many sub-Saharan nations (as well as other developing nations around the world) were forced to borrow even more money on the international financial markets simply to finance their increased interest expenses. Thus, as a result of circumstances over which they had no control, African nations were forced to borrow ever-increasing amounts of money while at the same time falling further and further into debt.

In terms of debt accumulation, the situation in sub-Saharan Africa is absolutely staggering. From 1985 to 1998, the total debt for all sub-Saharan nations rose from US$95 billion to $208 billion and although this increase is dramatic in itself, the figures for individual countries demonstrates an even greater problem. For example, in 1998 Congo's total debt equaled US$5.1 billion or 307 percent of the nation's Gross National Product, in Angola the debt was $12.2 billion or 297 percent of GNP, and in Zambia it was $6.8 billion or 217 percent. In other words, the amount of money owed to foreign creditors by these nations exceeded by two to three times the aggregate value of their total annual economic production. Other nations whose debts exceeded 100 percent of GNP included Sudan, Mauritania, Ivory Coast, Gambia, Guinea, Malawi, Mali, Mozambique, Burundi, Ethiopia, Sierra Leone, and the Democratic Republic of Congo.[52] Perhaps even more distressing than this, according to the United Nations' 1997 *Development Report*, six of the seven most heavily indebted nations in Africa pay more in debt service than what would be needed to "achieve major progress" against malnutrition, preventable diseases, illiteracy, and child mortality. If these governments could use the money they spend in debt repayment for human development programs, the UN estimates that approximately three million more children would live beyond their fifth birthday and a million more cases of malnutrition could be alleviated.[53]

With these statistics in mind, the debt crisis raises a number of poignant ethical questions for the world community as a whole. First, is it ethical to demand repayment from those who have not benefited from foreign loans in any real way? While borrowing money can be a valuable tool toward achieving economic development so long as it is used prudently, in the case of sub-Saharan Africa this has not been the case. As demonstrated, corruption has been a major stumbling block to many African development projects and the money received from foreign development loans has proved to be no exception. Corrupt government officials have either stolen large amounts of funds earmarked for development projects, diverted money to the purchase of arms, or used the funds for projects that aided only their ethnic tribes or political supporters. Foreign lending institutions themselves must take some blame for the African debt crisis because when the original loans were made there was little, if any, evaluation of specific loan requests and even less monitoring of how the money was actually spent.[54] Thus, due to corruption, mismanagement, and a lack of oversight on the part of the international financial community, relatively little of the money borrowed by African governments actually has been used to aid the African people.

Second, is it ethical to demand repayment for loans when the money used to service them could be better spent on vital social projects? It has been already noted that millions of children's living conditions could be dramatically improved if the money used to service debt could instead be used to fight malnutrition, disease, and illiteracy. Because many African nations spend more for debt service than for health care and education combined, debt repayment is a fundamentally ethical issue. It involves the well-being of families, the survival of the poor, the health of the community, and the future prosperity (or lack thereof) of millions of African people.[55]

Finally, the question must also be asked whether it is ethical to demand repayment for debts that in effect have already been repaid. The debt crisis as it exists today is really the result of increases in interest rates, not default on principal. With all the money African nations have been paying to their creditors over the last twenty years the original loan principal has been repaid many times over, it is the effect of compounding interest that fuels the vicious circle of debt. Once again, is it ethical for the international community to demand repayment for debts that exist primarily as a result of increases in interest rates, a situation over which the people of sub-Saharan Africa have had no control?[56]

4. Structural Adjustment

Because of the compounding effects of balance-of-trade deficits, rising interest rates, and foreign debt, by the early 1980s many African economies had virtually stopped growing and in some cases actually experienced decline. As a result, sub-Saharan nations were experiencing great difficulty securing loans and other sources of financial assistance necessary to generate economic growth. In response to this situation, the World Bank and International Monetary Fund (IMF), the two dominant international financial institutions, decreed that aid would be continued only if the receiving nations accepted serious and fundamental reforms in both their political and economic structures. In other words, the international financial institutions agreed to continue financial support for sub-Saharan nations, but only if these nations agreed to what is commonly known as structural adjustment.

According to Charles Harvey, a Fellow at the Institute of Development Studies at the University of Sussex, there are two primary reasons for structural adjustment. The first is that in order for macroeconomic policy changes to bear fruit, sub-Saharan nations must drastically reduce their huge budget deficits. The primary way to do this is to reduce the size of government which in turn entails reducing the size of the civil service and selling-off unprofitable government-owned businesses. A second reason for structural adjustment is the belief that the private sector is "seriously inhibited from recovery" so long as these reforms have not taken place. Stated differently, both the IMF and World Bank believe it is the private sector and not government that should play the primary role in African economic life.[57] The private sector needs a functioning banking system and the services it provides, it needs reform in the "parastatals" so that it does not have to pay artificially inflated prices for the inferior products and services of the state-owned corporations, and it needs the number of civil service personnel to be reduced because the state tends to hire the best educated and best qualified people to fill government positions. So long as government remains the dominant player in the economic realm, the private sector has little or no chance of assuming its rightful role.[58]

The reform programs of the IMF and World Bank may be classified under two categories: stabilization in that they first seek to stabilize the existing situation in the short term (primarily the goal of the IMF), and adjustment in that they then make the necessary structural changes to ensure long-term economic growth (primarily the goal of the World Bank). Specific policies employed by the two institutions include the following. First, because public spending has to be drastically reduced, they both insist that sub-Saharan governments sell all unprofitable parastatals, reduce the size of the civil service by firing large numbers of employees (a practice referred to as "retrenchment"), and remove all subsidies on consumer goods and services including food, education, and health care. Second, they insist that African governments devalue their currencies so that exports will become more attractive to foreign buyers thus bringing more "hard" currency into the nation. Related to this, the financial institutions also require that African governments repeal both their import tariffs and quotas and thus open their markets to greater international trade. Third, the IMF and World Bank insist that African governments end the practice of setting artificial prices for domestic goods and allow the market mechanism to accomplish this task on its own. This practice will not only allow the law of supply and demand to "accurately" set prices, but it will also reduce the political leaders' ability to arbitrarily distribute state resources and also force them to rely on economic performance (and not pay-offs) to maintain popular support.[59] In short, the logic of structural adjustment is that it promotes the "de-politicization" of the economic sector, allows autonomy in the economic realm, promotes both economic efficiency and productivity (especially in the private sector), and "eschews" rent-seeking.[60] Its rationale is that once spending and inflation are brought under control and the gap in balance-of-payments begins to close, investment will begin to increase, job creation and income generation will also increase, and governments will then be able to generate sufficient resources to both service their debts and provide necessary social services for their people.[61]

It should be noted that because both stabilization and adjustment programs often employ similar policies to achieve needed reforms, the distinction between them is not always apparent. According to David Sahn, an associate professor of development economics at Cornell University, the reasons for this are two-fold. First, although trade policies, liberalization of markets, and reforms in private enterprise are strictly adjustment policies, depreciating currency, limiting the money supply, reforming interest rates, cutting government spending, and adjusting taxes are all measures that can be effectively used by both stabilization and adjustment programs. As a result, both the IMF and World Bank utilize similar policies to achieve their desired aims. Second, because neither the economies themselves nor the various factors that influence them are static, policy needs in any given nation can and do change over time. In fact, what may begin as a policy of stabilization in a particular nation may by necessity have to shift to a policy of adjustment. Therefore, although adjustment focuses on resource allocation and economic efficiency while stabilization focuses on restraining demand, in reality the two programs are "inextricably intertwined" because many of the same reform measures are found within each.[62]

Notwithstanding the supposed "virtues" of present-day structural adjustment programs, there have also been many problems with them as well. While virtually every economist and political scientist consulted for this study agrees that major reform is needed in most sub-Saharan nations, there is an increasing belief among many of them that the adjustment policies of the IMF and World Bank have been either ineffective or have actually done more harm than good.[63] The figures from the United Nations Development Programme presented at the beginning of this chapter would seem to bear this out. By forcing governments to end price subsidies for consumer goods and services, the international financial institutions have caused a dramatic increase in the cost of living which in turn has forced many people to forego food, basic education, and health care services. Also, by forcing governments to trim their budgets, the IMF and World Bank have caused governments to lay-off or "retrench" large numbers of civil service employees without providing them with any retraining or alternative employment opportunities. In addition, because any monies gained by African governments must be put toward debt reduction, adjustment means less money is available for the maintenance of infrastructure (including drinking water and sanitation systems) and ecological concerns are almost completely ignored.[64]

As a result of the effects structural adjustment has had on the poor of sub-Saharan Africa, a number of economists and political scientists have begun to seriously question the viability of their continued implementation. Speaking of the need for development work to be done at the local level, Wilbert Gooneratne, coordinator for the African office of the United Nations Centre for Regional Development (Nairobi, Kenya), and R. A. Obudhu, a professor of geography at the University of Nairobi, claim that because the sub-Saharan region is so diverse in its social, economic, political and ecological realities, any uniform and centrally determined development plan is going to be unrealistic and irrelevant. In fact, because they focus "undue emphasis" on setting prices, achieving macroeconomic balances, and formulating "outward looking" strategies instead of "inward looking" approaches, present-day structural adjustment programs have actually exacerbated the African people's suffering by causing an increase in poverty, a continually widening income gap, and a further marginalization of the rural poor.[65]

Speaking of the efforts toward democratization on the African sub-continent, Julius Ihonvbere, an assistant professor of political science at the University of Texas-Austin, claims that because IMF and World Bank policies have generated "confusion, instability, and contradiction," attention has been focused away from the problems of people at the grass-roots level, away from the conditions necessary for democracy to survive, and away from the need for a strengthened civil society. Because Western institutions draw a direct link between democracy and economic development, they both praise the market mechanism as a solution in itself and impose political reforms that assume historically repressive African governments will suddenly demonstrate a respect for human rights. However, according to Ihonvbere, there is not one example of an African state where structural adjustment has led to greater democracy, political stability, or the provision of basic needs for growth and development.[66]

Senyo Adjibolosoo, an associate professor of business and economics at Trinity Wesleyan University, claims that most African development plans fail because the institutions formulating them do not adequately take into consideration the effects of their policies on real people. As an example, he claims that imposing structural adjustment on African economies is "tantamount to gross inefficiency" because the reform measures do not allow these economies to overcome chronic shortages in those goods that people need to survive. Furthermore, the

IMF and World Bank are so caught up in maintaining hegemony over sub-Saharan economies that they fail to recognize their reform policies are inadequate to bring about the conditions necessary for true economic recovery. In fact, Adjibolosoo claims the term "structural adjustment" really implies the IMF and World Bank artificially manipulating the production structures of sub-Saharan economies simply to serve the economic needs of the Western world.[67]

In the end, while proponents of structural adjustment contend that short-term difficulties will lead to greater long-term prosperity, critics claim that the macro economic and structural reform programs begun in the 1980s have failed because they concentrate on macroeconomic stability rather than addressing the underlying structural weaknesses of the African economies.[68] Also, critics argue that the stabilization and adjustment policies of the IMF and World Bank have focused too narrowly on the internal reasons for Africa's economic difficulties and have not taken enough consideration of the fact that many of the sub-continent's economic problems are a direct result of policies imposed upon them by the West.

It is only with this understanding of the present-day sub-Saharan economic situation that one can examine the contributions that the African Catholic bishops and theologians have made toward a theology of economic development. However, before doing so, one must first have an idea of what is actually meant by a theology of development. In the remainder of this first chapter I offer a brief overview of development theology by citing various theological justifications for participation in development-related activities, identifying the limitations inherent within any proposed theology of development, and offering my own definition of what development entails based upon Catholic social teaching.

Toward a Theology of Development

1. Theological Justification for Participation in Development Efforts

In speaking of a theology of development, it is important to first justify why Christians are even called to active involvement in development-related activities. Karl Rahner, SJ, maintains that the theological justification for this involvement lies in the integration of Christ's dual command to love both God and neighbor. For Rahner, real love of God can only be attained through the "total self-realization" and "radical self-transcendence" that is brought about by love of neighbor. Thus, true love for neighbor is ultimately love for God. He then argues that love for neighbor is not simply a task to be fulfilled within one particular aspect of an individual's life, but instead it is a "universal determinant of human existence" that must leave its mark on all that is "good." Then, after claiming religion (that which is expressed in worship) only discovers its true nature when it "abandons" itself to the worldly realization of love for neighbor, he states that love for God must to some extent "forget itself" within love for neighbor so that it (love for God) can both attain its "own full nature" and continually reach towards its eternal source. Rahner's ultimate point is that what at first may appear to be a "secular" love for one's neighbor is in reality the "source and sphere" for realizing true love for God.[69]

Josef Fuchs, SJ, argues that this theological justification is located in the fact that humanity as a whole is mandated to develop the world as a means to develop itself. Because the human person's primary function in the world is to be a human person, our development-of-self implies a "progressive humanization" of the world through which we realize our full personhood in relation to God. He claims that as we humans are historical beings, we cannot stagnate in a "time sequence" but must draw from both the past and present to plan for a "truly human future." In other words, as historical beings we must never adopt a "static attitude" in regard to the future of humanity, instead we must always look toward this future by attending to the development of both ourselves and the world around us.[70]

Similar to Fuchs, Philip Land, SJ, and Paul Abrecht[71] claim the theological justification for participation in development efforts (and, in fact, for constructing a theology of development) is located in what they term the "humanization of life." According to Land and Abrecht, many people view Christ's teaching to feed the hungry, clothe the naked, shelter the homeless, etc., in Matthew 25 as the primary justification for development-related activities.[72] However, since true development involves human progress and working towards "a more satisfying abundance" (understood as more than just meeting basic needs), then a new, more comprehensive justification is needed. Citing Colossians 1:15-20,[73] they claim that as everything on earth realizes its origin and "reconciliation" in Christ, Christ can be understood as both the "beginner" and "finisher" of any human effort toward development. Stated differently, while God reaffirms the "goodness" of creation through Christ's "sanctifying" work, humanity nonetheless is still called upon to create, shape, and bring order to this creation so as to allow human beings to become more fully human. In this sense, material progress is good because not only can it afford individuals a decent standard of living, but it can also allow them to become who they are meant to become through God's design. Thus, for Land and Abrecht, development understood as an element in the "humanization of life" actually possesses religious value in itself.[74]

I present these three justifications not only because they are the products of prominent Christian theologians, but also because they offer clear theological rationales for both individual and church-based involvement in development related efforts. Manifesting love of God through love of neighbor, working for the "progressive humanization" of the world, and seeking the fulfillment-of-self through communal service are all vital elements that must be included in any proposed theology of development. Although in the following chapters I may not specifically cite Rahner, Fuchs, Land, and Abrecht, the foundations to which they refer underlie the theological contributions that many African bishops and theologians have made to the issue of economic development.

2. Limitations to a Theology of Development

While justifications certainly exist for pursuing a Christian theology of development, there are also a number of limitations as well. The first concerns how one employs biblical texts. Economist Charles Elliott argues that because there are no specific references to development within the Bible, one cannot use it as a "case book" that offers unambiguous technical guidance in development-related efforts nor simply quote it to justify one's own judgments concerning present-day temporal affairs. He claims that not only is it an abuse of the Bible's integrity to directly apply its narratives to modern-day examples of injustice, but it also violates almost every accepted principle of biblical interpretation to propose that it speaks to a temporal reality beyond that of its original authors.[75] Theologians

Zoltan Alszeghy, SJ and Maurizio Flick, SJ, closely echo Elliott by arguing that as development theology is not a "reality" to which God ever spoke in the Scriptures, we do not remain "faithful" to God's Word if we directly or uncritically employ it to justify temporal actions. In fact, claiming that God's Word leads directly to doctrinal statements about present-day development is also to claim the biblical writers experienced a world that corresponds both scientifically and technologically to the one we experience today. For Alszeghy and Flick, this notion is obviously false.[76]

A second limitation concerns the question of whether one can construct a single, comprehensive theology of development that encompasses the human reality as a whole. C. B. Peter claims that because theological reflection on economic (and other) issues varies according to one's location in the world, by definition any theology of development is going to be contextual. He also maintains that because development theology's socio-economic concerns transcend both national and cultural boundaries, one realizes very quickly that there is not one single development theology but only numerous theolog*ies*.[77] Further complicating the issue, Bernard Lambert, OP, argues that as the world continually presents new challenges to which Christian theological reflection must respond, no theology of development can ever be considered "complete." He claims that at best, development theology can only be regarded as a "theology in the making" or a "theology in process." He continues by stating that not only does a theology of development not exist today, it will in fact never exist. However, for Lambert, this is actually good news because if one were ever to claim a "completed" theology of development, it would become an "arrested" theology and not one of a "reality in process of being achieved."[78]

A third limitation to any proposed theology of development concerns the danger of confusing theology with ideology. Charles Elliott once again argues that because ideology is the "ordering of a system of independently determined ideas" while theology is the "ordering of a system of ideas based upon beliefs about the revelation of God," any scientific analysis that ignores the realities of God and about God does not do justice to the entirety of truth. While Christians should certainly be open to the analysis of secular ideology insofar as its findings correspond to divine truth, when ideology and theology are confused the result is "bad ideology and even worse theology."[79] Similarly, Alszeghy and Flick argue that because scientific "truth" is oftentimes illusory, the theologian must be careful about basing theological reflection on the findings of the secular sciences. What happens when the theologian employs scientific findings as a foundation for theological reflection and twenty, fifty, or even one hundred years later these scientific findings are disproved? Once again, this is not to say that theologians should disregard the findings of the secular sciences (particularly in the socio-economic realm), however theologians must realize that any conclusions drawn will only remain valid if the "pre-theological" ideas supporting them are also valid.[80]

With these limitations in mind, I repeat once again that my goal in this study is not to construct a comprehensive theology of development for sub-Saharan Africa. In fact, these limitations would seem to indicate that this is an impossible task. Instead, I more modestly propose that through their contributions over the past thirty-plus years, both the African bishops and theologians have identified some of elements necessary for any proposed Christian theology of economic development.

3. Development Defined

A final issue that must be clarified in speaking of any proposed theology of development is how one actually defines the term "development." During the 1960s and early 1970s when modernization theory was in force, development was generally understood within the social sciences as the capacity of a previously stagnant economy to both generate and sustain a five-to-seven percent annual rate of growth in its gross national product (GNP). However, while during this period a number of African nations were achieving this five-to-seven percent rate, standards of living remained basically unchanged and thus this growth was not making a difference in people's everyday lives. As a result, in the mid to late 1970s when dependency theory was emerging, new definitions were proposed that incorporated the reduction or elimination of poverty, disease, unemployment, and inequality, along with providing for greater political stability, social organization, military strength, and technological advancement as necessary elements of any viable development program.[81] Thus, economic development came to be understood as more than a simple increase in gross national product, it also had to entail the enrichment of people's everyday lives.

Many of the same elements in this "revised" understanding of development can be found in present-day definitions as well. George Akeya Agbango, an associate professor of political science at Bloomsburg University (Bloomsburg, PA), claims that economic development must entail the ability of a nation to adopt policies that reduce unemployment, eliminate poverty, and improve quality of life through the provision of goods and services in the areas of health care, education, transportation, and communication.[82] Similarly, Senyo Adjibolosoo claims that while the goals of any economic development program must include the eradication of poverty, illiteracy, disease, urban squalor, malnutrition, economic injustice, and all forms of prejudice, these programs must also foster the "humanness" of every person, the right to the freedom of choice based on the "universal principles of life," and the means to peaceful coexistence. For Adjibolosoo, the acid test of any economic development policy is its effectiveness in creating an environment where the poor and disadvantaged are offered the ability to feed, clothe, and shelter themselves, and one where all people believe they belong to a "humane society."[83]

Interestingly, many of these perspectives on economic development from the secular social sciences reflect similar perspectives from within Catholic social teaching. In his 1961 encyclical *Mater et Magistra*, Pope John XXIII maintains that there can be no true development without respect for human dignity, the human person must always remain the "foundation, cause, and end" of any social institution, and within any program of economic development the people in less developed nations must remain the ones primarily responsible for their own progress.[84] In its 1965 *Gaudium et Spes*, the Second Vatican Council claims that while advances in agricultural production, industrial output, and human services all foster the "growth" of humanity as a whole, the "fundamental purpose" of these advances must never be simply to increase profits. Instead, because the economy is always at the service of humanity, it must be judged on how it satisfies not only material needs but also intellectual, moral, spiritual, and religious needs as well. According to the Council, although economic life operates under its own "laws and methods," it must always be carried out "within the limits of [Christian] morality."[85]

Further perspectives on development arise from Church officials in Africa. Joseph Cardinal Malula, Archbishop of Kinshasa, Zaïre,[86] claims that African nations must not simply accept the development programs of the West, but must construct their own programs to promote the originality, creativity, and "indigenous-ness" of the African people. In terms of the Church's role in these efforts, he claims it must above all "serve in truth" which means that it must continually proclaim the "permanent demand of progress" and also work to make human life "more human."[87] The French-speaking West African bishops (Conférence Episcopale Régionale de l'Afrique de l'Ouest) maintain that development has both economic and sociological aspects because it concerns the increase of humanity's creative powers in every domain of earthly life. These domains include, but are not limited to, material wealth, human relations, spiritual values, and the expression of one's own personality. However, the bishops also recognize that development in the economic sense is not possible without a corresponding transformation of both the people's mentalities and ways of life. In order for true development to occur there must be an "interior" modernization of not only African economic structures, but also of the political, administrative, and cultural structures of African society as well.[88]

Notwithstanding these and numerous other contributions, the most comprehensive definition of development within Catholic social teaching is articulated by Pope Paul VI in his 1967 encyclical *Populorum Progressio*. According to the pope, in order for development to be "authentic" it must not be limited simply to the economic realm but be "integral" in that it promote the good of all people in every aspect of their lives. He also claims that because service to humanity is the ultimate goal of any program to increase economic production, to speak of development really means to be as concerned with social progress as with economic growth. As such, any development program must aim to reduce poverty, combat discrimination, free people from servitude, and enable them to become instruments of their own spiritual advancement. Finally, in speaking of aid to the poor, the pope claims that simply spending money to fight poverty is not sufficient in itself. Instead, what is needed is the construction of a world where every person can live a "fully human life," one where everyone is free from "imposed servitude" and from the oppression caused by forces over which they have no control. In the end, Paul VI dreams of a world "where freedom is not an empty word and where the poor man Lazarus can sit down at the same table with the rich man."[89]

Based on these theological contributions, a Christian vision of development may be summarized as any concrete effort, action, policy, or program on the part of an individual or group that seeks to meet basic human needs and whose intention is to foster the "human-ness" of earthly life. I recognize that this vision of development is much more encompassing than what can be addressed in this study and as such I restrict myself to examining development solely within the economic realm. Thus, I operationally define economic development as any effort, action, policy, or program on the part of an individual or group that, in addition to working toward the elimination of poverty, unemployment, and want of material necessities, offers individuals the economic conditions necessary to become self-sufficient and to fulfill themselves as human persons using the rights, talents, and abilities granted to them by God. I should note that this definition does not imply that society as a whole should necessarily supply all material goods (although this may be the case in situations of dire emergency) or that it has a duty to assure that all people are self-fulfilled; instead it simply means that true economic development can occur only when individuals are offered the conditions that make both self-sufficiency and self-fulfillment possible in their own lives.

Plan of the Study

The format for the remainder of my study is as follows. In Chapter Two I examine how the Roman Catholic Church has both helped and hindered the economic development of sub-Saharan Africa by focusing on both its colonial legacy and its relevancy in present-day African society. In Chapter Three I examine the contributions of three African liberation theologians to demonstrate how they not only emphasize anthropological poverty in their writings, but also echo the basic economic principles found within Catholic social teaching. In Chapter Four I examine various pastoral statements from episcopal conferences on the national, regional, and continental levels to demonstrate the contributions that the African Catholic bishops have made to the construction of a theology of development. I should note that as my overall aim is to demonstrate what both the bishops and theologians bring to the issue of African economic development, I reserve my criticisms of their works until the final chapter. Finally, in Chapter Five I synthesize the similarities in both the bishops' and theologians' teachings, present my own critiques of their contributions, and look toward the future by offering suggestions for further study and for the role of the Church in African development efforts. Overall, because they uphold the principles of Catholic social teaching, demonstrate that any development theology must balance universal Church teachings with the people's contextual realities, maintain the temporal function of Christian theology, and also speak to the effects of human sinfulness, I conclude that together the African Catholic bishops and theologians examined in this study make an invaluable contribution to the articulation of a sub-Saharan theology of economic development.

Notes

[1] I define economic development as any effort, action, policy, or program on the part of an individual or group that, in addition to working toward the elimination of poverty, unemployment, and/or want of material necessities, offers individuals the economic conditions necessary to become self-sufficient and to fulfill themselves as human persons using the rights, talents, and abilities granted to them by God. This definition will be more fully explained in the final section of this chapter.

[2] United Nations Development Programme, *Human Development Report 2000* (New York: Oxford University Press, 2000), 149, 160, 189, 283-285. For additional economic indicators, see the World Bank's *African Development Indicators 2000* (Washington DC: World Bank, 2000).

[3] Peter Lewis, "Political Economy: Crisis and Reform," in *Africa: Dilemmas of Developmentand Change*, ed. Peter Lewis (Boulder, CO: Westview Press, 1998), 359-362 at 359.

[4] According to Benedict Mongula, the International Monetary Fund and other foreign financial institutions point to the first four of these reasons and thus lay the blame for Africa's economic situation on the African governments themselves. For their part, the African governments point to the last three reasons as being primarily responsible for their situation. See Benedict Mongula, "Development Theory & Changing Trends in Sub-Saharan African Economics 1960-1989," in *African Perspectives on Development: Controversies, Dilemmas & Openings*, ed. Ulf Himmelstrand, et. al. (Nairobi: East African Academic Publishers, 1994), 84-96 at 85-86.

[5] World Bank, *Development in Practice: Taking Action to Reduce Poverty in Sub-Saharan Africa* (Washington DC: World Bank Publications, 1997), 4-8.

[6] Ecumenical Association of Third World Theologians (EATWOT), "African Report," in *Third World Theologies: Commonalities and Divergences*, ed. K.C. Abraham (Maryknoll, NY: Orbis Books, 1990), 28-56 at 29.

[7] For a chronological survey of the African colonial period including the dates when colonies gained independence, see Robin Hallett's *Africa Since*

1875: A Modern History (Ann Arbor, MI: University of Michigan Press, 1974), 37-77.

[8] Walter Rodney *How Europe Underdeveloped Africa* (Washington DC: Howard University Press, 1974), 165-166, 180-181. See also J. Milburn Thompson's *Justice and Peace: A Christian Primer* (Maryknoll, NY: Orbis Books,1997), 13. For a more detailed account of how the Belgian government planned, implemented, and executed its colonial policies in the Congo, see Adam Hochschild's, *King Leopold's Ghost* (Boston: Houghton Mifflin Company, 1998).

[9] Karuti Kanyinga, "Into the Land Question in Kenya: Alienation of Public Land and the Intensity of Landlessness," in *Alienation of Public Land in Kenya* (Nairobi, Kenya: Catholic University of East Africa, 2000), 10-17 at 14-15; and Rodney, 180-181.

[10] Rodney, 149-154, 164-165; and Thompson, 13.

[11] See O. N. Gakuru, "The Social Security Systems in Traditional and Modern Societies: The Concept of Social Security," in *Evolving Strategies for Alleviating Poverty in Kenya* (Nairobi, Kenya, Catholic University of East Africa, 1999), 1-27 at 13, 18-19; Robert J. Cummings, "Religious Belief and Economic Behavior in Contemporary Africa South of the Sahara: Linking Religion and Development," in *Religious Belief and Economic Behavior*, ed. Jacob Neusner (Atlanta: Scholar's Press, 1999), 119-168 at 155; Paul Gifford, *African Christianity: Its Public Role* (London: Hurst & Co., 1998), 4; and Rodney, 205-209.

[12] See Bénézet Bujo, *The Ethical Dimension of Community: The African Model and Dialogue Between North and South* (Nairobi, Kenya: Paulines Publications Africa, 1998), 171-172; and Peter Lewis, "Development and Change in Africa," in *Africa: Dilemmas of Development and Change*, ed. Peter Lewis (Boulder, CO: Westview Press, 1998), 1-11 at 2-3. Ian Ritchie adds that although the creation of these artificial borders remains a source of discomfort for Africans today, the Organization of African Unity upholds the necessity of these boundaries because if they were to be changed it would call into question every African boundary. This would likely lead to continual border wars throughout the continent. See Ian Ritchie's "African Theology and Social Change: An Anthropological Approach" (Ph.D. Dissertation, McGill University, April, 1993), 35.

[13] Gifford, *African Christianity: Its Public Role*, 8-9.

[14] Peter Henriot, SJ, "Development in Light of the African Synod: An Alternative to the Structural Adjustment Program," *Catholic International* 7 (1996), 286-287; and Rodney, 234-235.

[15] Henriot, 286-287 and Rodney, 234-235.

[16] Rodney, 224.

[17] This is a claim of J. Milburn Thompson, 13-14.
[18] Rodney, 95-103.

[19] Robin Law, *The Slave Coast of West Africa 1550-1750: The Impact of the Atlantic Slave Trade on an African Society* (Oxford: Clarendon Press, 1991), 219-224.

[20] Lewis, "Development and Change in Africa," 6-7.

[21] Donal Dorr, *Option for the Poor: A Hundred Years of Catholic Social Teaching*, Revised Edition (Maryknoll, NY: Orbis Books, 1992), 172-173.

[22] Lewis, 7-8.

[23] Ibid., 8-9.

[24] Cited in Gifford, 12.

[25] Leonardo A. Villalón, "The African State at the End of the Twentieth Century: Parameters of the Critical Juncture," in *The African State at a Critical Juncture: Between Disintegration and Reconfiguration*, ed. Leonardo A. Villalón & Phillip A. Huxtable (London: Lynne Rienner Publishers, 1998), 3-25 at 11-14.

[26] Joseph C. McKenna, *Finding a Social Voice: The Church and Marxism in Africa* (New York: Fordham University Press, 1997), 38.

[27] Lewis, 4.

[28] Ayittey is also the founder and President of the Free Africa Foundation, a Washington DC-based human rights and lobby organization.

[29] George B. N. Ayittey, *Africa In Chaos* (New York: St. Martin's Press, 1998), 21, 73-76.

[30] Ibid., 151-154. See also Jean-Marc Éla's *Afrique: L'irruption des pauvres: Société contre ingérence, pouvoir et argent* (Paris: Éditions L'Harmattan, 1994), 144-146.

[31] Gifford, 5-8, 12-13.

[32] Jeffrey Herbst, "The Structural Adjustment of Politics in Africa," in *Africa: Dilemmas of Development and Change*, ed. Peter Lewis (Boulder, CO: Westview Press, 1998), 431-449 at 432-433. Here, Herbst cites the World Bank report, "Accelerated Development in Sub-Saharan Africa," 1981, 38.

[33] Herbst, 433-434.

[34] Ibid, 434-435.

[35] McKenna, 38-39. Factors leading to tribal "idolatry" include: 1) forms of the African world-view whereby one only "sees" the world through one's own tribe or one's perspective is limited to one's own tribe; 2) the view that the African person is not primarily an individual but a member of a community, thus first loyalties must always be toward one's own people; 3) the "tribe as family" mentality in that when one person rises in social status the benefits accrued are not for the individual alone but are to be shared by the entire family or tribe which has now been given a favored standing in society. Because tribal links are more important than merit, oftentimes people are appointed to government positions not because they are competent to do the job but because their "brother" is in a position of power. The ineptitude which results from this practice is one of the reasons for the many African ethnic divisions and wars. See Tatah H. Mbuy, "The Rwandan Nightmare: A Source of Great Pain for the Synod Fathers," *African Ecclesial Review* 37 (1995), 53-56.

[36] Ken Omolo, "Peace and Conflict Resolution in Kenya," in *Promoting Economic Development through the Strategy of Self-Reliance* (Nairobi, Kenya: Catholic University of East Africa, 1999), 5-18 at 8-9.

[37] For clarity, corruption is defined as "the utilization of official positions or titles for personal or private gain, either on an individual or collective basis, at the expense of the public good, in violation of established rules and ethical considerations, and through the direct or indirect [intervention] of one or more public officials whether they be politicians or bureaucrats." Kempe Ronald Hope, "Corruption and Development in Africa," in *Corruption and Development in Africa: Lessons from Country Case Studies*, ed. Kempe Ronald Hope & Bornwell Chikulo (New York: St. Martin's Press, 2000), 17-39 at 18.

[38] Hope, 20-24; and Ayittey, 199-200

[39] Mutahi Ngunyi, "Risks of a Bandit Economy: New Study Shows that Crime and Corruption Generate More Money than Formal Economy," *Sunday Nation* (Kenya), July 9, 2000, p.9.

[40] Hope, 19-23. See also Gervase Maipose's "Aid Abuse and Mismanagement in Africa: Problems of Accountability, Transparency, and Ethical Leadership," in *Corruption and Development in Africa*, 87-103 at 92-93; and Charles Harvey's "Constraints on Sustained Recovery from Economic Disaster in Africa," in *Constraints on the Success of Structural Adjustment Programs in Africa*, ed. Charles Harvey (New York: St. Martin's Press, 1996), 130-151 at 134-138.

[41] Hope, 23-25. See also George Ayittey's "Combating Corruption in Africa: Analysis and Context," in *Corruption and Development in Africa*, 104-118 at 104-108.

[42] "Balance of trade" is a term used to describe an equilibrium between a nation's imports and exports. If a nation imports as much as it exports it is said to have an equal balance of trade. If exports are greater than imports the nation has a balance of trade surplus and if exports are less than imports the nation has a balance of trade deficit.

[43] Louis O. Osuji, "Structural Adjustment and Persistence of Economic Crisis in Africa," in *Globalization and the New World Order: Promises, Problems, and Prospects for Africa in the Twenty-First Century*, ed. Felix Moses Edoho (Westport, CT: Praeger, 1997), 83-98 at 86-89.

[44] Ayittey, *Africa in Chaos*, 132-135.

[45] McKenna, 36-37 and Ayittey, 31. For further information on the limitations of foreign trade, see Philip Land, SJ's "What is Development?" in *In Search of a Theology of Development: A SODEPAX Report* (Lausanne, Switzerland: Imprimerie La Concorde, 1969), 180-203 at 189-191.

[46] See Felix Moses Edoho, "Overview: Africa in the Age of Globalization and the New World Order," in *Globalization and the New World Order*, 1-25 at 15; and Ayittey, *Africa in Chaos*, 10-11.

[47] See Appendix A "Net Aid Flows to sub-Saharan Africa" in Carol Lancaster's *Aid to Africa: So Much to Do, So Little Done* (Chicago: University of Chicago Press, 1999), 69; and Ayittey, *Africa In Chaos*, 275-277.

[48] Nicholas Van de Wall and Timothy A. Johnson, *Improving Aid to Africa* (Washington DC: Overseas Development Council, 1996), 48-70. See also Ayittey, *Africa In Chaos*, 275-284; and Lancaster, 220-233.

[49] Osuji, 85-86.

[50] International Cooperation for Development and Solidarity (CIDSE) "Putting Life Before Debt: A Catholic Guide for Reflection on the International Debt," *Catholic International* 9 (August, 1998), 359. Figures come from Osuji, 86.

[51] Thompson, 38-39.

[52] United Nations Development Programme, 221-222.

[53] CIDSE, 359.

[54] See Thompson, 38 and CIDSE, 359.

[55] Posing the debt question as an ethical question forms the basis for Archbishop Medardo Mazombwe's (Lusaka, Zambia) argument that Zambia should refuse to pay its debts. See Mazombwe's "A Pastoral Perspective for Africa on International Debt," *Origins* 28 (November 12, 1998), 384.

[56] For more information on the ethical issues surrounding debt repayment, see the Pontifical Commission for Justice and Peace's "An Ethical Approach to the International Debt Question," *Origins* 16 (1987), 601-611; the United States

Catholic Conference Administrative Board's *Relieving Third World Debt: A Call for Co-Responsibility, Justice, and Solidarity* (Washington DC: USCC, 1989); the Catholic Fund for Overseas Development's "The Human-Development Approach to Debt Relief," *Origins* 27 (1998), 760-764; and Roger Cardinal Mahoney's "The Cost of International Debt in Human Terms," *Origins* 27 (1997), 387-390.

[57] Underlying these structural adjustment programs is the assumption by the IMF and World Bank that a free market economy is in the best interests of developing African nations, an assumption that reflects the philosophy of these two dominant players in the world economy. One must question, however, whether the free market system is the best vehicle for sub-Saharan economic growth, especially when most of the nations in question are not democratic and, for the most part, have experienced only "negative" effects from the capitalist system.

[58] Harvey, 134-142. Interestingly, the rationale for present-day sub-Saharan structural adjustment programs can be found in two major reports issued by the World Bank during the 1980s. In its 1981 "Accelerated Development in Sub-Saharan Africa: An Agenda for Action," the World Bank claimed that the main cause of Africa's economic difficulties lay in the deficient internal policies of its national governments. In short, it claimed that African economic policies acted as obstacles to efficient resource allocation, weakened market functions, and caused economies to be especially vulnerable to external influences. It then suggested that true growth and development in Africa could only come about through programs that stressed readjusting overvalued exchange rates, improving agricultural price incentives, and both limiting the role of and improving the performance of the public sector. In conclusion, the World Bank claimed it needed to take a more active role and to exert greater influence over economic policy through the various "lending instruments" it offered to African nations. In 1989, the World Bank issued a second report, "Sub-Saharan Africa: From Crisis to Sustained Growth," in which it claimed the single most important factor to successful economic recovery was the liberalization of African political systems. Arguing that poor governance was the main cause of Africa's continued economic crisis, it proposed sweeping political reforms including the introduction of multi-party politics, constitutional reform, public sector transparency and accountability, free and fair elections, free speech, a free press, and a greater respect for human rights. In this report, the World Bank claimed political reform and state reconstruction were the first steps toward ending economic crisis and providing

the environment within which economic growth and development could take place. See John Mukum Mbaku, "A Balance Sheet of Structural Adjustment in Africa: Towards a Sustainable Development Agenda," in *Preparing Africa for the Twenty First Century: Strategies for Peaceful Coexistence and Sustainable Development*, ed. John Mukum Baku (Aldershot: Ashgate Publishing, 1999), 119-149 at 129-130; Ben C. Chikulo, "Structural Adjustment and the New Conditionalities: Towards Development in Africa," in *Structural Adjustment, Reconstruction and Development in Africa*, ed. Kempe Ronald Hope (Aldershot: Ashgate Publishing, 1997), 24-34 at 24-26; and Osuji, 84.

[59] See Thomas M. Callaghy, "Between Scylla and Charybdis: The Foreign Economic Relations of Sub-Saharan African States," in *Africa: Dilemmas of Development and Change*, 382-399 at 388-393; William Freund, *The Making of Contemporary Africa: The Development of African Society since 1800* (Boulder, CO: Lynn Rienner Publishers, Inc., 1998), 253-256; Mbaku, 130-132; and Chikulo, 24-26.

[60] Daniel Greene, "Ghana: Structural Adjustment and (Re)Formation," in *The African State at a Critical Juncture*, 185-211 at 189-190. "Rent" is understood as monopoly profits. "Rent-seeking" then is the effort to acquire access to or control over the opportunities to earn these rents and is part of an overall process through which either individual citizens and/or public officials seek private gain. Rent-seeking is often synonymous with corruption. See Jacqueline Coolidge & Susan Rose-Ackerman's "Kleptocracy and Reform in African Regimes: Theory and Examples," in *Corruption and Development in Africa*, 57-86 at 57.

[61] Lancaster, 26.

[62] David E. Sahn, "Economic Crisis and Policy Reform in Africa: An Introduction," in *Adjusting to Policy Failure in African Economies*, ed. David E. Sahn (Ithaca, NY: Cornell University Press, 1994), 1-22 at 12; and "Economic Reform and Poverty: An Overview," in *Economic Reform and the Poor in Africa*, ed. David E. Sahn (Oxford: Clarendon Press, 1996), 3-26 at 6, note 7.

[63] See David Sahn, "Economic Crisis and Policy Reform in Africa: Lessons Learned and Implications for Policy," in *Economic Reform and the Poor in Africa*, 373-381; Julius Nyang'oro and Timothy M. Shaw, "The African State in the Global Economic Context," in *The African State at a*

Critical Juncture, 27-42 at 28-30; Mbaku, 133-138; Chikulo, 26-33; and Osuji, 94-95.

[64] Henriot, 289-290.

[65] Wilbert Gooneratne and R. A. Obudhu, "Introduction," in *Contemporary Issues in Regional Development Policy: Perspectives from Eastern and Southern Africa*, ed. Wilbert Gooneratne and R. A. Obudhu (Aldershot, England: Avebury Ashgate Publishing Ltd., 1997), 1-14 at 2-3.

[66] Julius Ihonvbere, "Democratization in Africa: Challenges and Prospects," in *Issues and Trends in Contemporary African Politics: Stability, Development and Democratization*, ed. George Akeya Agbango (New York: Peter Lang, 1997), 287-320 at 296-299. In addition to this, Mahmood Mamdani, a Professor of Political Science at Makerere University (Kampala, Uganda), argues that the IMF restructuring programs undermine not only attempts to create independent, self-regulating economies, but also movements toward democracy. According to Mamdani: "Democracy is not just political, it is also cultural and economic. My argument has been that in the economy the need of the hour is for large-scale institutional changes, for major democratic transformations that will give peasants security of tenure and control over cooperatives ... That is why the conception of privatization, like that of the IMF, which leaves out of consideration the interest of the vast majority in society, has to be resisted. The property that needs liberalization today is not that of the [upper classes] who continue to appropriate the labour of the majority for their own unproductive consumption, but that of the peasantry whose property is the result of the labour of that majority. Privatization, IMF-style, is anti-democratic." See Mahmood Mamdani, "A Critical Analysis of The IMF Programme in Uganda," in *African Perspectives on Development: Controversies, Dilemmas & Openings*, eds. Ulf Himmelstrand, et. al. (Nairobi: East African Academic Publishers, 1994), 128-136 at 136.

[67] Senyo Adjibolosoo, *The Human Factor in Developing Africa* (Westport, CT: Praeger, 1995), 42-47.

[68] Sahn, "Economic Reform and Poverty: An Overview," 6.

[69] Karl Rahner, SJ, "Theological Justification of the Church's Development Work," in *Concern for the Church: Theological Investigations*, vol. 20, trans. Edward Quinn (New York: Crossroad, 1981), 65-73 at 67-68.

Rahner continues by stating: "For both the authority and the people of the Church (also as such) are charged with the task of active love: a love that goes out to the other person in the 'world' and is not understood as a means to something else, however sublime; a love that carries with it a will to justice and, today at least, also has sociopolitical tasks; a love that carries with it as its condition and ultimate ground God's love for us as it became eschatologically irreversible and victorious in Jesus Christ and our love for God in Jesus Christ. But this is a love that can become so 'worldly' precisely because it has to be given to our neighbor purely and simply, and not only to those who belong to the household of faith, because it must be extended as widely as God's love for man is itself extended. In a word, it is love seen from the Christian standpoint: not merely an inward disposition, but something that must be realized in action in which alone a person really gets away from himself ... The other person, who is loved, is the sacrament in which we receive God" (70-71).

[70] Josef Fuchs, SJ, "Moral Aspects of Human Progress," in *Theology Meets Progress*, ed. Philip Land, SJ (Rome: Gregorian University Press, 1971), 145-169 at 148-150.

[71] I should note that Paul Abrecht is not Roman Catholic but writes from the Baptist tradition.

[72] See Matthew 25:31-46.

[73] "He is the image of the invisible God, the firstborn of all creation. For in him were created all things in heaven and on earth, the visible and the invisible, whether thrones or dominions or principalities or powers; all things were created through him and for him. He is before all things, and in him all things hold together. He is the head of the body, the church. He is the beginning, the firstborn from the dead, that in all things he himself might be preeminent. For in him all the fullness was pleased to dwell, and through him to reconcile all things for him, making peace by the blood of his cross [through him], whether those on earth or those in heaven" (NAB)

[74] Philip Land, SJ, and Paul Abrecht, "Common Christian Convictions about Development," in *World Development: Challenge to the Churches*, ed. Denys Munby (Washington DC: Corpus Books, 1968), 137-146 at 137-142. Land makes similar observations about the benefits of economic development in his "What is Development?" 194-195.

[75] Charles Elliott, *The Development Debate* (New York: Friendship Press, 1971), 74. Elliott served as a Lecturer in Economics at the University of Nottingham, a Senior Research Fellow at the United Nations' Institute for Social Development and the Assistant Secretary of SODEPAX, the joint Roman Catholic/World Council of Churches Commission on Society, Development, and Peace.

[76] See Zoltan Alszeghy, SJ and Maurizio Flick, SJ, "Theology of Development: A Question of Method," in *Theology Meets Progress*, ed. Philip Land, SJ (Rome: Gregorian University Press, 1971), 105-143 at 112-114.

[77] See C. B. Peter's "Beyond a Theology of Development," *African Ecclesial Review* 35 (1993), 63-64. One might apply the same logic to critique the debt reduction and structural adjustment programs of the IMF and World Bank.

[78] Lambert was a professor of moral theology at Laval University, Quebec. See Bernard Lambert, OP, "A Personal Report on the Consultation," in *In Search of a Theology of Development: A SODEPAX Report* (Lausanne, Switzerland: Imprimerie La Concorde, 1969), 36-50 at 46.

[79] Elliott, 74-75. Further on in this work, Elliott claims: "[I]t is precisely the job of theology to continuously to review and challenge the normative premises of the ideological matrix. It is to enable us to see the facts of man in the light of God, to review the situation of life today in the perspective of eternal life. It is this dialectic relationship between ideology and theology which can enable to see, not a perfect scheme of God's ideas on development, but rather a Christ-like way of looking at *all* the relevant facts" (80).

[80] Alszeghy and Flick, 133-134. Philip Land offers a similar warning by claiming: "Surely we are not here entitled to underestimate the extent to which sin ... accounts for the disorders of modern society. But neither may we equate all disorder with sin – at least personal sin. Men can at times be disorderly because they have not yet known how to establish codes of behavior adapted to new and complex circumstances ... Many conflicts rest unresolved only because convergence of interest cannot be determined. But to find these [convergences] in the tangle of highly complex and dynamic situations requires experience beyond what we presently possess. The same is true of justice ... In our complex economic order, with its international dimensions, no one can pretend to arrive at anything better than approximations to justice, socially

acceptable for the moment, subject to reappraisal with the changing situation of tomorrow." See Land's "What is Development?" 200.

[81] George Akeya Agbango, "Political Instability and Economic Development in Sub-Saharan Africa," in *Issues and Trends in Contemporary African Politics*, 13-51 at 14-15. In offering these definitions, Agbango quotes Claude Ake's *A Political Economy of Africa* (New York: Longman, 1981), 141; and Michael Todaro's *Economic Development in the Third World* (London: Longman, 1985), 83. For more information on the various "processes and designs" of development, see Philip Land's "What is Development?" 181-185.

[82] Agbango, 36-37

[83] Adjibolosoo, 13.

[84] Pope John XXIII, "Mater et Magistra: Christianity and Social Progress," in *Catholic Social Teaching: The Documentary Heritage*, eds. David J. O'Brien & Thomas A. Shannon (Maryknoll, NY: Orbis Books, 1995), 84-128 at nos. 151, 215, and 219.

[85] Second Vatican Council, "Gaudium et Spes: Pastoral Constitution on the Church in the Modern World," in *Catholic Social Thought: The Documentary Heritage*, 166-237 at no. 64. The bishops continue by claiming: "Economic development must be kept under the control of mankind. It must not be left to the sole judgment of a few men or groups possessing excessive economic power, or of the political community alone, or of certain especially powerful nations. It is proper, on the contrary, that at every level the largest possible number of people have an active share in directing that development" (no. 65).

[86] Zaïre is now known as the Democratic Republic of the Congo.

[87] Joseph Cardinal Malula, "Pour un développement authentiquement Africain," *La Documentation Catholique* 1570 (1970), 823-824.

[88] The West African bishops' contributions are taken from Charles Valy Tuho's "L'Afrique," in *Ethique, économie et développement: L'enseignement des évêques des cinq continents* (1891-1991), ed Roger Berthouzoz and

Roberto Papini (Fribourg, Switzerland: Editions Universitaires, 1995), 101-125 at 106-107.

[89] Paul VI, Pope, "Populorum Progressio: On the Development of Peoples," in *Catholic Social Thought: The Documentary Heritage*, 240-262 at nos. 14, 34, and 47.

Chapter Two

The Role of the Catholic Church in Africa

With an understanding of the economic challenges facing the African sub-continent and both the justifications and limitations involved with proposing any theology of development, I now turn to the role of the Roman Catholic Church. In this second chapter, I begin with a brief overview of the positive contributions the Church and Church-sponsored organizations have made toward the development of the sub-Saharan people. Following this, I demonstrate how the colonial missionaries actually supported the secular colonial enterprise, undermined the religious and social fabric of traditional African society, and contributed to the present-day syncretism that exists within the African Catholic Church. Moving then to present-day issues, I demonstrate how both the financial dependence of the African Church and its authoritarian model of clerical formation work to separate the clergy from the laity, relegate many bishops and priests to a state of silent obedience, and undermine Church efforts toward economic development. The chapter concludes with calls by various African theologians for the Church to refocus its temporal mission in order to actively combat the injustice and oppression suffered by the African people, a refocusing these theologians claim is necessary to assure that the Church remains a relevant force within African society.

The Catholic Church and African Development Today

Throughout its history in sub-Saharan Africa, the Roman Catholic Church has maintained an influential presence, one that many believe is becoming even stronger today as a result of the fact that the numbers of African Catholics is steadily growing. From 1970 to 1998 (the last year for which figures are available), the estimated number of Catholics on the African continent grew from 39.7 million to 116.6 million, an increase of 193 percent, with the greatest growth being seen in sub-Saharan nations. This rapid growth is most evident in more recent years given the fact that from 1989 to 1998 the estimated number of Catholics increased from 85.6 million to 116.6 million.[1] In a number of sub-Saharan nations, Roman Catholics constitute a very high percentage of the national populations. In both Rwanda and the Democratic Republic of Congo, over 50% of the population is Catholic, in Angola 58% is Catholic, in Burundi 62%, Equatorial Guinea 86%, Seychelles 90%, and Cape Verde 96%.[2] In addition to these increases in the total numbers of Catholics, there have also been marked increases in the numbers of ordained clergy and religious. While in other parts of the world the number of priests has remained steady or has fallen, since 1993 the number of priests in Africa has increased at a rate of approximately 600 per year. This increase is mainly due to the fact that from 1993-1998 the number of ordinations per year rose from 737 to 1,071, an increase of over 45%. In the same period, the numbers of women religious also rose from 46,224 to 51,304, an increase of 11%.[3]

In terms of education and health care, two primary focus areas for any development strategy, the Catholic Church plays a vital role on the African continent. As of December, 1998, the Catholic Church maintained 29,824 primary or elementary schools serving 9.6 million children, 6,754 secondary schools serving 1.9 million high school-aged students, and its universities and institutes of higher education had over 62,000 students enrolled. As with population figures, a majority of these educational institutions are located in sub-Saharan Africa. In the Democratic Republic of Congo there are 6,502 primary and 2,074 secondary schools, in Kenya 5,117 primary and 1,139 secondary, and in Uganda 3,466 and 664 respectively. In addition, enrollment in Catholic universities and institutes of higher education stood at 23,485 in Kenya, 11,577 in Rwanda, and 6,409 in the Democratic Republic of Congo.[4] Because of its ongoing, influential presence in the education of African youth, it has been claimed that without the Church the sub-Saharan educational situation would be "lamentable."[5]

In the area of health care, the Church maintains a large number of hospitals (in some nations more than does the government) and has concentrated its facilities in rural areas where the need is often greater than in the cities. In 1998 there were 817 Catholic hospitals on the continent, 705 orphanages, and 504 homes for the elderly, chronically ill, invalids, and handicapped. Again, as with population figures and the number of educational institutions, a large percentage of these health-care centers are located in sub-Saharan nations. There are 167 Catholic hospitals in the Democratic Republic of Congo, 141 in Nigeria, 59 in Kenya, 46 in South Africa, and 45 in Tanzania. Of the 705 orphanages on the continent as a whole, 122 are located in the Democratic Republic of Congo, 85 in Kenya, and 56 in South Africa. Finally, of the 504 homes for the elderly, chronically ill, invalids, and handicapped that are administered by the Church, 364 are in Tanzania, 207 in Nigeria, 195 in Uganda, 131 in the Democratic Republic of Congo, and 112 in Rwanda.[6]

In addition to its major focus on education and health care, the Catholic Church is also heavily involved in other development-related activities. In various regions of the sub-continent, the Church supports agricultural projects that help local farmers increase production and it also sponsors credit unions which, although small in comparison to national and international financial institutions, offer individuals access to capital to finance projects that will help them move toward self-sufficiency.[7] Aided by the efforts of Church-sponsored organizations such as Caritas International, the African Catholic Church is also heavily involved with crisis relief efforts and has been influential in the growth of so-called "micro-projects" where local communities assume responsibility for installing running water, replanting forests, and providing specialized services for women and children. Furthermore, in some nations the Church is actively involved in "holistic" development programs that teach people how to cope with the changes in their lives, encourage them to think positively about their own talents and abilities, and empower them to take charge of their own futures.

Along with these "behind-the-scenes" efforts, Church officials and Church-based organizations are also becoming more vocal in speaking out against economic injustice and are taking on more active roles in the economic affairs of their respective nations. As will be more fully developed in Chapters Three and Four, many African theologians, individual bishops, and bishops' conferences have spoken out against economic dependency, the forced repayment of foreign debt, and the imposition of structural adjustment. As a concrete example of the contribution made by a Church-based organization, the Jesuit Center for Theological Reflection (JCTR) has served as a prime resource for the Zambian bishops' Justice and Peace Commission in its statements concerning land reform, agriculture, and inflation. Located in the Zambian capital of Lusaka, the JCTR publishes a quarterly bulletin that seeks to "broaden an understanding of the social, economic, political, and cultural issues of the day and promote response to these issues in light of the Church's social teaching."[8] Perhaps even more important than this, the JCTR runs a monthly feature in the Zambian national newspaper where it calculates the monthly cost of living for a typical Zambian family. In calculating this figure, the JCTR clearly demonstrates the ever-increasing cost of living as a result of externally imposed structural adjustment programs, and also the virtual impossibility of an average wage earner to adequately meet the material needs of his or her family. In fact, the JCTR is so well respected in Zambia that other Christian organizations will not speak publicly about economic issues without first checking their figures with it.[9]

However, even with the positive influence it has had on sub-Saharan development, the Church has been a negative force as well. Beginning with the practices and teachings of the missionaries in the colonial period and continuing today with its financial dependence and perceived superiority within society, the African Catholic Church has both consciously and unconsciously undermined efforts at economic development. In the following section I discuss the legacy of the Catholic colonial missionaries and demonstrate how the effects of this legacy continue to haunt the African Church even to this very day.

The Catholic Church and Colonialism

1. Cultural Inferiority

In speaking of the Catholic Church's colonial legacy in sub-Saharan Africa, the primary focus is not on economics but culture. According to Zaïrian[10] theologian Bénézet Bujo, when Catholic missionaries first came to the sub-continent to preach the gospel of Jesus Christ, they, along with their Protestant counterparts, very quickly adopted an attitude of condemnation concerning practically every aspect of traditional African culture. Practices such as polygamy, ancestor remembrance, and virtually any traditional rituals were viewed to be anti-Christian and thus had to be suppressed. Because the African people also did not demonstrate any system of writing or attempt to challenge their teachings in any real way, the early European missionaries mistakenly assumed the indigenous people possessed neither a viable culture nor a viable religion and thus took it upon themselves to teach a faith expression which they believed would bring the African people proper dignity and civilization. As a result, African converts were forced to refute both their culture and their traditional ways of life in order to be accepted into the Christian Church.[11]

Bujo also points out that one of the reasons why Christian missionaries maintained this notion of African cultural inferiority stems from an interpretation of Genesis 9:18-27 where Ham is cursed by his father Noah.[12] As African blacks were believed to have descended from Ham and because Caanan, the son of Ham, was cursed by Noah because of Ham's sin, all black Africans were understood to be cursed as well. Thus, the text from Genesis was interpreted to mean that as blacks were inferior to whites and that every aspect of their lives needed to be "Christianized." As further evidence of this triumphalistic mentality, in 1873 the Council of Indulgences accepted the following prayer for the conversion of Ham's followers in Africa, a prayer that was eventually approved by Pope Pius IX: "Let us pray for the most miserable Ethiopian peoples of Central Africa, who form a tenth of humanity, so that God almighty may take away from their hearts the curse of Ham and give them the blessings of Jesus Christ, our God and Lord." With this prayer in mind it is not difficult to understand how cultural inferiority and the brutal treatment of black Africans (including the slave trade) was, in a sense, "legitimated" by the Catholic Church.[13]

Another stinging critique of the missionary impact on traditional African culture is offered by Cameroonian theologian Fabien Eboussi Boulaga. Eboussi Boulaga repeats that the Catholic and Protestant missionaries who came to Africa simply viewed the indigenous people as pagans who needed to be "humanized," a process that could only happen through introduction of the Christian faith. In fact, he maintains that one of the primary elements that aroused missionary enthusiasm in Africa was the belief that they could assuage the "distress of the retarded pagan peoples" by converting them to Christianity. In order to accomplish this task, Eboussi Boulaga claims the Christian missionaries used a language of derision to ridicule the gods of the "pagan" native Africans, a language of refutation to negate their traditional belief systems, a language of demonstration to teach the Commandments and Christian sacraments, a language of orthodoxy to present the "true" faith to the African people, and a language of conformity to "remodel" the African's understanding of both time and space.[14] Because of the perceived primitive condition of the native peoples, the missionaries believed Africans were "morally incompetent" and thus required protection from themselves. It is precisely because of this perceived incompetence that Eboussi Boulaga believes Christian evangelization and secular colonization can be viewed as complementary phenomena in Africa. Although the two had different origins, participants, and ultimate objectives, each maintained the common goal of rehabilitating the "retarded, fallen" African person.[15]

Eboussi Boulaga's claims are echoed by both historians and other theologians who underscore the often intimate relationship between the Christian missionaries and the secular colonial authorities. Bujo claims the proper functioning of any European colony depended in large measure on the interrelationship between government, commerce, and mission; an interrelationship so important that in colonies where these elements worked together the potential success of the colonial enterprise was greatly enhanced. Thus, in the battles against polygamy,[16] the ancestor cult, and so-called witchcraft or sorcery, the secular colonial authorities had a powerful ally in the Christian missionaries because both believed the traditional belief systems were at odds with the Christian faith and with those social systems which they (the colonizers) believed underlay the well-being of society. In order to have a well-functioning and orderly society both the secular and religious leaders believed the traditional African community had to be transformed into a Western, Christian community. As such, the Europeans took every opportunity to tear down the beliefs and practices of traditional African society and replace them with their own.[17] Historian John Baur adds that Christian missionaries also maintained the colonial assumption of white superiority over the black, an assumption that fostered an attitude of condescension toward the indigenous people and did not allow them to take responsibility for the growth and administration of their own churches. Because of this misguided assumption, the early Christian missionaries oftentimes did too much *for* the African people and not enough *with* them.[18]

There is also evidence that both the colonial secular and religious leaders used each other to strengthen their respective positions on the African sub-continent. Historian Adam Hochschild claims that as the Catholic missionaries in the Belgian Congo were for the most part loyal supporters of Belgium's King Leopold II, they agreed to uphold Leopold's economic and political policies (and also deploy themselves in areas where the king wished to increase the Belgian influence) in exchange for monetary subsidies.[19] Baur adds that at times the Christian missionaries also enlisted European military support both to help them secure specific territories and to protect them from the "advances" of other Christian denominations. As examples, he claims that while Catholic missionaries along the Congo River called upon the French military so that their converts would not fall into the hands of the "heretical Protestants," Presbyterian missionaries in Malawi were calling upon the British to thwart the advances of the "Romish" Portuguese.[20] Because the Christian missionaries relied on secular economic and military support, lent an "aura of respectability" to the overall system of colonialism, and acted as accomplices in the loss of African cultural identity, it can be accurately claimed that in colonial Africa "the cross and the sword arrived together."[21]

2. Christian Missionary Education

Further compounding the negative impact of the colonial Christian missionaries was the educational system they imposed on the African people, one that in many ways mirrored the system imposed by the secular authorities. In the secular realm, the primary purpose of colonial education was to train Africans to fill low-level administrative positions in the European dominated "governments" or to fill similar positions in local private companies. It was not a system that grew out of the African cultural reality nor one that was designed to teach young Africans how to better manage their resources or instill in them a sense of confidence.[22] African students were taught European history and geography while the only mention of Africa itself came in references to the Europeans' victories over its native kings and chiefs. As a result, African youth were taught to admire the colonizers who in fact had "freed" them from the evils of their traditional life. Furthermore, the colonial educational systems taught that Westernization was the means to human advancement because true progress could only occur when Africans abandoned their cultural traditions, their history, and in fact themselves as a people.[23]

It is important to note that the secular educational system was one of the primary means through which the colonial powers impressed upon black Africans that they were inferior to European whites. According to Bujo, black dependence had to be promoted not only in the economic, political, and social structures of colonial Africa, but also in the "psychic sense" of cultural inferiority or the belief among the African people that they were helpless in the face of colonial rule. The reason for this was that the success or failure of the entire colonial enterprise rested on whether the Europeans could maintain a sense of irreversible inferiority within the African people. If at any point the black Africans began to see themselves as equals to the white Europeans, the future of the entire colonial system would be seriously threatened. Thus, the methods of enforcing black inferiority, methods that included education, had to be maintained as an important way of guaranteeing the continued economic success of the colonies.[24]

Unfortunately, these shortcomings within the secular educational systems were also present within those of the Christian missionaries. Historian Walter Rodney claims that because one of Christianity's primary roles in Africa was to "preserve the social relations of colonialism," the missionaries helped to promote the subjugation of the indigenous peoples by emphasizing to them the "virtues" of humility, docility, and acceptance of the prevailing social order. He further maintains that as a condition of their very presence on the African sub-continent, the Christian missionaries as a whole never taught the African people about their fundamental equality before God.[25] For Ugandan theologian Kodwo Ankrah, the deficiencies of the overall missionary program can be summarized under four headings. First, Africans were taught that what really mattered was not this world but the next one, that earthly life simply provided the background to work toward individual salvation and that with "fear, trembling, and patience" they should silently endure the trials and tribulations they encounter. Thus, the colonial Christian missionaries actually "blessed" the oppression of the prevailing social structures. Second, in speaking of divine providence, the missionaries taught the African people that suffering was "permitted" by God as part of the overall plan to bring them to salvation. As such, they were taught to turn the other cheek in the face of oppression, to not be angry or dissatisfied with their lot in life, and to eschew work for revolutionary change in the belief that all things would be rectified in the next world. Third, Africans were taught that because it reflected the relationship between God and humanity, the master/slave relationship was also a part of God's overall plan. In other words, the understanding of "divine lordship" was extended to legitimatize the unequal relationship between Africans and Europeans. Fourth, the doctrine of original sin was presented in such a way that African Christians were never taught to relate the preaching of Christ's gospel with the establishment of justice. Because they were taught that sinful human nature could only breed injustice, Africans learned to overlook societal inequalities and refrain from seeking to bring about justice in the world. As a direct result of these four general trends in its educational programs, colonial Christianity effectively maintained the status of the powerful while promoting the submission of the powerless.[26]

Speaking specifically of Catholic missionaries, the religious education they presented was in many cases "elementary" in that those who embraced the Christian faith were not taught to think for themselves but simply to memorize and repeat its basic tenets. As a result of this inadequate formation, newly-baptized African Catholics often had difficulty defending their faith against the challenges of both the secular universities and other religious traditions (especially Islam). In fact, because they could not adequately respond to these challenges, many African Catholics became disillusioned and even abandoned the faith.[27] In other cases the catechism used by the missionaries to teach the African people was not one that stressed the vitality of the gospel message in their lives, but one that was primarily concerned with how one should live a moral life. Cameroonian Jean-Marc Éla claims the Christian message taught to the indigenous people neglected any historical dimension of God's plan for humanity and reduced the gospel to a text where "every aspect of Christian life was interpreted in moralizing terms." Stated differently, the Catholic missionaries obscured the true gospel message in favor of emphasizing its moral laws and obligations, a practice that both reduced the Word of God to a series of commandments and relegated the faithful to the "demeaning task" of simply receiving these commandments and passing them on in society.[28]

One final shortcoming of Christian missionary education as a whole was that it failed to take into consideration both the African people's traditional world-view and their understanding of the divine. According to Eboussi Boulaga, before colonization and the influence of the Christian missionaries, religion was a metaphor for African life. It entailed people accepting their surroundings and conditions, their place in society, their attachment to the earth, their sense of belonging to a particular group, and how they existed in relationship with both God and life itself. The introduction of Christianity changed all this because the missionaries presented their understandings of the "religious" in terms the native Africans could not easily comprehend. Instead of being expressed through their everyday lives, Africans were taught that the "religious" was contained in a holy book, in an unintelligible creature, and in the transcendent. They were taught to "understand" the divine through concepts they could not comprehend, concepts that taught them life as they understood it was meaningless and what really mattered was an "object of esteem" that could not be physically experienced in this world. As a result of the fact that their "testimony of the senses" was renounced, their "substance of life" was rendered meaningless, and their "devotion" was reduced to an abstract and unintelligible being, Eboussi Boulaga maintains that African acceptance of colonial Christianity was simply an act of voluntarism.[29]

3. Present-Day Results of Catholic Missionary Education

While the shortcomings of missionary educational programs are normally presented within the context of the colonial period, a number of their effects can still be seen today. According to Bishop Peter Sarpong (Kumasi, Ghana), not only is the relevance of the Catholic faith being questioned today by the "enlightened elements" in African cities, but the Church itself "does not appear to be speaking" to the common person nor does it maintain the "same grip" on them as do the traditional African religions. The reason for this is that for a large percentage of African Catholics the faith instilled by the Church has remained only superficial or "skin-deep." In other words, because it is presented in a way that does not engage the totality of the African person, many Africans who profess to be Catholic lack both the knowledge and the religious foundation to allow it to actually take root in their lives. Sarpong further claims that as a result of this superficiality, the faith taught by the Church remains inferior to the influences of the traditional African religions, an inferiority best evidenced by the fact that in times of crisis many of the so-called "faithful" abandon the Church and revert back to their "traditional magico-ritualistic devices" such as diviners and witchdoctors for assistance.[30] Thus, it can be said that a syncretism exists within the African Catholic Church, a syncretism expressed in the fact that while many Africans faithfully attend mass and receive the sacraments on Sundays, as soon as they return to their homes they revert back to the beliefs, practices, and rituals of their traditional religions.[31]

Tanzanian theologian Laurenti Magesa also speaks to this syncretism by claiming it exists as a result of a fundamental tension between what he terms "official" and "popular" forms of Christian expression. According to Magesa, "official" Christianity is the faith expression found in the churches, seminaries, and institutes of higher education; yet a vast majority of the African faithful can only incorporate this "official" Christianity into their lives through their traditional cultural expressions, expressions that include the African Traditional Religions. Thus, while many African faithful want to respond to their Christian calling, they feel compelled to do so only if it means not denying their own culture and abandoning both the conception and understanding of the life that defines them as Africans. Magesa also points to the universal character of the Catholic Church as a further reason for the existence of this syncretism or, as he terms it, "dual religious consciousness." Because it is so focused on its universal nature and because its teachings (particularly those concerning moral matters) are understood to be binding on all Catholics, the Church cannot take into consideration all of the unique situations facing the local African communities. As a result, when people are faced with a difficult decision they have the choice of either following the practices of their traditional religions, practices that are both understandable and relevant to their own situations, or they can follow the teachings of Rome that do not spring from their own reality and that may or may not be relevant for the particular situation at hand.[32]

In connection with this problem of syncretism, Bishop Sarpong and British theologian Aylward Shorter both claim that the lack of connection between the Christian faith and people's everyday lives has caused many African Catholics to leave the Church in favor of the many sects (both Christian and non-Christian) that in recent years have sprung up on the sub-continent. These sects have been very successful in attracting new members because they offer their followers practical solutions to complex problems and also provide them with security, cultural identity, and a true sense of community. Both Sarpong and Shorter recognize that because the number of people joining these sects is only expected to increase in the future, the exodus of the faithful quite possibly poses the greatest challenge to the future of the African Catholic Church.[33]

One final present-day effect of the Christian educational legacy concerns the sense of individuality the missionaries helped to instill in their African converts. According to theologian Eugene Hillman, C.S.SP., the heavy emphasis the missionaries placed on the individual (an emphasis that reinforced the individuality of the secular educational systems) was a "disintegrating" force on African culture because it helped to negate the essentially social nature of traditional African society. In short, both the secular and religious educational systems taught Africans to become more competitive and also increased the sense of "every man for himself." Hillman argues that although these individualist "virtues" may be representative of the West, they are not representative of traditional African society and they are not the virtues Jesus taught his followers; a reality that may indicate that Western culture is less congenial to the Christian faith than is the culture of traditional African society.[34]

In concluding this brief discussion of the Catholic Church's colonial record in sub-Saharan Africa, one can rightfully claim that its legacy (as well as the legacy of Christianity in general) is at best dubious. Although the Church did help to bring Christianity to the African sub-continent, many of its practices and teachings have undermined both human dignity and efforts to fully inculturate the Christian faith into the everyday lives of the people. While the overall effects of colonialism are still being felt in the African Catholic Church today, other more contemporary issues also play an important role in determining the Church's role in sub-Saharan economic development. In the following section I demonstrate how the African Church's financial dependence along with the formation and focus of its clergy undermine its relevancy in present-day African society. This question of relevancy is especially important because if the African faithful do not believe their Church is either concerned with or willing to speak to the realities they face in their everyday lives, then they will not recognize it as a viable agent to help bring about true economic development.

Relevance of the Present-day African Catholic Church

1. Financial Dependence

The first area where the Catholic Church has a relevancy problem in sub-Saharan Africa concerns its own financial dependence. As a whole, the African Catholic Church is so dependent upon foreign donations that should financial assistance be cut-off or even significantly reduced it would seriously threaten the Church's very existence.[35] The primary reason for this dependence is that for the most part Church membership consists of poor peasants who have very little (if anything) to contribute in terms of financial resources. Thus, simply as a result of the poverty endemic to the continent as a whole, many local churches are dependent upon the contributions of foreign donors.

However, continental poverty is only one reason for this dependency. A second and more controversial reason concerns the standard of living enjoyed by members of the Catholic clergy. On the whole, this standard is significantly higher than that of the common person, it is beyond the financial means of the Church to support, and it is one that can be maintained only through the support of foreign donations.[36] Former Malawian bishop Patrick Kalilombe claims that one reason for this higher standard of living is what he terms the confusion between *unity* and *uniformity*, the belief that in order to maintain unity with their Catholic counterparts in the rest of the world the local African churches must imitate them in every detail. According to Kalilombe, the local churches maintain a "model" which they believe is the standard for what they should be and as such feel "inferior" or "substandard" if they cannot conform to it. Since they perceive clergy members in other parts of the world to be well fed, well clothed, and generally lacking no material need, the local African churches believe they must do the same. As a result, these churches burden themselves with providing trappings for the clergy that they (the churches) cannot afford. Unfortunately, by providing these trappings, the churches needlessly consume valuable resources and thus further deepen their dependency on foreign financial sources.[37]

A second relevancy problem regarding the inflow of foreign money concerns the gap or sense of separation it creates between clergy and faithful. Because they often drive fancy cars, live in nice homes, and generally enjoy a higher standard of living than does the average lay person, the African Catholic clergy is viewed by many in society as an exclusive club or social "caste" that has set itself apart from those it is entrusted to serve. In fact, their material wealth causes many African faithful to view the priest as a member of the upper class who no longer regards the lives of the common people as his primary concern.[38] Tanzanian Spiritan Rogath Kimaryo, C.S.Sp., claims this sense of separation also exists as a result of a "deformed mentality" within many Africans concerning the function of both the white missionary and the native African priest. The white missionary is viewed as autonomous, lacking for no material need, and one who maintains a seemingly endless supply of money to build churches, schools and hospitals so long as the people profess faith in his own religious tradition. A similar type of mentality exists in regards to native Africans who are ordained to the Catholic clergy. Because most Africans (including some seminarians) do not understand how a priest receives his income or how he supports himself financially, they believe that as a result of his ordination he moves into a "special mystery clan" and thus becomes a "mystery" to both his family and his community.[39] Further contributing to this sense of separation is the perception that it is the clergy themselves who benefit most from the infusion of foreign aid. Nigerian Elochukwu Uzukwu, C.S.Sp., maintains that when African bishops and missionaries travel to Europe and the United States to collect money for the "Church's work," in reality they are collecting money that will be used primarily for the upkeep of the clergy and those in religious life. The needs of catechists, hospitals, schools, and the poor themselves remain secondary because they only receive funds after the "major needs" of the clergy have been met.[40]

One additional reason why foreign dependence has helped to create a gap between clergy and faithful concerns the mentality of privilege maintained by many within the African Church. Laurenti Magesa argues that as a result of its monetary power, its "tiers of entitlement and rank," and also because the early European missionaries adopted a "complex of superiority," from its very beginning in Eastern Africa the Catholic clergy has maintained a mentality of privilege within society. This mentality of privilege continues today through clergy members who assume privileged sociological and theological understandings of themselves in relation to those who do not hold leadership positions within the Church.[41] One recognizes this mentality through the various attitudes the African faithful maintain toward the ordained clergy, attitudes that include: "You have finally made it!", "You are not like us!", and "Tell us what to do."[42] According to Magesa, this mentality of privilege is a major cause of discontent within the East African Church because it hinders practical creativity and also fosters a paternalistic clergy/laity relationship instead of one that is characterized by learning, sharing, and mutual cooperation.[43]

A third relevancy problem for the African Catholic Church regarding the inflow of foreign financial assistance concerns the conformity it breeds with the Church of Rome. Uzukwu maintains that because African seminarians are not taught to provide for their own material needs (in fact all material needs are provided for them), dependency is ingrained within candidates for the priesthood from day-one. In other words, because their seminary training does not teach them to be self-sufficient, when the candidate is ordained he is not able to adequately care for himself and therefore remains dependent on external donors for his day-to-day existence. This ingrained dependency also functions as a system of control because the priest knows that if he offends his benefactors he runs the risk of jeopardizing or even losing his external financial support. For Uzukwu, this is the main problem with foreign financial dependency. So long as members of the clergy (especially bishops) are concerned primarily with the reactions of foreign donors, they remain incapable of seeing, judging, and acting in a responsible manner toward the many problems facing both Church and society. Thus, foreign dependency assures that subservience and obedience are the "first law in the administration of the church," and also ensures the continuation of the Church's "pyramidal command structure."[44]

Aylward Shorter agrees that financial dependence is a "serious handicap" for the local African Churches, however he adds that in cases where there has been disagreement or differing points of view, the Church of Rome has also used both the granting and withholding of aid to manipulate African church leaders, religious communities, and development directors to adopt its (Rome's) own policies. Shorter also cites situations where African bishops have exercised a form of censorship over the African Catholic press because they (the bishops) believe any printed material that maintains the title "Catholic" must exclusively reflect the teachings of the papal magisterium. Therefore, just as secular forms of foreign aid include "conditionalities" to promote the donors' own particular interests, clerical dependency contributes to the inequality between the churches of Africa and those of the West because it effectively silences voices for reform and also "keeps the reins of Church power firmly in Western hands."[45]

A final consequence of foreign financial dependency concerns what might be best termed the "authentic-ness" of the African Catholic Church. Laurenti Magesa claims that because the Church of Rome (along with other Western churches) has continually provided necessary financial support, it has been able to shape both the structures of the African Church and the expression of African Catholicism into what it (Rome) believes they should be. Unfortunately, although many Africans would prefer to organize their churches and express their faith in ways that are different from what Rome commands, because of this financial dependence the African hierarchy is very hesitant to discuss, much less implement, any significant changes. Therefore, for Magesa, the "true cost" of financial dependence is that it has caused the African Church to express a faith that is not its own, organize itself in ways that are foreign to the African experience, and in reality "remain predominately an object and not a subject of its own history."[46]

Other theologians agree with Magesa's claim. Jean-Marc Éla holds that financial dependence is one of the primary elements in the overall "unjust relationship" between the African churches and those of Europe and North America. Because the African Catholic Church was founded by white missionaries and continues to be supported, maintained, and directed today by predominately white Westerners, Éla questions the true relevance it can have in the lives of the African people. Can white Westerners authentically root the gospel message in black African culture or can they really know what is necessary for the Christian faith to take hold in the lives of black Africans? Although these questions are asked rhetorically, Éla's obvious implication is that they cannot. He continues by claiming that because Latin Christianity maintains such a heavy influence on the orientation and practice of pastoral theology and because local churches almost completely lack the initiative to both reflect upon and research the "problems of faith" from the African perspective, the African Church also suffers from what he terms a "genuine underdevelopment in theology." In fact, Éla argues that so long as the African churches are not able to take on their own personality, Christianity will remain a religion of the "whites."[47]

Elochukwu Uzukwu also echoes Magesa by claiming in a rather provocative statement that the type of foreign aid currently being received by the African Catholic Church may not be in the best interests of sub-Saharan Africa. While admitting this may sound somewhat irresponsible at first, he claims that the aid the Church receives only allows it to practice a form of "ambulance ministry" for the poor, one that only provides for temporary relief. In a more fundamental program for action, he believes the Church must start looking toward the root causes of the sub-continent's social problems, plunge itself into a critical analysis of the African reality, and then, based upon its own social teachings, clearly state the necessary "principles of reflection, norms for judgement, and directives [for] action."[48]

2. Formation and Focus of the Clergy

In addition to its financial dependence, further relevancy questions facing the African Catholic Church concern both the formation of its clergy and the issues upon which it tends to focus its attention. Because they are educated in a universally standardized program (the same as would be any European or American) and thus never learn about traditional African culture, religion, or society, newly ordained African priests are oftentimes rendered "irrelevant" to the people they are supposed to serve. In other words, when these priests are "resocialized" into a local community following their ordinations they are incapable of functioning with people who still maintain traditional customs and beliefs.[49] Also, the pre-Vatican II model of formation that still exists in most African seminaries tends to instill a sense of fear among seminarians, a fear that inhibits both personal and spiritual growth and teaches them not to take initiative but to obey their superiors without question. In addition, the African model of clerical formation does not train the future priest to work in collaboration with parishioners or help him to empower people to assume responsibility for their own development. As such, it is not a model that teaches seminarians to employ their own particular talents and take responsibility for the future mission of the Church.[50]

Further undermining the Church's relevancy in African society are the issues upon which the clergy often focuses its attention, a problem that is manifested on both the universal and local levels. On the universal level, Jean-Marc Éla claims the Church of Rome runs the risk of marginalizing the problems of the Third World[51] as a whole because it is too preoccupied with its "three-dimensional universe" centered on the doctrines of sin, grace, and the sacraments. While not claiming sin, grace, and the sacraments are unimportant, he argues that Rome focuses on them to the detriment of the issues that preoccupy the churches of the Third World, namely poverty, hunger, and oppression. Similarly on the local level, Éla claims the "sensitive topics" that "raise questions of conscience" for the African clergy are topics that have little or no relevance for the common person. The clergy focuses its attention on maintaining religious rites and customs while the common person is primarily concerned with access to a balanced diet, safe drinking water, and both adequate healthcare and education. Éla further claims that when determining how a local Church will act in a particular situation, clergy members rarely make an effort to see what is actually happening within a particular area. Instead, by continually trying to insert universal Church teachings into specifically African situations, they ignore the real needs of the common people, reproduce models of the Church's hierarchy that have never been examined in specific African contexts, and reduce the role of the laity to simply obeying what is decreed to them "from above."[52]

3. The Church and Ethnic Tensions: The Case of Rwanda

One cannot conclude any overview of the Catholic Church's history in sub-Saharan Africa without at least briefly mentioning the role it played in fostering the ethnic tensions that culminated in the 1994 Rwandan genocide. Throughout its modern history the population of Rwanda has consisted of two primary ethnic groups, the Hutus and the Tutsis, yet in spite of this its population has remained predominantly Catholic.[53] This high percentage of Catholics was due in large measure to first German and then Belgian missionaries who converted large numbers of people during the early years of European colonization and then played a major role in forming the emerging Rwandan nation. However, instead of working to mitigate tensions between the two ethnic groups and teaching them to work together for the common good, the missionaries' actions actually exacerbated the differences between them. As the secular colonial powers concentrated wealth and power in the hands of the Tutsi rulers even though they only accounted for fifteen percent of the population, the missionaries (particularly the Belgians) also singled out the Tutsis as "natural overlords" and thus further solidified the divisions between them and their Hutu rivals. This situation remained intact from the late nineteenth century until the end of the 1950s, a period in which the minority Tutsis increasingly strained ethnic tensions by favoring their own interests and increasingly excluding the majority Hutus from educational and employment opportunities.

However, by the late 1950s many Catholic missionaries were becoming increasingly distressed by the injustices of the Tutsi leadership and began to actively promote the interests of the Hutus. The missionaries worked to better educate Hutus and also supported them in their successful revolt (1959-1962) in which they seized power from the Tutsis. As a result of both this aid and support, from 1959 to 1994 the Rwandan Catholic leadership enjoyed the favor of the Hutu government and maintained very close relationships with its high ranking political officials. Unfortunately these relationships would remain intact even in light of the injustices which began to be perpetrated by the now-ruling Hutus. For example, the first Hutu president Gregoire Kayibanda, a former editor of the Catholic-sponsored newspaper *Kinyamateka* and director of "Trafipro," a Catholic cooperative, enjoyed the seemingly unquestioned support of the Church even though his regime openly appealed to ethnic hostility in an effort to strengthen its political power. Under Kayibanda's rule, Tutsis were increasingly forced out of their government offices, their political organizations were dissolved, and some of their leaders were even executed. After rival Hutu Juvenal Habyarimana came to power (as the result of a July, 1973 coup d'etat), support from the Church remained intact even though by the mid 1980s the Rwandan economy was in a shambles, ethnic tensions between the Hutus and Tutsis were running high, and Habyarimana was favoring his own home region in terms of both creating jobs and benefiting from government expenditures (once again clientelism).[54]

In light of these Hutu injustices, from the late 1980s to early 1990s the Rwandan Catholic hierarchy issued a number of pastoral statements in which it criticized the government's ethnic and regional biases, its nepotism, and its misuse of public funds. However these statements were greeted with a fair degree of public cynicism because they remained vague, non-specific, and refused to name those responsible for injustices even though it was widely known who was responsible. In addition, these statements appeared to treat prejudice, violence, and corruption as "aberrations" rather than as systemic problems and also presented President Habyarimana as an advocate of good government, democracy, and national unity when in fact he participated in ethnic violence, corruption, and resistance to democratic change. One probable reason for the Church's lackluster criticism is the fact that both church and state leaders oftentimes shared similar interests concerning the "control" of Rwandan society, a situation demonstrated by the fact that until 1985 the Archbishop of Kigali (the Rwandan capital) served as a member of the Hutu ruling party's central committee and also acted as the personal confessor to President Habyarimana's wife. It is also argued the Church turned a blind eye to government injustices in return for the prestige and influence that came with having almost unquestioned control over education, health care, and development within the nation as a whole.[55] Further adding to these difficulties was the fact that ethnic tensions were also prevalent within the Church itself. Rwandan bishops who were predominately Hutu tended to dominate a clergy that was mostly Tutsi, and in the months leading up to the 1994 genocide some Church leaders openly aligned themselves with one ethnic group against the other.[56] Thus, although the Rwandan Catholic Church was not directly responsible for the 1994 genocide, it was not an innocent bystander either. Through its colonial preference for the Tutsis, its post-colonial preference for the Hutus, its relative silence when confronted with injustice, and its inability to address ethnic divisions within itself, the Catholic Church has arguably caused more harm in Rwanda than it has accomplished good.[57]

So what can be done? What can the African Catholic Church do to make both its teachings and its presence more relevant to the common African person? In the final section of this chapter I present the responses of four African theologians who address these very questions. In short, they believe the key to the Church's continued relevance lies in practical action.

Toward the Future: The Church and Practical Action

For a number of African theologians, one response to the question of relevance lies in the belief that the Church must become more intimately involved in the concrete lives of those it is mandated to serve. Laurenti Magesa claims that while there is certainly an important role for the numerous theological, pastoral, and catechetical statements that have emanated from the East African Church over the past thirty years, these statements are limited in that they can only underscore the theoretical aspirations the Church maintains in the region. In other words, if one wishes to speak of how the Church truly fulfills its vocation to the world, focusing solely on these statements will be neither sufficient nor very useful. Instead, Magesa claims that in order for true evangelization to occur, the Church must focus on practical action because it is only through acting concretely in the lives of the people that true evangelization can take place. If the work of evangelization remains solely in the theoretical realm it has no chance of taking root in the actual lives of the people. Without practical action, true evangelization is next to impossible.[58]

Other African theologians echo Magesa's concerns. South African Emmanuel Martey claims the transformations of African society from rural to urban and agricultural to industrial pose profound challenges for Christian theology because both transformations have led to greater poverty, inequality, and exploitation of the masses. In addition, the policies imposed by the World Bank and International Monetary Fund also pose challenges for Christian theology because by being so focused on reducing government spending and restructuring foreign debts, Western bureaucrats fail to take into consideration the social and economic impacts their policies have had on real human beings. Martey holds that instead of leading to development, many of these policies appear to have been designed to further aggravate dependency, poverty, inequality, subservience, and vulnerability within the African sub-continent. In the end, he argues that because of the sheer scale of poverty that exists in Africa today, one cannot "do" theology in Africa without taking into consideration the actual conditions under which its people live.[59]

Taking this claim one step further, Bishop Peter Sarpong believes that what the African Catholic Church truly needs is a theology with two new foci. First, it needs a theology that is based on the African reality, one that has the ability to "touch the heart" of the simple, common person. He claims this new focus is necessary because so long as its theology remains grounded in Aristotelian Thomism, the Church will continue to "talk over the heads of the faithful" and thus remain removed from those at the grass-roots level. Second, Sarpong also claims the African Church must refocus its theology so that it speaks to the African people in their "existential condition." In other words, the Church needs to better demonstrate how its theology relates to the people's actual living conditions, and also how God's Word contains a reassuring message for those who suffer from hunger, poverty, oppression, and disease.[60]

Speaking then of the interrelation between poverty, hunger and disease (the so-called "trinity of human evils"), Sarpong claims: "Here the rigid dichotomy between evangelization and human development, the sacred and the profane, spirit and matter, becomes artificial." In other words, because of the realities faced by the African people, he rejects any claim that the Church's sole mission is to prepare people for salvation in the next world. Instead, the Church's overall mission must also include a deep concern for this world and thus it must work for real, concrete change in people's temporal lives. Sarpong's rationale for this position is that because humanity is comprised of body, soul, mind, and spirit, and because to "truncate" or "dismember" any of these elements is to destroy the human person's very essence, then the African people's deplorable economic situation necessarily affects their spiritual lives in a profoundly negative way. In light of this reality, it is vitally important for the Church to help improve the economic situation of the African people, to liberate them from oppression, and to help them rebuild those aspects of their spiritual lives that have been stunted or destroyed by the poverty they endure on a daily basis. As such, he claims "the religious function of the Church in Africa must go hand in hand with a genuine effort at improving socioeconomic conditions for the masses of people," otherwise the Church's influence and credibility will be "shattered to pieces."[61]

Finally, Jean-Marc Éla argues that the reality of post-independence Africa poses a profound challenge to the Church and in fact forces the Church to redefine itself in light of the social difficulties faced by the African people. In light of the oppression, exploitation, and even murder that is rampant on the continent, he claims the Church cannot sit back and be content with the number of people it has baptized or with its liturgies that employ native languages and customs. Instead, its message must be one that challenges domination because the "locus of rediscovering the Gospel nature of the Church" can only be found in liberating people from oppression.[62]

In a strikingly poignant paragraph that captures the heart of his teaching, Éla claims that as a result of the "irruption" of poverty on the African continent, any discussion of the Church's temporal mission must include practical action at the grassroots level:

> Evangelizing people shaped by a certain culture must go hand in hand with their struggle for development in all aspects of their lives. Hence, the work of our faith must be understood in reference to the overall situation in Africa today. We must deal with down-to-earth questions, and get back to ground level where the Kingdom of God is built day by day. For the hope for a new world that is built in the framework of justice, peace, and freedom is the heart of the Christian message. We must get involved in this experience and use it as our

> starting-point for a radical critique of all that is happening before our eyes. This is the only source of energy that will impel us to interpret Christian responsibilities in the current context of black Africa."[63]

Thus, Éla believes the Church can not simply "look down" upon conflict in the world and remain isolated from the struggles that will help to shape both its own future and the future of humanity as a whole. Instead, in order for it to be credible in the eyes of the people, the Church must combat injustice by confronting the "forces of inertia in society," and in doing so it must be willing to become, as Christ was when he challenged the prevailing powers of his own time, an object of intimidation and threats. Although the Church's primary mission is "other-worldly," the reality of African life today demands that it challenge any unjust institution, structure, ideology, or social category. Only in doing so will it both preach and embody a faith that is credible in the eyes of those whom it is mandated to serve.[64]

With an understanding of the economic difficulties facing sub-Saharan Africa and the influences (both positive and negative) that the Catholic Church has had in the region, I now turn to the main focus of this study: the African Catholic Church's contribution to the construction of an African theology of economic development. In the next chapter, I concentrate on the contributions of theologians Engelbert Mveng, SJ, Jean-Marc Éla, and Laurenti Magesa to demonstrate how their three expressions of African liberation theology speak to the concrete economic realities of present-day African life.

Notes

[1] Population figures taken from the *Annuarium Statisticum Ecclesiae* (Vatican City: Libreria Editrice Vaticana) 1970, 1989, and 1998 editions. In the 1970 edition see the population table on page 57; in the 1989 and 1998 editions see Table I-a: "Estimates of Population and Catholics," page 18 in both editions.

[2] *Annuarium Statisticum Ecclesiae*, 1998 edition, 64-65.

[3] Ibid., 78, 81, 171-172 and 208-209.

[4] Ibid., 271-271.

[5] Peter K. Sarpong, "Setting Priorities for the Church: A View from Africa," in *American Catholic Identity: Essays in an Age of Change*, ed. Francis J. Butler (Kansas City, MO: Sheed and Ward, 1994), 250-266 at 260.

[6] *Annuarium Statisticum Ecclesiae*, 1998 edition, 344-345.

[7] Sarpong, 260. See also Paul Gifford, *African Christianity: Its Public Role* (London: Hurst & Co., 1998), 65-66 and 224-226.

[8] See the mission statement of the JCTR Bulletin which is available on-line at *http://www.jctr.org.zm/bulletin.*

[9] Gifford, 225-226.

[10] At the time when he was writing the works cited in this study, Bujo's native country was still known as Zaïre. Today it is the Democratic Republic of the Congo.

[11] See Bénézet Bujo's *The Ethical Dimension of Community: The African Model and Dialogue Between North and South* (Nairobi, Kenya: Paulines Publications Africa, 1998), 137, 162; and also his *African Theology in its Social Context*, translated by John O'Donohue (Maryknoll, NY: Orbis Books, 1992), 44-45.

[12] "When he (Noah) drank some of the wine, he became drunk and lay naked inside his tent. Ham, the father of Canaan, saw his father's nakedness, and he told his two brothers outside about it. Shem and Japeth, however, took a robe, and holding it on their backs, they walked backward and covered their father's nakedness; since their faces were turned the other way they did not see their father's nakedness. When Noah woke up from his drunkenness and learned what his youngest son had done to him, he said: 'Cursed be Canaan! The lowest of the slaves he shall be to his brothers.'" (NAB).

[13] Bénézet Bujo, *The Ethical Dimension of Community*, 135. See also John Baur's *2000 Years of Christianity in Africa: An African Church History* (Nairobi, Kenya: Paulines Publications Africa), 421.

[14] Fabien Eboussi Boulaga, *Christianity Without Fetishes: An African Critique and Recapture of Christianity*, translated by Robert R. Barr (Maryknoll, NY: Orbis Books, 1984), 30-43.

[15] Ibid, 20-21.

[16] According to Eugene Hillman, C.S.Sp., an American theologian long active in Africa, one of the main reasons why polygamous marriages existed in traditional African society concerned economics. The family needed many children in order to perform the various tasks (farming, hunting, etc.) necessary for survival. Because children acted as the family's primary labor force, the economic viability of a family was directly proportional to the number of children it had. Because of the high child mortality rate, families would have to produce many children simply to assure that enough would survive to adulthood. Having more than one wife helped a man ensure an adequate number of children to maintain the family. See Hillman's *Polygamy Revisited: African Plural Marriage and the Christian Churches* (Maryknoll, NY: Orbis Books, 1975), 88-93.

[17] Bujo, *African Theology in its Social Context*, 41-43.

[18] Baur, 422. See also Rodrigo Mejia SJ's "Foreign Missionaries at the Eve of the African Synod," *African Ecclesial Review* 35 (1993), 145.

[19] Adam Hochschild, *King Leopold's Ghost* (Boston: Houghton Mifflin Company, 1998), 134.

[20] See Baur, 420.

[21] These are the conclusions of both Africanist theologian Eugene Hillman, C.S.Sp., and the Third General Assembly of the Ecumenical Association of Third World Theologians (EATWOT). See Hillman's *Toward an African Christianity: Inculturation Applied* (Mahwah, NJ: Paulist Press, 1993), 8; and EATWOT's "The Statement of the Assembly: A Cry for Life," in *Spirituality of the Third World: A Cry For Life*, eds. K.C. Abraham & Bernadette Mbuy-Beya (Maryknoll, NY: Orbis Books, 1992), 203.

[22] Walter Rodney, *How Europe Underdeveloped Africa* (Washington DC: Howard University Press, 1974), 240-241.

[23] See Bujo, *The Ethical Dimension of Community*, 138; Hillman, *Toward an African Christianity*, 8; and J. Milburn Thompson, *Justice and Peace: A Christian Primer* (Maryknoll, NY: Orbis Books, 1997), 14. For more information on the colonial education system see Jan Vansina's "A Clash of Cultures: African Minds in the Colonial Era," in *African History: From Earliest Times to Independence*, ed. Philip Curtin et. al. (New York: Longman, 1995), 469-489 at 480-485;

[24] Bujo, *African Theology in its Social Context*, 43.

[25] Rodney, 252-253. See also Vansina, 470-473.

[26] Kodwo E. Ankrah, "Church and Politics in Africa," in *African Theology En-Route*, eds. Kofi Appiah-Kubi & Sergio Torres (Maryknoll, NY: Orbis Books, 1979), 155-161 at 157. It should be noted that Ankrah is not speaking specifically of Catholic missionary education but of Christian missionary education as a whole. For further information see Damaris K. M'mworia's "Theological Basis for the Church Involvement in Social Justice," *African Ecclesial Review* 40 (1998), 281; and Marie Giblin's "Taking Africa Seriously: The Challenge of Liberation Theology," *African Ecclesial Review* 30 (1988), 291.

[27] Joseph C. McKenna, *Finding a Social Voice: The Church and Marxism in Africa* (New York: Fordham University Press, 1997), 62.

[28] Jean Marc Éla, *My Faith as an African*, translated by John Brown and Susan Perry (Maryknoll, NY: Orbis Books, 1988), 163-164.

---

[29] Eboussi Boulaga, 27-28.

[30] Sarpong, 251-254. As another example of this syncretism, Steven Bwana claims that oftentimes either right before or right after a Catholic wedding ceremony the marrying couple will have another ceremony performed which "observes the traditional rites" of their particular African society. See Steven Bwana's "The Impact of the New Code in Africa," in *Canon Law-Church Reality: Concilium, 185*, ed. James Provost and Knut Walf (Edinburgh: T&T Clark, 1986), 103-109 at 106-107.

[31] I understand syncretism as the practice of combining nonconforming African and Christian teachings or practices. Seeking out and following the advise of a witchdoctor would be a practical example of syncretism. This differs from inculturation whereby Christian teachings and practices are introduced into African society (and vice versa) in a manner that does not theologically compromise either's teachings or practices but instead demonstrates the complementarity between them.

[32] See Laurenti Magesa's *African Religion: The Moral Traditions of Abundant Life* (Maryknoll, NY: Orbis Books, 1997), 9-10; and "Africa's Struggle for Self-Definition During a Time of Globalization," *African Ecclesial Review* 40 (1998), 326.

[33] See Sarpong, 256-257; and Aylward Shorter, "The Roman Catholic Church in Africa Today," in *Christianity in Africa in the 1990s*, ed. Christopher Fyfe and Andrew Walls (Edinburgh: Centre of African Studies, 1996), 22-38 at 25-26. Jean-Marc Éla adds that after more than a century of missionary work on the sub-continent there are few Africans who really feel at home in the Church. Although many people profess faith in a church where the catechism is taught and the sacraments are practiced, this church is nothing more than a "frame" or an "empty shell" because the Christianity introduced by the missionaries remains unintelligible to the African masses and supplies few, if any, answers to the practical problems of everyday life. See Jean Marc Éla, *My Faith as an African*, 33-34.

[34] Hillman, *Toward an African Christianity*, 22.

[35] It should be noted that these "foreign donors" consist of more than simply the Vatican. In fact, Paul Gifford claims that most of the money that

reaches the African Catholic Church comes from the personal contacts of Church officials and from Western foundations or agencies. See Gifford, 311.

[36] Shorter, 24.

[37] Patrick A. Kalilombe, "Self-Reliance of the African Church: A Catholic Perspective," in *African Theology En-Route*, eds. Kofi Appiah-Kubi & Sergio Torres (Maryknoll, NY: Orbis Books, 1979), 36-58 at 43-44, 55.

[38] See Shorter, 24 and Gifford, 312. Paul Gifford also claims that as both economic conditions and employment opportunities on the sub-continent have steadily deteriorated over the past twenty years, the priesthood and religious life have become increasingly attractive options for many African males even if they do not have the necessary faith commitment. In making this claim, Gifford cites Rev. Timothy Njoya, a Presbyterian minister who claims that over ninety percent of the clergy in Kenya do not have a true calling but have joined the ministry because they could not have had a better secular career. See Gifford, 345.

[39] Rogath Kimaryo, C.S.Sp., "A Call to Africa to Shake Off The Dependent Syndrome," *African Ecclesial Review* 39 (1997), 32-33.

[40] Elochukwu Uzukwu, C.S.Sp., *A Listening Church: Autonomy and Communion in African Churches* (Maryknoll, NY: Orbis Books, 1996), 90. See also Telesphore George Mpundu's "The Church's Life Style in the Context of Africa's," *African Ecclesial Review* 37 (1995), 275.

[41] Laurenti Magesa, "The Church in Eastern Africa: Retrospect and Prospect," in *How Local is the Local Church? Small Christian Communities and Church in Eastern Africa*, ed. Agatha Radoli, SOM (Eldoret, Kenya: AMECEA Gaba Publications, 1993), 3-35 at 9-11.

[42] For these and other attitudes of the faithful toward the clergy, see Peter Kanyandago's "Ordained and Non-Ordained Ministry In the Local Churches of Eastern Africa," in *How Local is the Local Church?* 139-162 at 143-147.

[43] Magesa, 11-12.

[44] Uzukwu, 95-98.

[45] Aylward Shorter, 24, 28-29, 31. See also Adrian Hastings' *African Catholicism: Essays in Discovery* (London: SCM Press, 1989), 134. Related to this issue of foreign control, Hastings claims that during the late 1960s the Vatican was becoming increasingly alarmed with the radical nature of reforms being proposed by the African Church. Because many of these reforms were being proposed by foreign bishops, the Vatican began a process of systematically replacing the "radical" foreigners with native bishops, bishops the Vatican believed would be obedient and who could be controlled (he specifically cites the "forced" resignations of Bishops Patrick Kalilombe of Lilongwe, Malawi and Emmanuel Milango of Lusaka, Zambia) . The strategy, Hastings claims, worked because as the 1970 progressed the numbers of "radicals" in positions of authority gradually waned and the African Catholic Church became a "Church of silence" (131).

[46] Magesa, 14-15.

[47] See Jean-Marc Éla's *African Cry*, translated by Robert R. Barr (Maryknoll, NY: Orbis Books, 1986), 105-112; and "Le droit à la différence ou l'enjeu actuel des églises locales en Afrique noire," in *Civilization noire et Église catholique: Colloque d'Abidjan 12-17 Septembre, 1977* (Paris: Presence Africaine, 1978), 204-217 at 211.

[48] Uzukwu, 89.

[49] See Hastings, 13 and Hillman, 42-44. Nigerian Chukwudum Okolo agrees by stating that because seminarians focus on academic theology (biblical criticism, Patristics, Medieval studies, the Reformation, and modern-day philosophy and ethics) instead of on the real needs of the people, most newly ordained priests are in fact irrelevant. According to Okolo: "It is no small wonder that such clergymen who are officially designated to 'serve' their people become more dominated by ideas, principles and all sorts of legislations from Rome, America, and Europe than by the sufferings and undeserved predicament of the poor in their native land largely because their formation and educational system are a betrayal to their world. These have geared them to aim at a Western "ideal" of Christianity and priestly training. This no doubt is the capital crisis in the African Church today." See Okolo's "Diminished Man and Theology: A Third World Perspective," *African Ecclesial Review* 18 (April, 1976), 85.

[50] See British theologian Cecil McGarry, SJ's "Formation of the Agents of Evangelization for the Realities of Africa Today: Its Urgency and Importance," *African Ecclesial Review* 41 (1999), 203-204; and "The Implications of the Synod Discussions for the Church in Africa," *African Ecclesial Review* 37 (1995), 21. For a more detailed overview of the challenges facing the African clergy, see J. N'Guessam Sess, SJ's "Formation of Priests and Religious for a Church that is Family," in *What Happened at the African Synod*? ed. Cecil McGarry, SJ (Nairobi, Kenya: Paulines Publications Africa, 1995), 96-114.

[51] Éla himself uses the term "Third World."

[52] Éla, *My Faith as an African*, 98-99, 120. See also Éla's "Christianity and Liberation in Africa," translated by Robert R. Barr, in *Paths of African Theology*, ed. Rosino Gibellini (Maryknoll, NY: Orbis Books, 1994), 136-153 at 137. Magesa echos Éla here by claiming that as an issue of human dignity the African Catholic Church must more fully welcome the participation of the laity because if they (the laity) do not participate in the Church's decision-making processes they will remain second-class citizens. For Magesa, "To emphasize the hierarchical nature of the Church to the exclusion of practical collegiality and collaboration is to deny the nature of the Church as simultaneously hierarchical as it is a fraternal and sisterly community of believers." See Magesa's "The Church in Eastern Africa: Retrospect and Prospect," 17-18, 23.

[53] Depending upon the source, the percentage of baptized Catholics in Rwanda ranges from fifty to sixty-two percent of the population.

[54] See Gifford, 54-55; and Timothy Paul Longman, "Christianity and Democratization in Rwanda: Assessing Church Responses to Political Crisis in the 1990s," in *The Christian Churches and the Democratization of Africa*, ed. Paul Gifford (Leiden: Brill, 1995), 188-204 at 189-190. For an overview of the Rwandan situation see J. Milburn Thompson's *Justice and Peace: A Christian Primer*, 127-131.

[55] Longman, 194-200.

[56] Gifford, 54-55 and Thompson, 131.

[57] Wolfgang Schonecke, Secretary of the Association of Member Episcopal Conferences of Eastern Africa (AMECEA), claims the Rwandan massacres demonstrate how the Church must always maintain a balance between involvement in politics and distance from the actual political process. In fact, he claims, "The events in Rwanda reinforce a lesson in Church history: a Church too closely aligned with a regime shares its fate." See Schonecke's "Are We Both 'Simple as Doves and Cunning as Serpents?': What Does the Rwandan Tragedy Say to the Church in Africa?" *Catholic International* 5 (December, 1994), 563.

[58] Magesa, "The Church in Eastern Africa: Retrospect and Prospect," 4-5. Chukwudum Okolo underscores Magesa by claiming that as "the aim of the Church's commitment to the poor in Africa is to create a just and equitable social order ... in Africa, too, evangelization has to be seen beyond its vertical dimension, that is to say, in the relationship of individuals to God. The increasing problems of social injustice in the continent make it imperative for the Church to carry on at the same time the twin tasks of humanizing and Christianizing Africans, of freeing them from poverty, ignorance, violence, and disease as well as transforming unjust social structures which breed them." See Okolo's *The Liberating Role of the Church in Africa Today: Spearhead 119* (Eldoret, Kenya: AMECEA Gaba Publications, 1991), 63-64.

[59] Emmanuel Martey, *African Theology: Liberation and Inculturation* (Maryknoll, NY: Orbis Books, 1993), 50-53.

[60] Sarpong, 257-258. Interestingly, Sarpong also points out that many Africans who have gained material wealth through morally objectionable or illegal means are prominent members of the Catholic Church, a situation that is the source of much disillusionment in society and one that causes many to leave the Church (253-254).

[61] Ibid., 263.

[62] Éla, *African Cry*, 7-8

[63] Éla, My *Faith as an African*, 91.

[64] Ibid., 131-134 and *African Cry*, 38.

Chapter Three

Development and African Liberation Theology

South African Emmanuel Martey maintains that there are two primary schools of thought dominant within African theology today, inculturation and liberation. In short, inculturation theology is mainly concerned with integrating the Christian faith into both African cultural life and traditional ways of thinking; liberation theology concerns itself with freeing the African people from any and all forms of anthropological and social oppression. He claims that after the Pan-African Conference of Third World Theologians in 1977, the distinction between the two schools became pronounced resulting in a sense of rivalry between those African theologians who favor inculturation and those who favor liberation. "Inculturationists" believe liberation cannot be the sole expression of African theology because liberation focuses on sociopolitical issues at the expense of indigenization and thus ignores the culture of those it aims to defend. By charging that they focus exclusively on freeing people from oppression in the economic and political realms, inculturationists claim liberation theologians lose sight of the fact that in order to be relevant the Christian faith must first engage people in their cultural realities. For their part, "liberationists" charge that inculturationists often become so "methodologically obsessed" with culture that they fail to recognize the many other dimensions of the present-day African reality. Because inculturation theology focuses so narrowly on how Christianity must appropriate African culture, liberationists charge that inculturationists ignore the oppressive reality of everyday African life.[1] Now, while no reputable African theologian would ever claim that one model should be employed exclusively or that one or the other model is irrelevant to the formation of an African theology of development, the two schools are distinct and should be identified as such.

In presenting the contributions that African theologians have made to the issue of economic development, I focus primarily on three theologians who write from the liberation model. I agree with the liberationist claim that in order to be relevant, any Christian theology must begin by addressing the concrete situations that people face on an everyday basis. Specifically in terms of economic development, the purpose of theological discourse must be to identify the ethical shortcomings associated with both past and present-day economic structures and policies and then offer well-grounded theological arguments whose aim is to empower people to take control of their own economic futures. As such, I concur that the liberation model is the one that can more effectively accomplish this task. This is not to say that African inculturation theology is unimportant or inferior to African liberation theology. In fact, concerning both dialogue with African traditional religion and discussion on specific issues such as liturgy, clerical celibacy, and marriage-issues that pose unique challenges to the African Catholic Church-it is crucial. However, when speaking of economic development, I do not find inculturationist arguments to be either theologically convincing or forceful enough to effect necessary, relevant change.[2]

Therefore, in this chapter I focus on three African theologians who speak from the liberationist model: Engelbert Mveng, SJ (Cameroon), Jean-Marc Éla (Cameroon), and Laurenti Magesa (Tanzania). I aim to demonstrate how their understandings of liberation can be applied to the theological discussion concerning economic development. I focus on these particular theologians for two reasons. First, as I was researching African theology as a whole in preparation for this study, the work of these three theologians continually kept resurfacing, even in the works of other authors. Second, in an article published in 1988 in which he presented an overview of African theology, Nigerian Justin Ukpong, C.S.Sp., identified Mveng, Éla, and Magesa as the primary proponents of African liberation theology.[3] I first examine the work of Engelbert Mveng who demonstrates the importance of a biblically based "spirituality of liberation," establishes the notion of anthropological poverty, and differentiates between the African and Latin American understandings of liberation. Next, I examine the works of both Jean-Marc Éla and Laurenti Magesa to demonstrate how they develop their biblical foundations for liberation, apply their understanding of liberation to specific issues of economic development, and explain the implication of these applications for both the individual Christian and the Church as a whole. In concluding the chapter, I offer my own evaluation of their contributions and suggest which elements might be included in the articulation of an African theology of development.

An African Theology of Liberation: Engelbert Mveng, SJ

1. Definition and Biblical Foundation

In speaking of how African liberation theology speaks to specific issues of economic development, it is important to gain an understanding of what African liberation theology entails. Perhaps the best example of a Catholic theologian who "defines" the African notion of liberation and then describes its relationship to African theology as a whole is the late Cameroonian Jesuit Engelbert Mveng.[4] According to Mveng, there are a number of aspects to consider when speaking of black African theology. First, it should be understood as a theology of the people in that it expresses both their faith and hope and also illustrates the actual experiences of real Christian communities in Africa. As such, black African theology is not "academic" theology, but instead it arises from the realities of people's everyday lives. Second, because it is a theology of the people, black African theology is by definition contextual. One cannot "do" theology in Africa without taking into consideration the domination and oppression of both the slave trade and colonialism, nor also ignore the present-day realities of neo-colonialism, famine, political corruption, instability, and the disregard of basic human rights. Stated differently, black African theology can be understood only within the context of the specific challenges people face in the cultural, political, and economic realms of their lives.[5]

Following from this, Mveng maintains that at its core black African theology is a struggle for spiritual liberation, a struggle that recognizes its theological foundation in the spirituality of the gospel Beatitudes. The true message of the Beatitudes is the proclamation that God's Kingdom characterized by truth, freedom, justice, and love will one day be established atop the "ruins" of this present world, a world characterized by injustice, domination, oppression, and death. However, while awaiting the establishment of this Kingdom, the

Beatitudes call upon people in the Third World[6] as well as the First to adopt a spirituality of liberation, a spirituality that will allow them to choose the "freedom" associated with the building of God's future reign over the "servitude" associated with an acquiescence to this world. In other words, humans are called to embody the Beatitude virtues in their daily lives in order to free both themselves and others from the forces of oppression in the world. Mveng continues by claiming the spirituality of the gospel Beatitudes should not be understood simply as the "eschatological result" of liberation theology, but instead as its foundation. The reason for this is that while one recognizes the spirituality of liberation within liberation theology, this spirituality also demonstrates the "universal character" of liberation theology and that liberation is *the* theology of both the individual Christian and the universal Church as a whole.[7]

In another work, Mveng further underscores this spirituality of liberation by speaking of how the individual strives to overcome evil in the world. In brief, the traditional African world-view recognizes the on-going tension between the "forces of life" (good) and the "forces of death" (evil) that are operative in the world, and also how the struggle between them is manifested in both society and the hearts of individual people. For Mveng, the only way to overcome these "forces of death" is for all people to reexamine their relationships with themselves and others, and then to recast these relationships so that they are not based upon the "arbitrary opinions" of humanity but upon the will of God. Within this recasting of relationships one grounds the liberation of the human person. As a model, Mveng again cites the Matthean Beatitudes whose spirituality he claims celebrates the victory of life over death, love over hate, freedom over servitude, and offers the key to understanding human suffering. The Beatitudes proclaim that the forces of death (poverty, hunger, injustice, humiliation, hate, and violence) will be overcome by the forces of love, and as such they also proclaim the ultimate victory of life over death. Thus, liberation within black African theology is not simply recognized in freedom from oppressive external structures. In order to be effective, liberation begins with the human person through the internal acceptance of the Beatitude virtues.[8]

2. Anthropological Poverty

With this understanding of the spirituality of liberation and how liberation is a vital aspect of black African theology as a whole, the question may be asked, "Liberation from what?" "From what do Africans need to be liberated?" For many African theologians, liberation theology is not seen primarily as a response to oppressive economic and political structures, but instead as a response to the perceived sense of anthropological poverty that prevails on the sub-continent today. As with the spirituality of liberation, this notion of anthropological poverty is best developed by Mveng. He claims anthropological poverty is not simply a lack of material goods but a state of "non-being" that occurs when a people are systematically stripped of everything that constitutes them as human persons. Stated differently, anthropological poverty refers not only to the privation of a person's "possessions" (including those of the material, intellectual, cultural, and sociological orders), but also the privation of everything that makes them a human being:

> When persons are bereft of their identity, their dignity, their freedom, their thought, their history, their language, their faith universe, and their basic creativity, deprived of all their rights, their hopes, their ambitions (that is when they are robbed of their own ways of living and existing) - they sink into a kind of poverty which no longer concerns only exterior or interior goods or possessions but strikes at the very being, essence, and dignity of the human person. It is this poverty which we call anthropological poverty. This is *an indigence of being*.[9]

For Mveng, the source of this anthropological poverty can be traced to both the slave trade and the period of European colonization. The slave trade entailed the "anthropological annihilation" of the African people because in addition to negating what is today termed human rights, its underlying purpose was to deprive Africans of their very humanity. Mveng claims Christianity must also be held partially responsible for this systematic anthropological annihilation because although Christianity's "participation" was indirect, it was the European Christian nations that were most heavily involved in the slave trade and that benefited the most from it. Similarly during the period of colonization from the late nineteenth to mid-twentieth centuries, this sense of anthropological poverty was underscored by the "ethnocide" perpetrated by the European powers. Mveng claims the European colonial policies of dictating to others their own laws, representing themselves as a "superior humanity," and acting as absolute masters over others in effect "grasps at insanity" and is the root cause for the alienation felt by many in sub-Saharan Africa today. Add to this the fact that colonial Christian missionaries refused Africans the right to their own sovereignty in religious/spiritual matters, and one can claim that Christianity acted as an accomplice to secular colonialism. Because each sought to "protect the black African in order to maintain him in a state of inferiority and absolute dependence," Mveng argues that both secular colonization (within which it is assumed he includes the slave trade) and Christian mission are the two primary causes for the anthropological pauperization of the African people.[10]

While anthropological poverty is rooted in Africa's past, it remains an essential factor in understanding the reality of African life today. Primary among these realities is culture. According to Mveng, there has never been a true dialogue between members of the First World and those of the Third World on any substantive issue, but only a monologue of arrogance and derision emanating from the First World to the Third. The reason for this is that Western culture has never accepted the existence of other cultures and in fact it actually reduces the rest of humanity, those of non-Western cultures, to being "simple instruments" in the realization of its own "projected undertakings." However, in addition to its prevalence in the secular realm, this cultural dominance is also evident in the anti-African bias of Western Christianity. Mveng claims that a major obstacle to dialogue between First and Third World Christians is cultural arrogance, a reality evidenced by the fact that Western theology has "monopolized" the Church, the Christian faith, and even Christ himself in an effort to proclaim a universal theology. Further underscoring this point, he maintains there is a flagrant contradiction between Christ's gospel and Western culture because while the gospel preaches compassion and deliverance, Western culture preaches domination and the subjugation of the African people.[11] Because culture is understood as the way one views the human person, the world, and God, and because it is only through one's own culture that both the categories and the language of faith can be grasped and understood, Mveng maintains that theological dialogue between the First and Third Worlds will not be possible until the First World acknowledges the validity of Third World, particularly African, culture.[12]

Another manifestation of anthropological poverty in the present-day can be seen in the way poverty is studied. Mveng argues that poverty has not been adequately addressed in the West primarily as the result of the fact that studies concerning it have centered on underdevelopment, a concept he claims is "nebulous" and one that if accepted by the African people necessarily condemns them to a state of self-imposed inferiority. Reasons for these claims are two-fold. First, when the term "underdevelopment" is used in Western studies it normally carries either a material or sociological connotation. However, because the African understanding of poverty also takes into consideration the "indigence of being," one cannot simply claim that the root cause of African poverty is material or social underdevelopment. In other words, Mveng is saying that in order to fully understand the extent of African *material* poverty, Western academics must first acknowledge the reality of *anthropological* poverty. Second, by accepting the notion of underdevelopment as the primary cause for their material poverty, the poor both relegate and condemn themselves to an inferior social position vis-à-vis those who are "developed." Stated differently, Mveng maintains that if the African people view themselves as "underdeveloped," they place themselves in a position "below" that which the West considers the base level of human dignity. In doing so, they reinforce the stereotype that they are incapable of taking care of themselves, further condemn themselves to a perceived sense of inferiority, and justify the actions of those who dominate and enslave them.[13]

Perhaps the most dramatic consequence of anthropological poverty is the spiritual void that it leaves within the African people. Echoing Bishop Sarpong's claim that prolonged poverty carries with it devastating spiritual consequences,[14] Mveng states that because many Africans have been stripped of their humanity they have become easy prey for the many worldly lures that militate against both the Christian message and the moral standards of traditional African life. Today, one recognizes this especially in the overpopulated African cities where people are forced to engage in prostitution and the drug trade simply to survive. This spiritual void is also manifested in the economic, political, and cultural "fragilities" of African life, and also in the moral downfall, corruption, and venality that erode both African institutions and African society as a whole. In response to this sense of spiritual void (and in fact to anthropological poverty as a whole), Mveng claims it is not enough for the Church to simply preach the gospel and make vague declarations while not getting involved in the realities of people's everyday lives. Because Christ's gospel is not neutral, the Church must work to afford Africans their true dignity, identity, freedom, and presence in the world. In short, the Church's mandate is to help rebuild the humanity of the African person, a mandate that can only be accomplished through the articulation of an authentic theology of African liberation.[15]

Although not necessarily employing the same terminology as Mveng, other African theologians have picked up on this theme of anthropological poverty. Zaïrean moral theologian Bénézet Bujo claims the concept of poverty must be extended to include culture, an area that he argues has been either overlooked or treated superficially in the struggles against economic poverty. According to Bujo, this poverty involves "a total loss of identity and a total alienation, since it involves a denial of humanity to the whole person, down to the cultural roots." This cultural understanding of poverty should be one of paramount importance because as an individual's dignity cannot be realized outside of his or her culture, human dignity cannot be respected if one's culture is not taken seriously. As a result, Bujo maintains that in terms of social ethics one might rightfully include culture as a form of property. Thus, to ignore another's culture or relegate it to an inferior status may well be the first violation of human rights.[16]

Employing the term anthropological pauperization, Emmanuel Martey claims that the sense of "non-being" experienced by many Africans today occurs at two distinct levels, the "politico-socioeconomic" level (concerning "what we have") and the "anthropologico-religiocultural" level (concerning "who we are"). Because these two mutually complementing dimensions are such a reality in African life, he maintains that the individual's struggle against them forms the basis for the entire African theological agenda. African theologians not only have to employ both African worldviews and thought forms to allow the people to creatively interpret the gospel message for their own realities, but they must also combat the domination and "belittling" of their culture(s) that have eroded African pride. In fact, Martey concludes that this struggle against anthropological pauperization forms the "pivot" upon which must rotate any relevant African theological interpretation or methodological consideration.[17]

Finally, the African delegation to the Second General Assembly (1986) of the Ecumenical Association of Third World Theologians (EATWOT) maintains that any serious study of African history demonstrates that "historical annihilation" is the main problem facing the African people. Colonial oppressors did not destroy black Africans *physically*, but rather they deprived Africans of both their identity and personality by systematically destroying the political, economic, and cultural structures of traditional African society. Unfortunately, independence has not brought about any real change. Under the guise of assistance, new structures of oppression have taken root in Africa (read Western development, debt-reduction, and structural adjustment programs), structures that have caused greater poverty and dependence in the political, economic, and cultural realms. According to the African delegates: "If pauperization consists of making people poorer and poorer by depriving them of what they have, what they are, and what they do, pauperization becomes anthropological when persons are deprived of their identity, dignity, essential rights, culture, [and] history." Today, this systematized anthropological pauperization characterizes Africa's relationship with the industrialized world, holds its leaders hostage, and reduces its political systems to being mere "puppet shows" of the West.[18]

3. African versus Latin American Theologies of Liberation

As a third point concerning the importance of liberation within black African theology as a whole, I wish to demonstrate how Mveng differentiates an African understanding of liberation theology from that of Latin America. According to Mveng, when speaking of a theology (or theologies) of liberation one cannot simply focus on the formulations emanating from Latin America as a model for the rest of the world. He states that while Latin American liberation theology is by far the most recognized and most popular, the primary reason for this is a misinformed world media that considers liberation theology to have been created in Latin America and assumes that "other" theologies of liberation emanating from Africa, Asia, and the rest of the Third World are its simple appendages. He argues that this understanding is false because in actuality liberation theology was born in sub-Saharan Africa as a direct result of European colonial racism (including what he terms a "failed and oppressive" Christianity) long before it was ever articulated in Latin America. In reality, African liberation theology arose out of an interpretation of the biblical message from the perspective of the Bantou people, an interpretation that led to the creation of independent Christian churches in the late nineteenth and early twentieth centuries.[19]

Interestingly, Mveng claims that as the Bantous were forming their own independent churches, they were also formulating the basic fundamental categories of present-day liberation theology. First, they practiced *contextualization* or reading the biblical message from the historical context within which they lived. Second, they did*analysis of context* in which, although not theorists, they identified and analyzed the characteristics of oppression, exploitation, and injustice in their relationships with the colonial powers. Third, these church founders offered a *liberating reading of Scripture* in that they "invented" an African manner of reading the Bible so as to offer a message of salvation to the oppressed. Finally, they demonstrated a *liberating praxis* which, although it is a term coined in Latin America, actually expresses what the oppressed black African Christians did in founding their own independent churches and establishing for themselves spaces of freedom and creativity.[20] Thus, while the "discovery" of these four elements of liberation theology are normally credited to Latin American theologians, Mveng claims they were actually practiced by sub-Saharan Africans more than a half century earlier.

Besides its "discovery," perhaps the most important difference between African and Latin American liberation theology is the focus of liberation itself. Mveng claims that Latin American liberation theologies are primarily concerned with freeing people from the effects of both material poverty and oppressive societal structures. As such, they focus their attention on the influence of Western capitalism and its resulting political-military imperialism. By contrast, African liberation theology is primarily concerned with freeing the African person from imposed depersonalization or poverty in its anthropological sense. Thus, although it speaks to specific issues in the economic and political realms, African liberation theology focuses on the cultural and spiritual aspects of human life. Mveng underscores this point by claiming that since theology is contextual in that one can understand the gospel message only within one's own historical situation, all the cultural bases of African life are "immediate consequences" of the fundamental questions concerning life and faith. Thus, although a similar "spirituality of liberation" exists between them, the overall expressions of African and Latin American liberation theology have different ends. Unlike its Latin American counterpart(s), African liberation theology is a call for freedom in all domains of human life, spiritual and cultural as well as economic and political.[21]

As a result of the fact that both the history and the focus of liberation is somewhat different for African and Latin American theologians, the methodology employed in constructing a theology of liberation for Africa is different from the methodology employed in the Latin American context. As one example of this, Mveng points to the use of Marxist analysis. In Latin America, he claims the focus of liberation is really class struggle, the poor South struggling against the economic and political oppression of the rich North. Since this struggle is viewed primarily in the economic and political structures of these Latin American nations, a Marxist analysis may be appropriate. However, since in Africa the focus of liberation is more broad in that it concerns how one conceives of the human person, the world, and God within one's own cultural reality, and also how one is to overcome the forces of racism and anthropological destitution, African liberation theology seeks a "revolution" (Mveng purposely employs this term) in the world's conception of both the African person and African culture. The problem with Marxist analysis is that it is too narrowly focused to take into consideration the entirety of the African situation. Economic and political oppression exist in Africa, but the reasons why these problems exist cannot be limited simply to the influence of Western capitalism as Marxists would claim. Instead, the root causes for oppression in Africa include racism, apartheid, and the anthropological pauperization of the masses, issues for which Marxist analysis contributes little. Because Marxist analysis as a critique of Western capitalism does not sufficiently account for the situation in Africa, and because it has little to offer to the problems of racism, culture, and understanding of the human person, Mveng argues that it does not "suffice" as a methodological tool and thus cannot be realistically incorporated into an African theology of liberation.[22]

As with his understanding of anthropological poverty, numerous other African theologians share Mveng's convictions concerning the differences between African and Latin American expressions of liberation and also the use of Marxist analysis.[23] As early as the first meeting of EATWOT in 1976 (Dar es Salaam, Tanzania), the African delegation had great difficulty accepting the notion of liberation proposed by the Latin American delegates primarily as a result of their differences in understanding the nature of poverty. For the Africans, the concept of poverty could not be understood simply in economic or political terms, instead poverty had to include "anthropological impoverishment" or the fact that Africans have been robbed of both their culture and their identity.[24] The "Final Communiqué" from the 1977 meeting of the Pan-African Conference of Third World Theologians (Accra, Ghana) claimed that African theology must be *contextual* in that it take into consideration both the actual contexts within which people live and also the freeing of the African people from "cultural captivity." In a brief summary of its position, the Conference stated: "We stand against oppression in any form because the Gospel of Jesus Christ demands our participation in the struggle to free people from *all forms* of dehumanization."[25] In other words, the conference claimed that African liberation theology must incorporate the entirety of the human person in struggles against the forces of oppression, no matter what these forces may be. Concerning the limitations of Marxist analysis, the African delegation to the Second General Assembly of EATWOT (1986) claimed that although it may be of some use to help identify specific situations of oppression, a Marxist analysis of African history cannot be a primary methodological tool for African theology. The reason for this is that Marxist analysis deals exclusively with the effects of capitalism while, as previously noted, the root causes for African oppression are much more broad. In fact, because the African struggle is a "struggle for life" instead of a "struggle of class," the delegation concluded by claiming the African concept of liberation is both more encompassing and more radical than the Marxist concept of revolution.[26]

With this overview of how Mveng views the biblical foundation for liberation, how African poverty is understood to be anthropological, and how African liberation theology differs from its Latin American counterpart, I now turn to the contributions of Jean-Marc Éla and Laurenti Magesa. I focus on these two theologians because they present a comprehensive theological analysis of the sub-Saharan economic situation and offer practical suggestions as to what the African understanding of liberation can bring to the development of the African people.[27] In presenting both Éla's and Magesa's contributions, I identify the biblical basis for their arguments, discuss what they believe to be the specific economic challenges facing the African people, and demonstrate how they view the role of African liberation theology in addressing these various challenges.

Liberation and Development: Jean-Marc Éla

Quite possibly the best example of an African Catholic theologian who writes from the liberation perspective is Jean-Marc Éla.[28] His writings on liberation in general and economic development in particular are not "systematic" in that they proceed from any specific theologies of liberation or other theological sources.[29] Instead, the impetus for his understanding of liberation comes from his own experience living and working with the Kirdi population of Northern Cameroon, a people who experienced famine, sickness, natural disasters, and exploitation at the hands of government and multinational corporations. As a result of experiencing their poverty and exploitation, Éla claims his work with the Kirdi people demonstrated to him the limitations of a purely academic theology and also caused him to rethink how the Christian faith is both understood and experienced in the lives of real people. Now he cannot view the gospel message without beginning with the situation of the marginalized and then assessing its impact on their everyday lives. Thus, Éla's theology of liberation is in part the product of his recognizing the realities faced by his people and applying what he terms an "African reading" of the Bible to their actual situations. In fact, he underscores this point in the introduction to one of his early theological works when he argues that liberation of the oppressed "must be the primary condition for any authentic inculturation of the Christian message."[30]

It is important to note that in a way similar to Mveng, Éla formulated his own theology of liberation apart from the influence of Latin American liberation theology. In a 1994 interview, he stated that in addition to his work with the Kirdis, his own theology of liberation grew out of reading the works of Aimé Césaire, Léopold Senghor, and Cheikh Anta Diop, the "fathers" of the Negritude movement.[31] From their analysis of the African situation he understood that there was a problem facing the sub-continent (presumably one of liberation) and that Christianity could make an important contribution to the "libération totale" of the African person. Later, after arriving in Strasbourg to pursue graduate theological studies, he took part in a formation program whose principal theme was the book of Exodus. From this, Éla further recognized how the Exodus message spoke to the African reality, a recognition that caused him to begin formulating his own understanding of what liberation actually entails. As a result of these experiences and the fact that the messianic "spirituals" he used to sing as a child contained many references to Moses and the liberation of the Hebrew people, he stated the goal of his pastoral work in 1980 was to evangelize in the spirit of Exodus. It was in formulating this pastoral plan that he was first introduced to the work of Latin American liberation theologians and recognized many of the similarities he shared with them.[32]

As a final point of introduction, Éla further emphasizes the importance of liberation by claiming that today one cannot focus solely on inculturation theology because inculturation is not sufficient in regards to the struggles of present-day African society. For Éla, the struggle against poverty and oppression forms the center of missionary engagement in Africa and also demands a veritable revision in the methods of analyzing societal problems. While at the 1977 Pan-African Conference of Third World Theologians (Accra, Ghana) the question was whether African theology should be one of adaptation (inculturation) or liberation, today this question is no longer relevant and in fact it is anachronistic. Because of the myriad forms of exploitation perpetrated by the West, liberation is the only choice for both African theology and Christianity.[33] I should point out, however, that for Éla, liberation is a multi-faceted issue because he equates Africa's need for liberation from Western exploitation with the African Catholic Church's need for liberation from Rome. In other words, just as the economic structures of the Western world hold Africa in a dual state of submission and dependence, so also do the ecclesial structures of the Vatican hold the African Catholic Church in a state of submission and dependence as well. Although my study focuses only on the economic aspect of liberation within his work, one should keep in mind that liberation from "oppressive" ecclesial structures is Éla's primary focus.[34]

1. Biblical Foundation for Liberation

Éla introduces his biblical understanding of liberation by claiming Christian faith is not abstract in that it can be understood a-temporally or a-historically. Faith grapples with the problems, tensions, and conflicts people face in their everyday lives and as such it can only be lived in the context of the events that make up human history. Because of this, any Christian theology that purports to deal with questions of faith must also be historically grounded and capable of being understood by real people. Thus, if the Bible is the foundation for both Christian faith and philosophy, then one cannot read it without taking into consideration the realities facing sub-Saharan Africa today. For Éla, the "core of the biblical faith" is the liberating message of Exodus, a living message that must be reread and reapplied to the concrete situations facing the African people today.[35]

Although liberation is foundational to Christian faith as a whole, Éla claims that for the past 100-plus years the Exodus message has been "terribly absent" from the African people. The reason for this absence is that the true message of Exodus calls into question not only the theology brought to Africa by the colonial missionaries, but also their ecclesial practices, forms of worship, and spirituality as well. In short, the God presented to the African people (the God of the colonizers) was one who showed no concern for the specific cultural and economic situations of the African people, remained both distant and unidentifiable to them, and in fact was a God who demanded both adaptation and submission to the existing order. By failing to speak of the "sociohistorical dimension of salvation" and by "hiding behind an apolitical disguise," the colonial missionaries failed to teach that the biblical understanding of salvation entails not only paradise in the next life, but also liberation in this life. In response, Éla claims that for any African religious movement the primary function of the Bible (and in particular the Old Testament) is to "express the reaction and revolt of African Christians to the institutional churches in which the despised, humiliated human person lives in relationship to God under the rubric of absence." The African churches must teach their followers that the God of the Exodus is intimately concerned with *their* world and in fact this God presents them with a theological justification to speak out against every form of oppression.[36]

Closely related to this, Éla continues by claiming that because God is intimately involved in human history, we cannot view justice, freedom, reconciliation, peace, and general human happiness solely in a "beyond" that has no connection to the realities of everyday temporal life. God's intervention in human history through the Exodus proposes a "collective project of communion and oneness," a project that recognizes both the importance of liberation and the fact that God's message of hope calls people to work for the transformation of the temporal world. In other words, God's revelation not only illuminates and interprets the existing reality of this world, but it also "introduces a contradiction" into this reality and "initiates a dynamism" whose thrust is toward the fulfillment of God's future promise. Thus, human history is understood as a journey by which we are at the same time moving toward God and moving toward a world as it ought to be.[37]

As a practical consequence for the present day, the liberating message of Exodus demands that the African Church better integrate the Christian faith into concrete projects that will allow the African people to move from servitude to freedom. Although the Church's mission is ultimately supernatural and thus other-worldly, in order to credibly present God's message to the African people it must speak of the here and now. Similar to his statements cited in the conclusion of Chapter Two, Éla maintains that it is not enough for the Church simply to maintain schools, hospitals, or orphanages, and to perform charitable functions in society. Instead, bolstered by the Exodus message of God intervening in human history, the Church is called to denounce oppressive and dehumanizing social structures, enter into greater solidarity with the poor, and intervene in all levels of society to protect the weak from the "arbitrary will" of the powerful.[38]

2. Liberation and Development

Based on his recognition of how the Exodus message calls for transformation in the temporal world, Éla then relates his theological understanding of liberation to concrete issues of sub-Saharan economic development. Writing in the early to mid-1980s,[39] Éla maintains that the economic injustices characteristic of the colonial period have not ended as a result of African independence. These injustices still exist but simply with new sources. As one example, he points to the situation in Cameroon where the Kirdis are forced to produce cacao and cotton for international export instead of the millet they need in order to survive. As described in Chapter One, the result of maintaining this form of cash-crop economy is that in addition to having multinational corporations reap virtually all profits, the workers are not allowed to cultivate adequate food staples to feed themselves, their families, and their fellow countrymen. Éla recognizes these shortcomings and claims the problem with this form of "development" is that multinational corporations do not allow the African people to either participate in or reap the benefits of their own economic activity. In reality, these corporations condemn the people to further destitution.[40]

Éla also points to the élites of African society, the government officials and their supporters, as a second source of economic oppression. Again as described in Chapter One, many African government officials exploit their political positions for personal gain and as a result create what Éla terms "oligarchies of the privileged." African nations receive revenues from the goods they produce but instead of being channeled back to the producers or being reinvested in the rural areas, a large percentage of these revenues disappears into the governmental machine. This governmental machine in turn uses the revenues to support a self-perpetuating "political-administrative" class, one that can only maintain its existence through exploitation of the peasant masses. For Éla, the people's true condition can only be understood with the recognition of a "local bourgeoisie living in connivance with the origins of plunder, ... a parasite class that lives on the crumbs of the exploitation of African countries."[41] Thus, instead of the colonial powers forcing the people to produce goods for the benefit of the mother nations, it is now the élites of African society who, along with the foreign multinationals, force the masses to produce goods for the benefit of their own (the élites') personal interests.

As a result of the policies of both the foreign multinationals and African leaders themselves, Éla maintains that reliance on cash-crop economies has not allowed the common person's standard of living to improve in any appreciable way. In fact, he claims that after twenty years of independence the so-called development programs of the West have not improved the people's lives but instead have only brought about "developed underdevelopment."[42] Because the economy is oriented toward export goods instead of self-sufficiency, because it deteriorates the environment, and because it disorganizes traditional economic relationships, so-called development programs have only exacerbated the oppression and economic dependence of the African people. In light of this situation, Éla poses a number of poignant rhetorical questions to those who unquestioningly support Western economic policies in Africa. How does one understand "development" within an economic system characterized by structures of dependency? Can the masses really have any hope of improving their standard of living in a system of planned dependency, one that is dominated by those who control all capital? With the transfer of cash-crop revenues to foreign bank accounts (capital flight), is there any real hope for development in the interests of the nation as a whole? What is the meaning of "popular sharing" in the planning, development, and execution of projects in areas where people have no financial resources and are not allowed to participate in these processes? Finally, since social and economic imbalances exist on both the national and international level, does not true development demand structural changes on both the national and global levels?[43]

While not offering direct responses to these questions, Éla does maintain that because the various development strategies imposed on the African sub-continent primarily favor the rich, the term "underdevelopment" is one that is grossly misinterpreted.

Underdevelopment is not a term that should be used to describe the African people or their economic situation because, echoing Mveng, it "disguises" the fact that the true hindrance to sub-Saharan development is neocolonial domination. Éla continues by arguing that if economic development means the transfer of profits to the privileged, if it involves further dependence upon the West which in turn places the nations of Africa under "foreign tutelage," and if the production of cash crops fails to raise the standard of living for the masses, then the whole concept of development must be reevaluated in terms of liberation. Will Africans continue to maintain "dependent development" where the multinationals and ruling classes take their profits at the expense of the masses, or will they work toward "autonomous development" where economic activity is actually directed toward serving the poor?[44]

With the connection between liberation and development having been made, the question now becomes, what is the role of Christian faith? Why should both the individual Christian and Christian theology as a whole be concerned with the issue of African economic development? For Éla, the justification for concern, as well as the impetus for response, is located in the communal or social understanding of the Christian faith. The question of development calls Christians to recognize that the "first duty" of the human person is to be fully a human person. In other words, Christians must teach and manifest a faith that is not simply a doctrine, but one that demands the freedom and subjectivity of each human person, directs individuals to take charge of their own destinies, and works to transform the entire world. Citing Pope John XXIII's emphasis on socialization (although not offering a specific citation), Éla claims the only type of development compatible with the Christian faith is one that promotes the common good because it is only through the "experiences of collective promotion" that God's design for the universe is entrusted to humanity. Furthermore, because the concept of development presumes that nothing in the world is sacred (particularly the structures of the international economic system) and because the task of development is humanity's "becoming" as intended by God's design, he maintains that the purpose of Christian faith is to both restore God's rightful place in the universe and to make sense of the fact that the meaning of our relationship with others is very much like our relationship with God.

As such, Christian faith must be rooted in the practical situations that Africans face and it must work to liberate them from any form of domination that hinders them from attaining their full creativity, community, and union. Because of these two complementary functions, Christian faith must be viewed as both a force for human liberation and a vehicle for change in the temporal world.[45]

Now the question becomes, how is this to be done? How in the pursuit of liberation does one translate a Christian faith, understood as relationship with God, into a world that is entrusted to human beings? Éla makes this connection by drawing upon the African (and biblical) understanding of the human person as a social creature. Because the human is not a "purely interior being" but instead is endowed with a social nature, Africans view salvation not only in terms of the individual soul but in terms of humanity as a whole. Put differently, the African understanding of liberation concerns the salvation of the entire world. African Christianity recognizes that the world entrusted to humanity by God is not complete and that the temporal purpose of faith is to recreate a world in tune with God's design for the human race. Christians are called to "reinvent" creation through activities influenced by the gospel message and to create a world that is "dis-alienated," one where people take responsibility for the future of their brothers and sisters, and one where all are able to realize both their own dignity and the fulfillment of their creative capacities.[46] Thus echoing-although not citing-Mveng's emphasis on anthropological poverty, Éla maintains that true liberation entails freeing people to become who they are meant to become.

Then, speaking directly to the issue of economic development, Éla claims that while liberation in its fullest sense entails the freeing of the person's entire "being," it entails freedom within societal structures as well. Because the Bible continually speaks of God intervening in human history and delivering God's people from economic, social, and political captivity, Christians cannot ignore development-related problems on the grounds that they are a "human affair." Instead the question of economic development poses a fundamental challenge to Christian faith:

> Faith is the demand for an incarnation of the Gospel in society in quest of itself, a society undergoing radical transformations. Faith is experienced, in living fashion, in an awareness of a human being to

invent and a world to build. Faith is the engagement of a community of men and women who, in the very act of looking to Jesus as a group, feel responsible for the Gospel ... [and] promote a new manner of being-in-the-world. In short, faith is verified and actualized in wherever the future is striven for and invented, in all of society's tension spots. *Unless it takes account of economics* as well as the realities of power and the corrective realities of powerlessness, faith is disincarnate."[47]

Concerning the specific role of the Roman Catholic Church in Africa's economic development, Éla claims that although through its schools, hospitals, and other social services it is heavily involved in development-related projects, this involvement may actually be hiding more deeply rooted problems. For example, he states that it is becoming increasingly evident that many Church-sponsored services can only be accessed by the rich and thus the Church seems to be maintaining its distance from those who are most in need of its aid. In addition, he claims the Church must recognize that its charitable acts may actually function to "placate its conscience" and thus close itself off to the effects of alienating social conflicts. In other words, by providing charity-based aid church officials believe they have "done their part" and thus fail to examine the underlying structural causes for African poverty. Furthermore, by focusing on charity-based programs, the Church has done little to gain the analytical tools necessary to act in light of the gospel message and it has also done little to create an "authentic ministry of Christian understanding" focused on current societal problems.[48]

Éla claims that the only way the Church can "reconcile" itself with African society is by more fully acknowledging the social functions of both faith and theology, actively promoting development at the grassroots level, and actively supporting the poor in their efforts to transform society. If it continues to view itself as "above" problems in the economic realm, it will "remain in the imperialist camp" and in fact help to further "integrate Africa into a system of domination."[49] Éla also believes that in the future the Church must reflect on how it can incarnate the gospel message into the "administrative milieus" where the political, economic, cultural, and social institutions of Africa will be formed. It must provide the motivation for present African leaders to transform society and must also focus on the educated youth who, as the future leaders, will shape the course of African history. In the end, he believes the only way the Church can build a bridge between itself and African society is if it makes a true commitment to both live out the gospel message and actively work to end oppression and inequality in all facets of African life.[50]

3. Liberation and Development Today

Although Éla first articulated his understanding of the relationship between development and liberation in the early to mid-1980s, today his message remains essentially the same. Sub-Saharan nations today face profound economic difficulties as a result of their continued reliance on cash-crop economics, the structural adjustment and debt reduction policies imposed on them by Western financial institutions, and also the phenomenon of economic globalization whereby Western powers exploit the global markets for their own benefit.[51] Speaking at the SEDOS (Servizio di Documenatzione et Studi) symposium in Rome during the 1994 Synod for Africa, Éla claimed that while the balance of Christianity is steadily moving towards the South, the most serious issue facing Africans today is that they are at the point of "crossing the dividing line" between poverty and exclusion. Because it is no longer strategically important for the world superpowers and because the "mechanisms of money" view the sub-continent simply as a means to gain ever-greater profits (profits gained at the expense of the native populations), sub-Saharan Africa has become virtually irrelevant on the world scene. Africans today have virtually no input in the decisions that effect their own economies, much less any voice in those that influence the world economic system as a whole. In light of this situation, Éla insists that in order to have any semblance of relevance in present-day society, the African Catholic Church must "rediscover the totality of liberation" to help free people from every form of economic, political, and social oppression. While for centuries the challenge for Western Christianity was to synthesize faith with reason, today the challenge for African Christianity is to synthesize faith with liberation.[52]

In two more recent although non-theological works, Éla, writing as sociologist, again criticizes specific economic policies imposed on Africa by the Western financial institutions. In his *Afrique: L'irruption des pauvres* (1994), he claims that because the structural adjustment programs of the IMF and World Bank force African nations to focus on short term economic issues (such as debt repayment) without looking toward more comprehensive transformations in the long term, the only true results of these programs have been the increasing economic gap between the North and South, the maintenance of inadequate and unjust political systems, and the further marginalization of the African people. Thus, the reform programs of the Western financial institutions have actually done more to accentuate African poverty than to alleviate it. As examples of the concrete effects these reform programs have had on the people of Cameroon, Éla points to the sharp reduction in salaries for public sector workers, the closing of universities (in fact, he claims Cameroon has been forced to "sacrifice" school age children to repay the debt), and the lack of access to proper medicine.[53] In response, he maintains the international financial institutions must recognize the "human dimension" of their policies and begin to reevaluate them in light of the consequences they have had on real human lives. Thus, even when writing in the sociological context, Éla maintains his theological position concerning the centrality of the human person in any development-related program. The economic difficulties facing the African people are "problêms humains" and it is only through "investing in the human person" that true development will ever take place.[54]

Similarly, in his *Innovations sociales et renaissance de l'Afrique noire* (1998), Éla offers a stinging critique of structural adjustment policies by claiming that they both undermine national sovereignty and take on an almost messianic role in African life. After again recounting the effects of structural adjustment on the African people, he argues that, because African nations need to liberalize their markets in order to secure foreign aid, it is the IMF and the World Bank who decide the future of millions of African men and women through the implementation of reform measures.[55] He argues that the "silent partners" of the IMF and World Bank have become so powerful that they actually take the place of the African state and reduce the state to an organization that simply mediates their own policies. Following this, Éla compares the liberal economic ideologies of the IMF and World Bank to a form of secular religion. Structural adjustment is so pervasive that it imparts what he terms a "dogmatism of the total market" to which African nations must "convert" in order to survive. In addition, because of their unquestioned leadership in all areas of research and reflection concerning African development, the international financial institutions have become "invested with a sort of infallibility," exercise an economic "magisterialism," and "assume the divine mission [of] taking 700 million Africans by the hand and leading them toward the promised land of the market." As a result of their almost unquestioned power, these institutions have become the "new Moses" who preach the "Ten Commandments" of Structural Adjustment:

> You shall adopt the measures of austerity; You shall reduce the role of the state; You shall privatize public corporations; You shall remove the fat from the civil service; You shall "dis-index" salaries (from the cost of living); You shall abolish subsidies; You shall devalue your currency; You shall submit yourselves to laws of the market; You shall abolish tariff barriers; You shall bless the vulgarization of agriculture.[56]

Liberation and Development: Laurenti Magesa

The third African liberation theologian whose contributions I examine in this chapter is Tanzanian Laurenti Magesa.[57] Magesa is included here not only because he is an outspoken critic of oppressive societal structures, but also because as a native of East Africa he demonstrates that many of the economic, social, and political problems experienced by his own people are the same as those experienced by West Africans (including Mveng and Éla). While not offering a biographical rationale for his focus on liberation as does Éla, Magesa also holds that one of the primary functions of the Catholic Church is to help free the African people from whatever hinders them from expressing their full humanity.

1. Biblical Foundation for Liberation

While many, if not most, African liberation theologians ground their theologies in either the book of Exodus or the gospel Beatitudes, Magesa is somewhat different. Magesa maintains that the biblical foundation for liberation is best demonstrated by Mark 2:1-12, the story of the paralytic man who was let into the home where Jesus was teaching by friends who opened the roof for him and lowered him down.[58] Recognizing the man's faith, Jesus tells the paralytic his sins are forgiven and then, responding to the murmuring of the scribes who question how he can forgive sins, he heals the man of his paralysis. For Magesa, this short account best demonstrates the biblical notion of liberation because within it one recognizes both the "summary and substance" of humanity's salvation history. First, by demonstrating how the crowds made it impossible for the paralytic to reach Jesus and how the Jewish leaders did not believe Jesus could forgive sins, the story identifies both the physical and psychic impediments to salvation. In other words, just as there were both physical and psychological obstacles to the paralytic man being liberated from his paralysis, so also are there physical and psychological obstacles for Africans to overcome in their struggle for liberation/salvation.[59] Second, this account also demonstrates what Magesa terms the "twofold condition" for salvation: "Your sins are forgiven" and "Get up and walk." Jesus' words here indicate that any authentic call for liberation must include *metanoia*, or the conversion of heart, as well as an empowering to self-reliance. Once again, just as the paralytic was freed of his sins *before* he was cured, so we must also be freed or liberated from our own prejudices, presuppositions, and sinfulness before we can "get up and walk" on our own and thus empower others to do the same. Magesa maintains that although the message of liberation is present in the Old Testament (particularly in Exodus), this message is only completed or fulfilled through Christ's teaching in this particular story. While the Old Testament places emphasis on the empowering aspect of liberation, through his words to the paralytic Jesus demonstrates the necessity of repentance in the liberating process and shows how "Your sins are forgiven" both balances and complements the command to "Getup and Walk!"[60]

Magesa further justifies this biblical interpretation by claiming the gospels and the New Testament epistles both demonstrate that repentance is not true repentance and faith is not true faith if they do not produce "tangible" and "appropriate" results in the world. Because the fruits of Jesus' incarnation and work on earth are manifested in the virtues of love, sharing, justice, helpfulness, and truth, any expression of repentance or faith that is void of "engagement in human life" is in fact meaningless. Echoing Éla, Magesa also holds that just as Christ's mission was to transform human life and make it more free in his own time, so also the task of any sincere Christian must be to liberate humanity from oppression and make it more free in our own time. Thus, the story of the paralytic's cure "dramatizes" the biblical process of liberation because it demonstrates humanity's transformation from the "inhuman condition of impotence to the attainment of potency and self-confidence;" a transformation that Magesa claims is befitting of all true sons and daughters of God.[61]

2. Anthropological Poverty

As with the previous two theologians examined in this chapter, Magesa also maintains that anthropological poverty or the perceived sense of "non-being" is one of the most pressing challenges facing the African sub-continent today. Like Mveng, he argues that the primary source for anthropological poverty was the loss of African cultural identity at the hands of the Europeans. Because an estimated 200 million Africans were forcibly removed from their native homes as a result of the slave trade, by the time European colonialism began in earnest in the late 1800s many African communities were lacking both the societal cohesiveness and stability necessary for their continued cultural development. In fact, he claims that by the time the colonial period began many African societies had become "culturally stymied." In the absence of necessary cohesiveness and stability, the African people began to adopt from the colonial powers both "ways of living" and "means of doing things" that were not their own; as a result they proceeded to alienate themselves from each other, from themselves, and from the traditional indigenous institutions that for centuries had influenced their lives.[62] Therefore, in addition to exploiting the native populations for their own economic ends, the European colonizers caused social discord in many African communities by introducing practices and customs that were foreign to traditional African culture.

Magesa also agrees with Mveng through his claim that the Christian missionary legacy has led to a "crisis of self-confidence" among present-day sub-Saharan Africans. His rationale for this claim is that while the secular colonial governments and systems of economic organization consciously intended to humiliate Africans and strip them of "any psychological acumen and punch," the white Christian missionaries actually accomplished the same thing (although in many cases unwittingly) through their denigration of traditional African culture. For Magesa, culture is the "interior conscious reflection" and "unconscious feeling" of a specific group of people concerning the "structures of life"-he specifically cites birth, marriage, and social organization-and because culture is handed down from generation to generation it acts as a source of continuity within African communities. However, when the Christian missionaries declared African culture to be primitive and barbaric, they undermined the values of traditional African society and in effect "dealt the coup de grace" to both the African understanding of the human person and the African notion of "is-ness." As practical consequences in the present-day, cultural domination by the Christian missionaries (one that worked hand-in-hand with domination by the secular powers) has led to the "emasculation" of the African people and has left them both "powerless" and "psychologically quite lame" in the face of their oppressors. Thus, whether by design or not, the present-day effects of both secular and Christian colonialism are the same: Africans have "lost their nerve," are mired in a "crisis of self-confidence," and no longer trust in their God-given power to bring about their own liberation.[63]

Magesa continues by stating a second reason for the African people's sense of anthropological poverty today is the phenomenon of globalization.[64] Similarly to Éla, he maintains that although globalization manifests itself in the various social, political, and cultural spheres of African society, its single most influential driving force is economics. The reason for this is that with the "demise of doctrinaire socialism" following the collapse of the Soviet Union, liberal capitalist economics has become the "engine" of a world-wide movement whose aim is to "uniformalize" the entire world. Africans most clearly recognize this movement towards uniformity in the IMF and World Bank which, through the "conditionalities" of their reform policies, have gained control of virtually every aspect of African life and in effect hold Africa hostage to their own "whims and desires."[65] However, in addition to the imposition of these conditionalities, economic globalization has had other negative effects on the African people as well. Globalization has helped to increase the number of trans-national corporations in Africa yet these corporations do not pay adequate attention to the social effects of their business dealings, effects that are particularly manifested in the growing levels of unemployment, crime, and pollution. Thus, as multinationals exploit the sub-continent to increase their own wealth, the common person is left to deal with the dehumanizing consequences of their actions. In addition, because the prices for African goods are set at levels that benefit Western business interests, African countries continually earn less income for their goods and thus become increasingly poor. Once again it is the common person who suffers the most from this situation. As national income declines health care services also decline, the quality of education falls, HIV infection rates increase, and children slowly starve to death. Because of its far-reaching and detrimental consequences on African life, Magesa concludes that the present-day phenomenon of economic globalization is characterized by a system of inherent unfairness and must be viewed as the primary reason for the pauperization of the African people.[66]

3. A Theological Response: African Socialism

To understand how Magesa views the role of Christian theology within the development process, it is important first to explain how he links theological analysis with political power. Magesa claims that in economically developing nations, theological analysis focuses on three principal elements in speaking to the concrete situations facing humanity: the economic, social, and political. While not completely neglecting the other two, Latin American liberation theology focuses primarily on economic analysis as its "controlling paradigm," Asian liberation theology focuses on the social-cultural, and in Africa the controlling paradigm is the political. The reason for African liberation theology's focus on the political is that politics is always associated with power and the past 300-plus years of African history is replete with evidence of different groups vying to exercise power over one another. For example, although many view economics as the "rationale" for the slave trade, Magesa argues that the underlying issue was actually the Europeans gaining control over the African people so as to exploit their labor for the Europeans' own benefit. During the colonial period the underlying issue was similar. The colonial powers had to gain and maintain power (or control) over the African people because, as noted in Chapter Two, if at any point the Africans began to realize their inherent equality with the Europeans the success of the entire colonial enterprise would be seriously jeopardized. Today in the neocolonial period, power remains a central issue specifically as a result of the conditionalities imposed by the IMF and World Bank. Because they manipulate African economies for the benefit of Western business and political interests, Magesa claims the main concern of many African nations today is how they can free themselves from the stranglehold of these financial institutions, a struggle that at its core is political because it involves the power of each nation to both direct and control its own future.[67] Therefore, any policy or program concerning sub-Saharan economic development must be understood in terms of politics and any relevant theological analysis concerning these same policies or programs must always take into consideration who maintains the power to affect them.

If politics is really the "controlling paradigm" of African theological reflection, the question then becomes, "what is an appropriate theological response to the economic difficulties facing the African sub-continent?" Or posed differently, "what legitimate means can Catholic theology adopt in order to help Africans assume the power necessary to direct their own economic futures?" Although first proposed over twenty-five years ago, one possible response to these questions may be found in Magesa's understanding of African socialism. Rooted in traditional African society, African socialism seeks to transfer the ideals or values of traditional society into present-day African life, and as its "common theme" it emphasizes cooperative living and "man-in-community." Magesa claims the "essence" of African socialism is the "practical acceptance" of human equality, an equality manifested in the belief that all people have a right to the basic necessities of life, to participate in both the formation and functioning of their governments, and to the best of their abilities contribute to the common good of their own communities. African socialism offers a viable model for African economic development because it demands that the ultimate end of any economic activity be the well-being of the human person. In other words, because of its emphasis on human equality, African socialism demands that the "primordial needs" of the people be the overriding priority of any development policy. Included in these "primordial needs" are nutritious food, potable water, and adequate shelter for all people; other development "priorities" such as building skyscrapers, paving roads, and purchasing luxury cars always remain secondary.[68]

In addition to this, African socialism also provides a response to the competing ideologies of capitalism and communism, ideologies that Magesa believes cannot be fully applied to the African context because they both contain fundamental "mistakes." As examples of these "mistakes," he claims capitalism simply "reduces" the entire concept of social justice to the right of private property and also relies on economic inequality in order to survive. For its part, communism or Eastern European forms of socialism fail to respect the individuality of the human person and in fact only view the human person as a means to a specific economic end. Although at the time (mid 1970s) he admitted it was still in its infancy, Magesa argues that African socialism seeks to overcome these fundamental mistakes by freeing people from oppressive societal structures, reducing the "gap of inequality" between the rich and poor, and proposing an authentically African ideology that empowers the African people to truly participate in world affairs.[69]

Magesa concludes his argument for African socialism by claiming that its primary tenets are in "full accord" with the social teachings of the Catholic Church. First, concerning the relationship between human liberation and structural change, he maintains that African Socialism echoes the teachings of *Rerum Novarum, Mater et Magistra, Pacem in Terris*, *Populorum Progressio*, and *Gaudium et Spes* because to varying degrees these documents each stress that human alienation can never be compatible with the Christian message and also call upon Christians to commit themselves to transforming oppressive societal structures. Next, citing various Church Fathers (Basil, Augustine, Gregory the Great, Bonaventure, and Albert the Great), the radio message of John XXIII (September 11, 1962), and the documents *Populorum Progressio* (no. 69) and *Gaudium et Spes* (no. 33), Magesa claims African socialism's understanding of private property also echoes the Church's teachings concerning both the common good and social nature of private goods. African socialism recognizes each person's right to own property, however this right is only "inalienable" to the degree that everyone enjoys the basic necessities of life. Third, as the overall goal of African socialism is to reduce the gap between rich and poor, it demands a sincere effort on the part of all people to both identify and "eradicate" the root causes of poverty. This effort entails teaching that poverty is not God's will but is in fact man-made, having government put pressure on the wealthy to give up some of their wealth for the benefit of the poor (here he cites *Populorum Progressio*, no. 33), and focusing on projects whose aim is the integral development of the people as a whole.[70]

In sum, African socialism is centered on a tri-partite respect for individual responsibility, human dignity, and the fulfillment of self-within-community. Because of its concern for the human person and because it emphasizes equality and justice in the economic, political, and social realms of African life, Magesa proposes that African Socialism is a means toward liberation in this life and in fact offers a "unique contribution" to the world as a whole.[71] Although Magesa does not specifically employ the term "power" in speaking of African socialism, the implication is readily apparent. Through its emphasis on both the human person and human equality, African Socialism seeks to free individuals from imposed servitude, offer them the opportunity to become self-sufficient, and empower them to take control of their own destinies. As such, African socialism offers a viable secular model for Catholic theological reflection.

4. A Theological Response: Christ as Liberator

While maintaining his previous teachings, Magesa in the 1990s also wrote of the difficulties facing sub-Saharan nations by advocating a Christological understanding of "Christ as Liberator." Echoing Éla once again, he claims that, in order for Christ's message to be relevant for Africans today, it must offer a voice to the voiceless, courage to the weak, and hope to the suffering and outcasts of society. Then, repeating his "Your sins are forgiven" and "Get up and walk" language from twenty years earlier, he states that Jesus' earthly life serves as a model for Africans of how to "cultivate" both a better person and a better world, and also how to reject the alienating structures of domination, corruption, and tribalism so prevalent in African society.[72]

However, in addition to providing his message with a greater measure of relevance, this portrait of "Christ as Liberator" has ramifications for present-day African ecclesiology as well. By claiming "Christ as Liberator," Magesa argues that we are really speaking of Christ's "assurance of solidarity" with humanity in the struggle to eradicate all forms of poverty; an assurance that is given to humanity primarily, although not exclusively, through the Church. In other words, although Christ's message of assurance can be understood to apply directly to specific individuals in specific circumstances, it is through the Church that this assurance is "particularly" offered. Thus, African Christology is really ecclesiology. Christ is *the* liberator and the Church is "ideally the agent and articulator" of his liberating message in the temporal world."[73] Then, returning to the story of the paralytic's cure, Magesa further claims that the Church itself must be the "enabler" in African society because to teach Africans to "Get up and walk" is in effect to fulfill its mandate from Christ. The Church only becomes Church when it liberates people from oppression and empowers them to meaningfully participate in societal life.[74]

What do these three expressions of African liberation theology bring to the construction of a proposed theology of economic development? In the final section of this chapter I respond to this question by identifying the commonalities within Mveng, Éla, and Magesa's expressions of African liberation theology and then by relating their contributions to the basic principles of Catholic social teaching.

Toward an African Theology of Development

Overall, I believe there are four common threads running through the works of Mveng, Éla, and Magesa that speak to a theology of economic development for the African sub-continent. The first and most obvious contribution is that theology has a temporal function. To those who would claim that the Catholic Church (and in fact any religious organization) should focus on preparing souls for the next world and not concern itself with earthly affairs, these three expressions of African liberation theology respond with a resounding "No!" Although its ultimate concern is humanity's eternal salvation, the Church has a mandate to speak out against sinfulness in this world, including that sinfulness associated with economic inequality and "faulty" development programs. Each of these three theologians believes that, in order to be authentic, Catholic theology must not remain theoretical but it must involve itself in the concrete relalities of everyday life.

Closely related to this concern for temporal life, the second common theme concerns the importance of contextuality. Mveng's claim that African theology as a whole is not particularly academic but arises from the concrete lives of the African people, Éla's claim that his understanding of liberation emerged primarily from his experiences with the Kirdis of Northern Cameroon, and Magesa's argument that the human person is the primary end of African socialism are all significant because they each point to the fact that in order to be relevant, any authentic African theology must both arise from and be grounded in the lives of the African people. In terms of this study, these three statements also demonstrate that in order to foster positive economic change, the rationales, foundations, methodologies, and conclusions of any development theology must be grounded in African contextual realities.

Theologically this focus on contextuality is important especially in light of applying basic tenets of Catholic social teaching to the African economic situation. Since the end of the 19th century the Roman Catholic Church has constructed a comprehensive body of teachings concerning economic affairs, teachings that include Pope Leo XIII's *Rerum Novarum* (1891), Pope Pius XI's *Quadragesimo Anno* (1931), the Second Vatican Council's *Gaudium et Spes* (1965), Pope Paul VI's *Populorum Progressio* (1967), and Pope John Paul II's *Laborem Exercens* (1981), *Sollicitudo Rei Socialis* (1987), and *Centesimus Annus* (1991). Through these documents the Church has proposed specific principles which it claims must be incorporated into any just economic system; principles that include human dignity, community, solidarity, participation, common good, subsidiarity, and the preferential option for the poor. Now although these principles have great relevance for the African situation and must be incorporated into any proposed development theology, one might rightfully question how they (and in fact all of the Church's social teachings) can be applied to the African context. As detailed in Chapter One, one of the main problems with many Western development programs is that in addition to not allowing for popular participation in their formulations, they are imposed without taking into consideration the values, beliefs, or mindsets of the African people. This same difficulty may also exist in applying the principles of Catholic social teaching. Because these principles were constructed within the context of Western (particularly European) philosophical and theological reflection, one cannot expect them to be clearly understood, much less wholeheartedly applied, if they are simply "imposed" upon the African people.[75] While in the following chapter I demonstrate how numerous African bishops' conferences actually ground their statements on economic development within the Church's social teachings, in this chapter I show how Mveng, Éla, and Magesa demonstrate that there must be a strong grounding in the actual lives of the people as well. In other words, in order to formulate an authentic theology of development for sub-Saharan Africa there must be a creative tension between the Church's universal teachings and the theological insights that arise from the African "sensus fidei."

The third and perhaps most important contribution of these three expressions of African liberation theology concerns their emphasis on anthropological poverty. As a direct result of the slave trade, the colonial legacy, and present-day neo-colonialism in the form of debt reduction and structural adjustment programs, Africans have come to view poverty as not only material privation, but also privation in the sociological, cultural, and spiritual realities of everyday life. For Mveng, anthropological poverty manifests itself in the cultural, academic, and theological arrogance of the West as well as in the "spiritual void" it leaves in the African people; elements that when combined render true development next to impossible. For Magesa, anthropological impoverishment is recognized today in both the dehumanizing results of economic globalization and in the "crisis of confidence" that renders many Africans powerless in the face of their oppressors. Although not specifically employing the term, Éla certainly alludes to the concept of anthropological poverty by demonstrating the debilitating effects of Western-imposed development programs and also by arguing that any true expression of the Christian faith must help Africans to both recognize their inherent dignity and fulfill their creative capacities as human persons.

In terms of constructing a theology of development for sub-Saharan Africa, this emphasis on anthropological poverty is significant because it provides a means for Africans to recognize and apply the basic principles of Catholic social teaching within their own contexts.[76] While in a previous paragraph I cautioned that the Catholic Church cannot authentically teach the basic economic principles of its social teachings without also taking into consideration the African contextual reality, I now propose that the emphasis on overcoming anthropological poverty actually allows this to occur. Even without employing its specific terms, African liberation theology's focus on anthropological poverty in the economic realm actually reflects the basic economic principles of Catholic social teaching. For example, in order to overcome the sense of inferiority and resignation so prevalent in many African communities, any authentic development program must begin with those whom it intends to serve. The ultimate end of any African development program must not be to promote the interests of those who propose, fund, or administer it (especially if it is proposed, funded, and administered by organizations outside of Africa). Instead, its ultimate end must be to promote the good of the African people themselves. In this sense, the emphasis on overcoming anthropological poverty closely reflects the Catholic social principles of human dignity and preferential option for the poor. Concerning human dignity, the Church teaches that because all humans are created in the image and likeness of God they maintain an inherent dignity that must be respected at all times. Respect for human dignity means that the African people must never be viewed simply as a means to an economic end, especially an end that is not their own. Instead, they must always be viewed as ends in themselves and in reality as the true rationale and purpose for any development-related program. Concerning the preferential option for the poor, the Church teaches that the poor of society maintain "the single most urgent economic claim on the conscience of [a] nation"[77] and that economic policies must be evaluated as to how their consequences directly affect them. Preferential option for the poor means that any economic program must be geared primarily toward helping the African poor meet their basic needs and move them toward self-sufficiency, not toward helping corrupt governments and multinational corporations earn ever-increasing profits at the expense of those they exploit along the way. In addition, preferential option for the poor also means that debt-repayment and structural adjustment programs must be constantly monitored to assure that their resulting effects do not cause greater harm to the poorest members of African society.

African liberation theology's focus on anthropological poverty also demonstrates that in order to be effective, any authentic development program must rely on Africans themselves. Again, although not stated explicitly, a common thread underlying Éla's and Magesa's understanding of development is that no one other than Africans themselves can better recognize both the shortcomings of past development policies and also what Africa needs for its future economic prosperity.[78] In this sense, African liberation theology's emphasis on overcoming anthropological poverty reflects the Catholic social principles of participation and subsidiarity. Concerning participation, the Church teaches that all people have the right to participate in those societal decisions that directly affect their lives, including those decisions that affect their economic prosperity. However, as even the most cursory reading of their history would show, the African people's participation in the formation, implementation, and evaluation of any economic or development-related program has been severely lacking. So long as Africans are denied their right to participate in the decision-making processes that determine their own economic well-being, any future development policy (whether Western-imposed or otherwise) will likely be doomed to failure. Concerning subsidiarity, the Church teaches that responsibility for maintaining the health and well-being of any society should remain at the most local level possible and that a "higher" authority can only step in when the "lower" authority loses its ability to perform this function effectively. Beginning with the colonial period and continuing to this very day, the West has repeatedly violated this principle by not allowing the African people to take any real responsibility for their own economic prosperity. In order for any sub-Saharan development policy to bear fruit, the responsibility for formulating, implementing, and administering it must be given, to the greatest degree possible, to the African people themselves.[79]

In somewhat more explicit terms, African liberation theology's focus on anthropological poverty also incorporates the principles of community, solidarity, and the common good. Concerning community, the Church teaches that because humans are intrinsically social creatures, it is only in relationship with others that they can express their full dignity and full humanity. Concerning solidarity, it teaches that because true growth and prosperity can only be achieved through human interdependence, all people must commit themselves to both serving and working toward the greater good of their neighbors. With these principles in mind, Magesa's claim that cooperative living is the "common theme" underlying any valid expression of African Socialism becomes that much more relevant. Similarly, greater relevance is also afforded to Éla's claim that because humans are social creatures, liberation/salvation must be recognized in terms of humanity as a whole and that in its temporal expression Christian faith calls on all people to "dis-alienate" themselves from their sisters and brothers.[80] Concerning the common good, the Church incorporates the principles of human dignity, participation, community and solidarity to teach that all people have both the right to participate in and the duty to contribute to the continual improvement of society as a whole. With this principle in mind, I repeat Éla's claim that the only form of economic development compatible with Christian faith is one that promotes the common good because it is only in the experience of "collective promotion" that God entrusts creation to humanity. I also recall Magesa's claim that African socialism recognizes the right of all people to the basic necessities of life before one can possess wealth "in excess," and also that within any development policy the "primordial needs" of food, water, and shelter must take precedence over any extraneous needs. Thus, because their emphases on both identifying and overcoming the effects of anthropological poverty provide a means to apply the basic economic principles of Catholic social teaching to present-day African life, Mveng, Éla, and Magesa each make an important contribution to the construction of an African theology of development.

Finally, on what may be a more "theological" level, I conclude this chapter by demonstrating how these three expressions of African liberation theology avoid two important criticisms leveled against liberation theology as a whole. Speaking primarily to its Latin American formulations, Joseph Cardinal Ratzinger, Prefect of the Church's Congregation for the Doctrine of the Faith, claims the "danger" of many liberation theologies is that by focusing so exclusively on freeing people from oppressive secular structures they fail to recognize that Christianity views liberation primarily in terms of liberation from sin. Stated differently, Ratzinger charges that some liberation theologians fail to recognize sin as the greatest "oppressor" from which humanity needs to be liberated and as such do not present their adherents with a complete understanding of what liberation actually entails.[81]

These three expressions of African liberation theology avoid this criticism by maintaining that in addition to working for external change in unjust societal structures, there must be an internal transformation as well. This call for internal liberation is best demonstrated by Magesa who argues that in curing the paralyzed man Christ coupled "Your sins are forgiven!" with "Get up and walk!" to demonstrate that both metanoia and forgiveness are necessary in order to empower one to self-reliance. Mveng also speaks of liberation from sin through his claim that the Beatitude virtues provide the model for a spirituality of liberation, one that enables people to make a conscious choice to live in accord with God's will rather than bow to the lures of the world. Although criticized for dealing almost exclusively with liberation from oppressive societal structures in his earlier works *African Cry* and *My Faith as an African*,[82] Éla indirectly upholds the centrality of liberation from sin in a more recent essay concerning the liberating function of the Church as a whole. Criticizing the shortcomings of the colonial Christian missionaries, he claims the "partial" and "incomplete" message they preached was focused exclusively on "freeing" the African people from their sinfulness while deliberately ignoring their liberation in the temporal realm. He also maintains that as part-and-parcel of its present-day mission the African Catholic church must "rediscover the totality of liberation in a context both socio-economic *and religious*," and that any comprehensive understanding of liberation must involve not only freedom in the spiritual order, but freedom in the temporal order as well.[83] From these statements it is evident that although the call for liberation from sin is not Éla's primary concern, it is clearly assumed. Éla does not deny the theological understanding of liberation, he simply claims the African Catholic Church has been *too* focused on preaching liberation from sin and not focused enough on working for liberation in the economic, political, and social structures of African society.[84]

African liberation theology also avoids a second major criticism, that of formulating theological systems based on secular ideologies. Once again criticizing Latin American liberation theology, Cardinal Ratzinger claims it is "theologically unacceptable" and "socially dangerous" to mix the Bible with politics, sociology, and economics because neither Scripture nor Catholic theology must ever be used to "absolutize" or "sacralize" any theory concerning the socio-political order.[85] In making this statement, Ratzinger is particularly targeting those liberation theologians who employ the class struggle and revolutionary elements of Marxist ideology in formulating their theological positions. Because Marxist ideology is always grounded in a socio-political order that is "contingent," he claims that anyone who mixes theology with ideology only succeeds in "producing a dreamy fanaticism" that in actuality can lead to even greater injustice and oppression.[86]

As with the previous concern, these three expressions of African liberation theology avoid this second "error" as well. In a direct (although unintentional) response to Ratzinger's cautions, Éla states that the very concept of development presupposes that no worldly institution or ideology is "sacred," and also that the true task of development is humanity's becoming what it is meant to become in accord with God's design. With these claims, Éla clearly maintains the "contingency" of the temporal order and also argues that the true purpose of any development program is to move humanity toward the ultimate fulfillment of God's will. Similarly, as it seeks first and foremost to free the individual from anthropological impoverishment, African liberation theology does not "absolutize" or "sacralize" any specific element of the temporal world but instead focuses on the liberation of human life itself. Therefore, just as the Congregation for the Doctrine of the Faith teaches that temporal liberation "involves all the processes which aim at securing and guaranteeing the conditions needed for the exercise of authentic human freedom,"[87] African liberation theology teaches that the African people must be afforded the dignity they deserve as human persons and then be freed to express this dignity in every aspect of their lives.

Furthermore, Mveng, Éla, and Magesa explicitly reject the totality of Marxist ideology as evidenced by the fact that each conspicuously distances himself from any expression of liberation theology that even remotely endorses it. Mveng does this by differentiating anthropological from material poverty and by claiming that because it is so narrowly focused on the oppression caused by capitalist political and economic structures, Marxist analysis really has little to offer to the plight of the African people. Éla claims that Marxist philosophy is not relevant for many of the difficulties facing the African sub-continent and that his own understanding of liberation was formed from reading the "fathers" of the Negritude movement, from his recognition of the realities facing the African sub-continent, and from his own pastoral work with the Kirdis of Northern Cameroon. Finally, Magesa distances himself from this criticism by claiming that although some of its elements might be relevant in specific struggles for justice, Marxism is an imported ideology and, particularly because of its "crude atheism," is one that does not truly speak to the reality of African life. As such, African Socialism "feel[s] no obligation" to Marx, "couldn't care less" about Marxism as a viable philosophical system, and explicitly rejects it as a model for African economic and social development.[88] Thus in their quest to overcome repressive societal structures, these three expressions of African liberation theology do not rely on the Marxist concept of class struggle or on any "scientific" understanding of human history. Instead, echoing the Congregation for the Doctrine of the Faith's further claim that the "logical consequence" of liberation from sin includes freedom in the cultural, social, political, and economic spheres of life,[89] Mveng, Éla, and Magesa maintain that the primary temporal function of African liberation theology is to free people to become who God intends them to be. In terms of constructing a theology of economic development, they each claim that it is only through prior anthropological liberation in the cultural, social, and spiritual realms of human life that true liberation in the economic realm can realistically take place.

Notes

[1] Emmanuel Martey, *African Theology: Liberation and Inculturation* (Maryknoll, NY: Orbis Books, 1993), 69-70, 122-124. It should be noted that Martey places feminist and black theology under the liberation category. For more on inculturation and liberation as the two main themes of African theology, see Chukwudum Okolo's *The Liberating Role of the Church in Africa Today: Spearhead 119* (Eldoret, Kenya: AMECEA Gaba Publications, 1991), 69-74.

[2] As an example of an African inculturation theologian who speaks of development-related issues, one whose argument I do not find convincing, see Elochukwu Uzukwu's *A Listening Church: Autonomy and Communion in African Churches* (Maryknoll, NY: Orbis Books, 1996), 66-103. I might add that while I certainly believe African inculturation theology maintains an important function even to this day, others are not so sure. In a scathing critique of how inculturation theology was "practiced" in Africa during the 1980s and early 1990s, Zaïrian Bénézet Bujo states: "No one could take seriously a theology which preached the necessity of inculturation but simply ignored surrounding social misery ... The theology of inculturation so often preached triumphantly in African churches is a pompous irrelevance, truly an ideological superstructure at the service of the bourgeoisie. It may be the cause of some satisfaction in that the African hierarchy has adopted a theology of incarnation as its official policy. So far, however, there have been more words than actions and one cannot help wondering how serious is the commitment of the bishops of Africa to a truly effective incarnation of Christianity in Africa." See Bénézet Bujo, *African Theology in its Social Context*, translated by John O'Donohue (Maryknoll, NY: Orbis Books, 1992), 70-71.

[3] See Justin Ukpong's "Theological Literature from Africa," in *Theologies of the Third World: Convergences and Differences: Concilium, 199*, eds. Leonardo Boff and Virgil Elizondo (Edinburgh: T & T Clark, 1988), 67-75.

[4] Born in 1930, Mveng joined the Jesuit order after completing his secondary education. He studied at the University of Dakar, Senegal, the Jesuit faculty of Fourvières in Lyons, France, and earned a doctorate from the Sorbonne. Mveng's scholarly work can be best described as interdisciplinary. Beginning in 1965 he taught in the history department at the University of Yaoundé, Cameroon (at various times serving as the department chairperson)

and wrote a two volume *Histoire de Cameroun* (1985). In addition, he was a consultant to UNESCO from 1963-1966, the head of Cultural Affairs for the Cameroonian Ministry of Education and Culture from 1966-1974, an avid artist, and also a member of both the Academy of Overseas Sciences and the Académie Française. As a theologian, Mveng served as the Secretary General of both the Ecumenical Association of African Theologians (1980-1994) and the Ecumenical Association of Third World Theologians (1981-1986), edited *Spiritualité et libération en Afrique* (1985), and wrote numerous articles on the African Catholic Church. Mveng was also an outspoken critic of the political leadership in Cameroon and although never proven, this criticism most likely led to his murder in April, 1995.

[5] Englebert Mveng, "African Liberation Theology," translated by Barrie Mackay in *Theologies of the Third World: Convergences and Differences,* 17-34 at 17-18.

[6] I should note that in this and other essays, Mveng employs the terms "First World" and "Third World." I am not introducing these terms into his work.

[7] Mveng also believes that black African theology incorporates both inculturation and ecumenism as well. Concerning inculturation, he maintains African culture itself must be evangelized by Christianity so that it (culture) can be "integrated into the eternal Christian heritage" and thus cause this heritage to become more "catholic." However inculturation also entails the Africanization of Christianity so that it (Christianity) can become a "constituent of the spiritual and cultural inheritance of Africa." In other words, inculturation must be viewed as a two-way street. One cannot simply claim that inculturation entails the influence or "augmentation" of African traditional culture by Christianity, it entails traditional African culture influencing and "augmenting" Christianity (and in particular the Catholic Church) as well. According to Mveng, it is to this second "element" of inculturation that liberation theology can make a significant contribution. Concerning African ecumenism, Mveng contends that it must not be understood as the "institutionalism of the division of (Western) churches;" instead African ecumenism entails the forces of reconciliation, unity, and solidarity that are rooted in the ancestor tradition of traditional African life. In other words, African ecumenism is grounded in the fact that all Africans whether Christian, Islamic, or followers of the indigenous religious all share a common heritage in the ancestor tradition. See Mveng's "African Liberation Theology," 18. For a brief yet informative discussion of the African

ancestor tradition and its possible application to the present-day African Catholic Church, see Bénézet Bujo's *African Theology in its Social Context*, 17-37 and 75-114.

[8] Mveng, "Spiritualité et libération en Afrique," in *Spiritualité et libération en Afrique*, ed. Engelbert Mveng (Paris: Editions L'Harmattan, 1985), 13-25 at 19-23. Interestingly, Theo Witvliet claims this struggle between the "forces of life" and the "forces of death" is the "determinative feature" of Mveng's theological writings as a whole. According to Witvliet, Mveng believes that humanity is involved in a "dramatic conflict" between life and death, that human life is the battlefield on which this conflict takes place, and that human persons are the "combatants" who must chose which path to follow. In the end, this conflict ultimately becomes meaningful in life's victory over death. See Theo Witvliet's *A Place in the Sun: Liberation Theology in the Third World*, translated by John Bowden (Maryknoll, NY: Orbis Books, 1985), 92.

[9] Mveng, "Impoverishment and Liberation: A Theological Approach for Africa and the Third World," translated by Robert R. Barr, in *Paths of African Theology*, ed. Rosino Gibellini (Maryknoll, NY: Orbis Books, 1994), 154-165 at 156; italics in original.

[10] Mveng, *L'Afrique dans l'église: Paroles d'un croyant* (Paris: Editions L'Harmattan, 1986), 203-207. See also Mveng's "De la sous-mission à la succession," in *Civilization noire et Église catholique* (Paris: Presence Africaine, 1978), 267-276 at 271-273.

[11] Mveng, "A Cultural Perspective," in *Doing Theology in a Divided World*, ed. Virginia Fabelle and Sergio Torres (Maryknoll, NY: Orbis Books, 1983), 72-75. Former Malwian bishop Patrick Kalilombe agrees with Mveng by claiming the task for the Third World (and for Third World theologians) is to denounce the true motives behind the present North/South relationship, expose the power, prejudice, and dominating attitudes of the North, and demonstrate the inherent hypocrisy in the relationship. However, he also claims that this is only half the task. What also needs to happen is the "annunciation" of a new vision for the relationship, a vision that is based on solidarity, communication, and cooperation and one that views the "other" not as an impersonal object for "study and manipulation," but as a subject in its own right with whom exchange is made for the benefit of all. See Kalilombe's

"How Do We Share 'Third World' Christian Insights in Europe?" *African Ecclesial Review* 40 (1998), 19.

[12] In a later publication, Mveng further defines culture as "The conception of the world, humanity, and God proper to a given people and starting from how the people try to organize their lives every day, organize the world in which they live, and organize their own system of thinking." It is only from this understanding of culture that true dialogue can take place. See Engelbert Mveng and B.L. Lipawing, *Théologie, libération et cultures africaines: Dialogue sur l'anthropologie négro-africaine* (Yaoundé, Cameroon: Editions CLE, 1996), 58. Commenting on the intimate relationship between respect for culture and authentic human development, Nigerian Chukwudum Okolo claims: "True development for Africa ... is through the resources of [the people's] own, not alien culture. So there is a strong connection between culture and *freedom*, because if people predominately reflect foreign elements in their culture they cannot be said to be really *free*. The struggle for *cultural freedom* by Africans is a reflection of their desire to recapture their culture and social ideals as the authentic path to self-identity, self-knowledge, and self-survival." See Okolo's *The Liberating Role of the Church in Africa Today*, 13 (italics in original).

[13] Mveng, "Impoverishment and Liberation," 154-155.

[14] See Chapter Two, at note 61.

[15] Mveng, *L'Afrique dans l'église*, 211-213.

[16] Bénézet Bujo, *The Ethical Dimension of Community: The African Model and Dialogue Between North and South* (Nairobi, Kenya: Paulines Publications Africa, 1998), 134-137.

[17] Martey, 38 and 130-131.

[18] Ecumenical Association of Third World Theologians (EATWOT), "African Report," in *Third World Theologies: Commonalities and Divergences*, ed. K.C. Abraham (Maryknoll, NY: Orbis Books, 1990), 28-56 at 47-48.

[19] Mveng and Lipawing, 28-31

[20] Ibid., 28-31. Mveng further claims that the first written manifestation of an African liberation theology was the 1956 publication of *Des prêtres noirs s'interrogent*; however, citing the works of Gustavo Gutiérrez and James Cone, it was not until the 1960s that liberation theology in both Latin America and North America came into its own. See his "African Liberation Theology," 30-31.

[21] Mveng and Lipawing, 33-34, 38-40. I must question Mveng here about his apparently narrow vision of Latin American liberation theology. While many expressions of Latin American liberation theology focus on overcoming oppressive political and economic structures, as a whole they do not completely neglect these "other" aspects of poverty. As an example, Gustavo Gutiérrez speaks to various dimensions of poverty in his *A Theology of Liberation*. According to Gutiérrez: "'Dominated peoples,' 'exploited social classes,' 'despised races,' and 'marginalized cultures' were formulas often used in speaking of the poor in the context of liberation theology. The point of these formulas was to make it clear that the poor have a social dimension. But the turbulent situation in Latin America has caused many to place an almost exclusive emphasis on the social and economic aspect of poverty (this was a departure from the original insight). I am indeed convinced that it is still necessary to call attention to this dimension of poverty if we are to do more than touch the surface of the real situation of the poor, but I also insist that we must be attentive to other aspects of poverty as well ... In the final analysis, poverty means death: lack of food and housing, the inability to attend properly to health and education needs, the exploitation of workers, permanent unemployment, the lack of respect for one's human dignity, and unjust limitations placed on personal freedom in the areas of self-expression, politics, and religion." Gustavo Gutiérrez *A Theology of Liberation*, 15th Anniversary Edition, translated by Sr. Caridad Inda and John Eagleson (Maryknoll, NY: Orbis Books, 1988), xxi.

[22] See Mveng and Lipawing, 32-34, 40-43 and also Mveng's *Afrique dans l'église*, 206-207. In addition to this criticism of Marxist analysis, Mveng also claims that because the methodology one employs in constructing a theology of liberation is contextual (in that it arises from one's own concrete situation), there is a real danger that the theologian may become "frozen" in his or her own experience and tend to generalize what liberation is even for those who do not share a similar context. As an example, he claims that in Latin America one finds liberation theologians who, proceeding from their own contexts, believe the root cause of their oppression is Western capitalism and thus make

"universal" claims that liberation is essentially economic and/or political without taking into consideration that there are other causes for oppression in other parts of the world. Because the exploitation of Western capitalism is the primary focus of Latin American theologians, they have not dealt with issues of racism, culture, and what it means to be a human person, issues that are profoundly relevant for Latin America but have not been adequately examined. In fact, Mveng claims there are serious, inexplicable lacunae in Latin American liberation theology because for decades it has "coexisted" with racial discrimination (he specifically cites the situation in Brazil) without sufficiently recognizing it or challenging it. See Mveng and Lipawing, 51-53, 59.

[23] In making this claim I must also note there are African Catholic theologians who do see the relevance of Latin American liberation theology for the African context. Nigerian Chukwudum Okolo identifies three themes of Latin American liberation theology that have relevance to the African situation. First, the notion of contextuality is very important for the African Church because if it is to become "decolonized" or free itself from the cultural captivity of the West, it must root itself and its theology in the fact that African Christians are, in fact, Africans. Second, the Latin American claim that Christian faith must take on practical meanings in people's lives demonstrates to the African Church how it must become more dynamic in its criticism of African society. For Okolo, there is a tendency with the African Church to make "sterile and ineffective denunciations" of the problems in African life without offering real solutions. If the faith is to become more dynamic and take root in people's lives, the Church must move beyond the spiritual realm and learn that working for people's material needs is an important aspect of preaching God's kingdom. Third, just as Latin American liberation theology views the human person as a subject or an active participant in history and not simply an object or passive observer, so the African Church must teach that Africans must take charge of their own destinies. Whereas "passive submission" rather than "active participation" characterizes the attitude of many African faithful, the Church needs to become one of dialogue, critical reflection, initiative, and participation. Nevertheless, although Okolo maintains that African liberation theology can follow in the general direction of Latin American liberation theology, the specific name or form it takes "should depend on the nature and experience of Africans." See Chukwudum Okolo's "Liberation Theology and the African Church," *Bulletin of African Theology* 4 (July-December, 1982), 174-186; "African Liberation Theology: Concept and Necessity," *Africa: Kairos of a Synod: SEDOS Bulletin* 94 (1994), 103; and *The Liberating Role of the Church in Africa Today*, 72.

[24] See the introduction by Simon E. Smith, SJ, to Jean Marc Éla's *My Faith as an African*, translated by John Brown and Susan Perry (Maryknoll, NY: Orbis Books, 1988), ix.

[25] Pan-African Conference of Third World Theologians, "Final Communiqué," in *African Theology En-Route*, eds. Kofi Appiah-Kubi & Sergio Torres (Maryknoll, NY: Orbis Books, 1979), 189-195 at 194; my emphasis.

[26] EATWOT, "African Report," 47. For more concerning the discussion of this conference on the limitations of both Marxist analysis and Latin American liberation theology as a whole, see Frank Chikane's "EATWOT and Third World Theologies: An Evaluation of the Past and Present," in *Third World Theologies: Commonalities and Divergences*, 147-169 at 150-159. At the time, Chikane was the General Secretary of the South African Council of Churches.

[27] I note once again that economic development is not the primary focus of either African liberation theology or of any of the specific theologians examined in this chapter. Nevertheless, because the African understanding of liberation encompasses all aspects of human life, African liberation theology recognizes the importance of true economic development.

[28] Éla was born in 1936 to a peasant farming family in southern Cameroon and grew up during the final years of the European colonial period. Under the tutelage of the Benedictines, he studied theology in Cameroon and in 1964 he was ordained a diocesan priest. He studied both theology and sociology in France and Belguim, completed a doctorate in theology at the University of Strasbourg in 1969, and completed a second doctorate in sociology in 1978. Éla worked for a number of years ministering to the Kirdi people of northern Cameroon, taught at the University of Yaoundé (Cameroon), and in August of 1995 fled to Canada following the murder of his colleague Engelbert Mveng, SJ.

[29] This point about the "unsystematic" nature of Éla's work is underscored by Philip Gibbs in his *The Word in the Third World: Divine Revelation in the Theology of Jean-Marc Éla, Aloysius Pieris, and Gustavo Gutiérrez* (Rome: Pontifical Gregorian University, 1996), 99. Éla himself states: "Faced with this situation (specifically, the forcing of Kirdi farmers to plant cash crops instead of food staples), I had to free myself immediately from a certain number of

constraints in order to get a fresh perspective on the problems of my mission. I did not feel called to become the manager of a form of decaying Christianity, bound up in its doctrine and discipline, so I decided to keep my distance from a model of church designed elsewhere by people who do not know the conditions of the mountain people." See Éla's *My Faith as an African*, 4-5.

[30] Éla, *My Faith as an African*, xvi-xviii. In making this claim, Éla cites Claude Geffré's *Théologie et choc des cultures* (Paris: Cerf, 1984), 10-11.

[31] Janet Vaillant, Associate Director of the Soviet and East European Language and Area Center Program at Harvard University, states that although Senghor credited Césaire with inventing the term *Negritude*, the two men actually "developed its significance" together. In short, they took French adjective for black, *nègre*, and transformed it into a noun by adding the suffix "*-itude*." For Senghor, Negritude meant "the manner of self-expression of the black character, the black world, black civilization." Césaire held that Negritude was "[the] recognition of the fact of being black, and the acceptance of that fact, of our destiny as black, of our history and our culture." Thus, from its very beginnings Negritude maintained two distinct meanings. For Senghor it was "an objective visible reality, namely black culture, style, and character." For Césaire it was "the acceptance by the black individual of the importance of his color and its significance for him in everything he did." According to Vaillant, Negritude was for Césaire an attitude while for Senghor it was an objective reality. See Vaillant's *Black, French and African: The Life of Léopold Sédar Senghor* (Cambridge, MA: Harvard University Press, 1990), 244.

[32] See Éla's interview in Philip Gibbs' *The Word in the Third World*, 351-352.

[33] Éla, "Globalization et paupérization: Un défi à la théologie africaine," in *Liberation Theologies on Shifting Grounds: A Clash of Socio-Economic and Cultural Paradigms*, ed. G. de Schrijver (Leuven, Belguim: Leuven University Press, 1998), 153-175 at 163-173.

[34] Particularly because of his calls for liberation from Rome, historian Paul Gifford states that Éla has been marginalized by both the Catholic Church in Africa and by Rome. While he taught at the University of Yaoundé (Cameroon) and at the Faculté Protestante, Éla celebrated very popular weekly Masses that were characterized by liturgical inculturation and "radical, socially

aware sermons." However, although he was always welcome to speak to students, he was never allowed to teach at the Catholic University in Yaoundé. Gifford claims the "official" reasons offered for Éla's marginalization include that he was a sociologist and not a theologian, that he wrote primarily for the West, and that his writings had no bearing on the life of people in the villages. See Paul Gifford's *African Christianity: Its Public Role* (London: Hurst & Co., 1998), 269-270.

[35] In fact, Éla claims theology "is nothing more than reflection fashioned of the stuff of lived experience" and that one can only gain an understanding of God's Word through an understanding of a people's historical situation. See Éla's *African Cry*, translated by Robert R. Barr (Maryknoll, NY: Orbis Books, 1986), 28-29; and *My Faith as an African*, 103.

[36] Éla, *African Cry*, 29-33. In making these claims Éla cites Jürgan Moltmann: "The God of the Exodus is a God of promise and of leaving the present to face the future, a God whose freedom is the source of new things that are to come ... His name is a wayfaring name, a promise that discloses a new future, a name whose truth is experienced in history inasmuch as his promise discloses its future possibilities." See Moltmann, *Theology of Hope: On the Ground and the Implications of a Christian Eschatology* (New York: Harper and Row, 1967), 30. Engelbert Mveng, SJ, agrees with Éla by claiming that an African reading of the Bible must overcome the interpretations of those who have "held captive" and "disfigured" the true biblical message. According to Mveng, the concepts of race, chosen people, and covenant have been effectively manipulated by "oppressors" to justify the racism and systems of domination that have existed since the dawn of the colonial period. In response, an African reading of the Bible must closely examine these concepts and demonstrate that each of them can only be understood within the context of salvation and freedom for the oppressed. In short, the biblical concepts of race, chosen people, and covenant paradigmatically serve as examples of God's preferential option for the poor. Thus the goal of any African reading of the Bible is to exorcise, demythologize, and rid these concepts of their mystery and then reconstruct them to their original meaning. See Mveng's "African Liberation Theology," 27-28.

[37] *African Cry*, 34-36.

[38] Ibid., 36-38. Interestingly, in only his second footnote to this entire discussion, Éla further justifies his claim for the Church's prophetic mission by

citing Jesus' quote of Isaiah (Luke 4:16-21): "The Spirit of the Lord is upon me, because he has anointed me to bring glad tidings to the poor. He has sent me to proclaim liberty to captives and recovery of sight to the blind, to let the oppressed go free, and to proclaim a year acceptable to the Lord" (NAB). For Éla, this quote of Jesus indicates what he (Éla) terms an "actualization of the Exodus" or a "recovery of the Exodus event for the present." He claims it is this Exodus tradition which "permeates" the entirety of the Old Testament and for Jesus was the "prototype" of both God's actions in history and the type of action God expected of God's people (142).

[39] Unless otherwise noted, Éla's contributions in this section are taken from his two most well-known theological works *African Cry* (1980) and *My Faith as an African* (1985). These books were originally published under the French titles *Ma foi d'Africain* and *Le cri de l'homme africain: Questions aux chrétiens et aux églises d'Afrique*.

[40] *African Cry*, 62-63. See Chapter One of this study for further examples of how colonial policies continue to effect African life today.

[41] Ibid., 63-64. Citing former Tanzanian President Julius Nyerere (although without providing a specific reference), Éla makes the same argument in *My Faith as an African*, 88-89, 96.

[42] *My Faith as an African*, 90. In fact, Éla defines development as "a destructive integration into the world market, creating a socio-cultural and political situation where the growing of cotton for export benefits only the traditional leaders, the ranks of administration, the dignitaries of the government party, and the multinational corporations" (95) He also claims the "vulgar ideology of development" is in reality "a plan that licenses whatever is used to starve a people, under the pretext of accumulating foreign exchange, for the profit of a club of the affluent" (97).

[43] *African Cry*, 85.

[44] Ibid., 64, 85-86.

[45] Ibid., 87-89. For further information concerning the emphasis Éla places on liberation, see Gibbs' *The Word in the Third World,* 127-130.

[46] *African Cry*, 89-90, 93, 98.

[47] Ibid., 90-92; my emphasis.

[48] *My Faith as an African*, 151, 154-155.

[49] Ibid., 151-152.

[50] *African Cry*, 74-78.

[51] In a 1994 essay "Christianity and Liberation in Africa," Éla both summarizes and restates his basic argument from *African Cry* and *My Faith as an African*. In short, he cites the dependency caused by both multinational corporations and the African élites, claims the "irruption of the poor" seriously calls into question the focus and praxis of African Christianity, restates that the Church must incarnate the gospel in Africa with a spirit of liberation, and emphasizes that the only way for Christianity to be credible is if it is willing to "get its hands dirty" and involve itself in the concrete issues facing the future of the African people. See Éla's "Christianity and Liberation in Africa," translated by Robert R. Barr, in *Paths of African Theology*, ed. Rosino Gibellini (Maryknoll, NY: Orbis Books, 1994), 136-153.

[52] Éla, The Church-Sacrament of Liberation," in *The African Synod: Documents, Reflections, Perspectives*, ed. Africa Faith and Justice Network (Maryknoll, NY: Orbis Books, 1996), 131-138. In making these claims, Éla cites the final statement of the 1971 International Synod of Bishops (Rome) and Pope Paul VI's *Evangelii Nuntiandi*.

[53] Recall from Chapter One how reductions in public sector salaries leads to increased corruption and also how money spent on debt repayment could be better used to fight illness, illiteracy, and malnutrition.

[54] Éla, *Afrique: L'irruption des pauvres: Société contre ingérence, pouvoir et argent* (Paris: Éditions L'Harmattan, 1994), 45-59, see also 194-197. Speaking further of the difficulties facing African development, Éla claims the World Bank's discourse on the current crisis in Africa demonstrates that it does not recognize how the socio-economic structures inherited from the colonial period remain one of the primary reasons for Africa's present-day economic difficulties (125).

[55] As demonstrated in Chapter One, in order to remain solvent African governments are dependent upon foreign financial assistance. However, to ever-increasing degrees, this foreign assistance carries with it "conditionalities" of reform, conditionalities that in effect allow the international financial institutions to control virtually every aspect of African public life.

[56] Éla, *Innovations sociales et renaissance de l'Afrique noir* (Paris: Harmattan, 1998), 360-368; my translations.

[57] Magesa holds both a Ph.D. and a Th.D. from St. Paul University (Ottawa, Ontario, Canada). He is a former professor of moral theology at the Catholic University of East Africa (Nairobi, Kenya), a former visiting Professor at the Maryknoll School of Theology (New York), and continues to teach summer courses at the Maryknoll Institute of African Studies in Nairobi. He is also a priest of the diocese of Musoma, Tanzania and is presently at Belcama Parish, Tarime, Tanzania.

[58] This same story is also found in Matthew 9:1-8 and Luke 5:17-26.

[59] Similar to Éla, Magesa includes temporal liberation within his overall understanding of salvation.

[60] Magesa, *The Church and Liberation in Africa: Spearhead 44* (Eldoret, Kenya: AMECEA Gaba Publications, 1976), 2-8.

[61] Ibid., 8-9.

[62] Magesa, "The Political Axis of African Liberation Theology," 130-152 at 137.

[63] Magesa, *The Church and Liberation in Africa*, 17-19. For further perspectives on the "psychological oppression" of both the slave trade and colonialism, see Magesa's "Am I not a Human Being and a Brother/Sister?" *African Ecclesial Review* 34 (1992), 95-114; and John Mary Waliggo's "The North and Africa: A Question of Justice," in *Africa, the Kairos of a Synod: SEDOS Symposium on Africa*, ed. Walter von Holzen, SVD and Seán Fagan, SM (Rome: SEDOS, 1994), 147-162 at 149-157.

[64] Magesa defines globalization as "the era of de facto universal linkage and interdependencies that intertwine and affect the lives of people

worldwide." See his "The Political Axis of African Liberation Theology," 139. In offering this definition, Magesa cites C. J. Collins' "Reshaping Africa: Effects of Economic Globalization," *Africa Faith and Justice Network* 401 (1996), 1.

[65] As explained in Chapter One, the conditionalities of structural adjustment and debt reduction programs include the retrenchment of public employees, the opening of local industries to foreign markets, and the reduction of public service programs such as heath care and education.

[66] Magesa, "Africa's Struggle for Self-Definition During a Time of Globalization," *African Ecclesial Review* 40 (1998), 321-325; and "The Political Axis of African Liberation Theology," 139-140. Magesa adds that globalization has also been a source of alienation in the cultural realm because not only does it bring the "glitter" of Western attitudes, behaviors, and consumer goods to Africa, but it also demonstrates to the African people that "Western is better." As examples, Magesa claims that because African are viewed by the international news media as consumers and not producers, most of the news about Africa is produced from outside the continent itself. Thus, Africans only receive news about themselves through foreign sources and often this news is skewed to fit the needs of the producers without portraying the true African reality. In addition, television has had a profound effect on African culture (especially among the youth) because Western programs have influenced sexual behavior and orientation, affected people's attitudes towards traditional cultural practices, and even cultivated a feeling of shame among Africans about the color of their skin. In fact, Magesa claims that because it portrays a reality that is not the African reality yet one that is accepted by Africans as real, Western television has done more in one decade to alienate Africans from themselves than it took colonialism over a century to do.

[67] Magesa, "The Political Axis of African Liberation Theology," 142-143. Engelbert Mveng, SJ, agrees with Magesa by claiming the issue of poverty is above all else a political problem, one that concerns the justification of the power of the oppressor over the oppressed. For Mveng, the relationship between poverty and power is best exemplified in the present-day African state: "Overwhelmed with debt, strangled by the claws of structural adjustment, prostrate before the International Monetary Fund, on its knees to the captains of cooperation and technological assistance, the black African state is today the most humiliating and shocking incarnation of the debasement of and contempt for black people." See Mveng's "Impoverishment and Liberation," 155, 157.

[68] Magesa *The Church and Liberation in Africa*, 21-23. In defining these specific elements of African Socialism, Magesa cites Julius Nyerere's *Freedom and Socialism* (London: Oxford University Press, 1968), 324-325; and Aylward Shorter's "Two Examples of Development and Continuity in Social Change," in *The African Contribution to World Church* (Kampala, Uganda: Pastoral Institute of Eastern Africa, 1972), 29.

[69] Magesa, *The Church and Liberation in Africa*, 25.

[70] Ibid., 23, 25-26. Speaking further to how private ownership is viewed in African society, Magesa claims in a more recent work that although African Religion emphasizes the communal nature of property, it does not completely forbid private ownership. Instead, the "ethical task" for African religion "is to establish a balance between exclusion and inclusion with regard to the acquisition and use of material resources; in other words, to establish a balance between the rights to private ownership of property and the human meaning of the resources of the universe. Thus, tradition usually indicates the parameters within which personal ownership may be exercised without harming the common good, which, in the end, is always primary. See Magesa's *African Religion: The Moral Traditions of Abundant Life* (Marykoll, NY: Orbis Books, 1997), 277-278. The understanding of private property within African traditional religion will be discussed more fully in Chapter Five.

[71] Magesa, *The Church and Liberation in Africa*, 23.

[72] Magesa, "Christ the Liberator and Africa Today," in *Faces of Jesus in Africa*, ed. Robert J. Schreiter, C.PP.S. (Maryknoll, NY: Orbis Books, 1991), 151-163 at 157.

[73] Magesa, "Christ the Liberator and Africa Today," 158.

[74] Magesa, "Christian Discipleship in Africa in the 21st Century," *African Ecclesial Review* 36 (1994), 294-295. Speaking to the Church's liberating function during the 1970s, Magesa argued that it has a "special role" to play in bridging the chasm between the theoretical need for greater "humanism" (which includes economic development) and practical action in the real world. In this sense, the Church must act as the conscience of humanity and arouse individuals to work toward justice and liberation for all people. In fact, Magesa further claims that if the Church fails in this mandate it "atrophies its mission"

and loses its reason for existence. See Magesa's *The Church and Liberation in Africa*, 10.

[75] In their various works both Éla and Magesa demonstrate that on issues such as clerical celibacy, polygamy, liturgy, and authority within the Church (areas of their work not covered in this study), ecclesial regulations "imposed" by Rome have been met with either indifference or outright opposition. The reason for this is that these regulations do not take into consideration the realities of African life.

[76] In making this claim I must note that as incredible as it may seem, the Church's social teachings remain largely unknown not only to the African Catholic laity, but also to graduate students in theology and even to many seminarians and priests. Thus, before even beginning to effect real change in African communities, the Church must first educate the African people as to what the Church teaches in terms of economic development.

[77] This formulation is taken from the United States Catholic Conference's "Economic Justice for All," in *Catholic Social Thought: The Documentary Heritage*, eds. David J. O'Brien & Thomas A. Shannon (Maryknoll, NY: Orbis Books, 1995), 572-680 at no. 86.

[78] One could probably include Mveng here even though in his work he does not specifically speak to economic development programs.

[79] I include the qualifier "to the greatest degree possible" with the recognition that given the sub-continent's present-day economic and political situations, in the short-term this call for African responsibility may not be possible. Instead, an African assumption of responsibility might be better recognized as a long-term goal of both African and Western development policy.

[80] Speaking to this sense of community, Engelbert Mveng states that the individual is not a human *person* as such, but in reality only an "outline sketch" of what he or she is to become through integration in society. As such, the human person is characterized by a network of interpersonal and cosmic relations and might in fact be better understood through the Old Testament concept of "corporate personality." See Theo Witvliet's *A Place in the Sun*, 92. Bénézet Bujo adds that not only is the "common ground and connecting thread" of any African ethic the sense of community it affords, but also that the validity

of any ethic is judged on how it upholds the communitarian dimension of African life. See Bujo's *The Ethical Dimension of Community*, 11.

[81] Joseph Ratzinger and Vittorio Messori, *The Ratzinger Report* (San Francisco: Ignatius Press, 1985), 173. The Congregation for the Doctrine of the Faith later underscored this criticism by claiming in its *Instruction on Certain Aspects of the Theology of Liberation* (1984) and *Instruction on Christian Freedom and Liberation* (1986) that the most radical form of slavery is slavery to sin and that any notion of human liberation must begin with the reality of human sinfulness. See the Congregation for the Doctrine of the Faith's *Instruction on Certain Aspects of the Theology of Liberation* (Washington DC: United States Catholic Conference, 1984), 3, 9-12; and also its *Instruction on Christian Freedom and Liberation* (Washington DC: United States Catholic Conference, 1986), 21-22, 28-33. It should be noted that Ratzinger's criticisms of Latin American liberation theology cited here were published before the release of the Congregation for the Doctrine of the Faith's *Instruction on Certain Aspects of the Theology of Liberation.*

[82] As one example of this criticism, Philip Gibbs states that in terms of his understanding of liberation, the sociological orientation of Éla's writing acts as both a strength and a liability. Although this sociological orientation grounds his work in the reality of people's lives and gives his work a true sense of immediacy, it also runs the risk of reducing God's Word to simply the economic, political, and social dimensions of human life. In other words, Gibbs maintains that the problem with Éla's use of sociological language is that it (the language) cannot take into consideration the theological subtleties needed to differentiate between secular liberation in the temporal realm and theological liberation in the spiritual realm. What Éla must do is further develop a faith language that speaks to sociological realities while remaining faithful to the theological concepts of transcendence and human freedom before God. See Gibbs' *The Word in the Third World*, 150.

[83] Éla, "The Church-Sacrament of Liberation," 134-137; my emphasis.

[84] In reality, this "working for liberation" in economic, political, and social structures actually entails combating sin and its resulting effects in African society.

[85] While it is true that in regards to the economic order Mveng, Éla, and Magesa do employ biblical teachings, as will be demonstrated in the following

paragraphs they never use these teachings to either "absolutize" or "sacralize" their own notions of a "properly" functioning economy.

[86] Ratzinger and Messori, *The Ratzinger Report*, 190. For further criticism concerning the use of Marxist analysis, see the Congregation for the Doctrine of the Faith's *Instruction on Certain Aspects of the Theology of Liberation*, 17-22.

[87] Congregation for the Doctrine of the Faith, *Instruction on Christian Freedom and Liberation*, 18.

[88] See Magesa's "Instruction on a 'Theology of Liberation:' A Comment," *African Ecclesial Review* 27 (February, 1985), 6-7.

[89] Congregation for the Doctrine of the Faith, *Instruction on Certain Aspects of the Theology of Liberation*, 3.

Chapter Four

Development and the African Bishops' Conferences

With an understanding of the contributions from three prominent liberation theologians, I now turn to the "second source" for an African theology of development, the African Catholic bishops. Of all the world wide episcopal conference statements concerning development written from 1891-1991, the African bishops as a whole rank numerically third in the world with approximately fourteen percent of all documentation attributed to them. While they lag far behind their European and Latin American counterparts (thirty-seven and twenty-nine percent respectively), they have out produced the bishops of North America (ten percent) and Asia (seven percent), and have written more concerning integral development, corruption, education, and economic goals than the bishops of any other region in the world.[1] Since the Second Vatican Council, the African Catholic bishops have issued over 170 statements concerning economics and development.[2] As it is impossible to examine all of these documents in this chapter, I will focus on a representative sample of them starting with the development statements from the continental assembly of African bishops (SECAM), followed by those from various national and regional episcopal conferences, and finally those from the 1994 Synod for Africa.[3] I conclude the chapter by detailing the common themes within the bishops' statements and then identifying their specific contributions to the formulation of a proposed theology of economic development for sub-Saharan Africa.

Development and SECAM

In the African Church today, there are nine regional episcopal conferences and one continent-wide body. The continent-wide body is the Symposium of Episcopal Conferences of Africa and Madagascar, commonly known as SECAM. Comprised of representatives from the nine regional conferences,[4] SECAM is not an episcopal conference in the juridical or canonical sense. Rather, it is a forum for exchanging ideas and experiences, for study and reflection, and for joint collaborative action amongst the nine regional conferences concerning pressing issues facing the African Church as a whole. SECAM has also been described as the "hinge" or linchpin between the papal magisterim and the local African churches because, while it promotes the universal Church's teachings, through its tri-part "fidelity" to the Word of God, African heritage, and the realities of the modern world, it also functions as the "animating force" for the Church in Africa. Thus, SECAM not only promotes solidarity, communion, and cooperation among the local African churches, but it also aims to promote solidarity, communion, and cooperation between African Catholics and their brothers and sisters from around the world.[5] In my first section of Chapter Four, I examine the SECAM bishops' early statements concerning economic development (1969-1974) and demonstrate how they carefully relate these statements to Catholic social teaching. I then examine in greater detail two important SECAM statements from the early 1980s to demonstrate how the African bishops understand the particular role the Catholic Church must play in the future economic development of the African continent.

1. SECAM 1969-1978: Continuity with Catholic Social Teaching

On the occasion of Pope Paul VI's apostolic visit to Africa in 1969, the First Assembly of SECAM convened in Kampala, Uganda. In their first (albeit very brief) declaration as a unified whole, the African bishops made clear their recognition that the Church has a vital role to play in the economic future of the African continent. According to the SECAM bishops, the primary problem facing Africa is the dual struggle for human development and peace. Because of the misery brought on by poverty and seemingly endless civil wars, they claim that they cannot ignore the hunger, sickness, ignorance, discrimination, and oppression that overwhelms so many in the Third World[6] (especially in Africa) without also "failing gravely" in their overall mission as shepherds of the Church. In other words, in light of the Second Vatican Council's call for the Church as a whole to become more open to the world, the SECAM bishops recognize their duty to both defend and speak for those who cannot defend or speak for themselves. The bishops continue by claiming the full "flowering" of the human person must include his or her "promotion" in the economic, political, cultural, and social realms of life, and that this flowering can only occur in the absence of all forms of discrimination and foreign domination. Furthermore, because the Third World poor are often the victims of injustices perpetrated by the "egoism" of the First World rich, any reform in world economic structures must take into consideration the Third World's right to true development. As such, aid packages must not contain "conditionalities" that are contradictory to human dignity nor must they offer "false solutions" that contradict the African values of family and respect for life.[7]

In making these claims concerning development and the Church's role in the overall process, the SECAM bishops were careful to ground their own teachings within those of the universal Church. Their claim that they cannot ignore the hunger, sickness, and ignorance of the African people without "failing gravely" in their mission reaffirms similar teachings from both the Second Vatican Council and Pope Paul VI. According to the Council's *Gaudium et Spes* (1965), although Christ did not mandate to the Church a "proper mission" in the economic, political, or social orders, the religious mission he did mandate to the Church can help to "structure and consolidate" human society according to God's divine law. As such, when situations arise where people are in desperate material need, the Church "can and indeed should initiate activities on behalf of all men ... particularly activities designed for the needy."[8] Similarly, Paul VI maintained in *Populorum Progressio* (1967) that the world situation demands "concerted action" based on a clear understanding of the economic, social, cultural, and spiritual aspects of human life. Because the Church exists within history and was founded by Christ to promote God's reign on earth, it can assist people to attain their "full flowering" by offering them her characteristic attributes, "a global vision of man and of the human race."[9]

In terms of the difficulties inherent with Africa's reception of foreign aid and its economic relations with the West, the SECAM bishops also echoed both the Second Vatican Council and Pope Paul VI. The Council bishops state that although the development of any nation depends on both human and financial assistance from foreign nations, the assistance of "experts" should not be rendered in "lordly fashion" but instead be offered in a spirit of mutual cooperation.[10] Paul VI states in his 1967 *Africae Terrarum* that even though many African nations have gained their independence, they fear that the financial and technical aid they receive from more developed nations will restrict their abilities to chart their own economic futures. Citing John XXIII's *Pacem in Terris* (no. 123) and his own *Populorum Progressio* (no. 65), Paul VI emphatically states that developing nations must never be regarded as "inferior," that the dignity of those who receive aid must be respected absolutely, and that nations receiving aid must remain primarily responsible for their own development.[11] Concerning equity in international trade relations, Paul VI recognizes in *Populorum Progressio* that because the prices for raw materials exported by developing nations are subject to wild and sudden fluctuations in the international markets, many developing nations cannot rely on these exports to ensure their future prosperity. He also perceives that because the "rule of free trade" often favors "rich" nations at the expense of "poorer" ones, it must not be the sole determinant of international relations. Instead, without completely abolishing the competitive market, social justice demands that international trade relations become more just and moral, and that they offer all participants a "certain equality of opportunity."[12]

In addition to reaffirming these earlier teachings, the SECAM bishops' claim that they "fail gravely" in their mission if they ignore the temporal needs of their people also foreshadowed a central (and controversial) teaching from the 1971 International Synod of Bishops in Rome.[13] Gathered from around the globe to discuss ever-increasing instances of injustice, the bishops' assembly issued "Justice in the World," a pastoral that called upon the Church as a whole to more fully commit itself to working for justice and peace. In perhaps the most often cited quotation from the entire text, the synod bishops maintain that "action on behalf of justice and participation in the transformation of the world fully appear to us as a constitutive dimension of the preaching of the gospel, or ...of the Church's mission for the redemption of the human race and its liberation from every oppressive situation."[14] The bishops justify this position by arguing that because our relationships with others are "bound up" in our relationship with

God, because every human person is a "brother of Christ" created in God's image, and because love "implies an absolute demand for justice," our own response to God's love is "shown to be effective" through our love and service of neighbor. Then, concerning the Church as a whole, they claim:

> The Church has received from Christ the mission of preaching the Gospel message, which contains a call to man to turn away from sin to the love of the Father, universal brotherhood, and a consequent demand for justice in the world. This is the reason why the Church has the right, indeed the duty, to proclaim justice on the local, national, and international level, and to denounce instances of injustice when the fundamental rights of man and his very salvation demand it. The Church, indeed is not alone responsible for justice in the world; however, she has a proper and specific responsibility which is identified with her mission of giving witness before the world of the need for love and justice contained in the Gospel message, a witness to be carried out in Church institutions and in the lives of Christians.[15]

Thus, although the SECAM bishops' statement that they "fail gravely" in their mission if they ignore the temporal needs of their people is not specifically cited in this synodal text, the implication is certainly present. Even before the publication of "Justice in the World," the SECAM bishops clearly recognized the vital role the Church must play in efforts to bring about a more just world.

The African bishops' recognition of the Church's role in development efforts was restated three years later at the 1974 International Synod of Bishops in Rome. Gathered once again with their counterparts from around the globe to discuss evangelization and how the Catholic Church could best fulfill its missionary mandate, the African delegation spoke to the development question in its report "Experiences of the Church in the Work of Evangelization in Africa." Citing the fact that Christ himself is intimately concerned with the salvation of the *entire* person, the delegation holds that participating in development efforts and providing social services are not "alien task[s]" of the African Church, but an "integral" element of the gospel message it is called to proclaim. It continues by claiming that just as the Church is mandated to proclaim Christ's prophetic mission and defend "authentic human values," so also must it be willing to confront any social system (or individual) that undermines human dignity or perpetrates injustice. In fact, the Church's prophetic function is rendered "meaningless" if it is not supported by practical involvement in efforts to liberate people from oppression. The African delegation concludes by maintaining that the Church must not be simply a "partner" with the state in promoting development activities, instead it must function as the "soul" of these activities by promoting the spiritual values that both "animate" development and give it its "full human dimension." By defending the values of love, justice, cooperation, and respect for human dignity, the Church promotes temporal progress and also provides the "spiritual corrective" needed to assure that development programs are in accord with gospel teachings.[16]

Once again, the African delegation's contributions were reflected in the final declaration of the 1974 synod as a whole. In their "Evangelization of the Modern World," the synod bishops recognize the "intimate connection" between evangelization and liberation and, citing Luke 4:18,[17] they teach that as part of its overall mission the Church must both announce and actively work to bring about humanity's "integral salvation." Concerning how this is to be accomplished, they claim the Church must draw from the gospels those "profound reasons" and "ever new incentives" that promote service to humanity (especially to the poor, weak, and oppressed) and also eliminate the "social consequences of sin" that are manifested in unjust social structures. Thus, the bishops closely link evangelization with liberation.[18] True Christian evangelization demands practical action in the temporal world.[19]

Drawing upon the work of both the African delegation and the synod as a whole, in 1975 Pope Paul VI promulgated *Evangelii Nuntiandi*, a document that would be heavily cited in future SECAM statements concerning the Church's role in African development efforts. After establishing that the "kernel and center" of Christ's message is the proclamation of salvation and the liberation of humanity from all forms of oppression, the Pope argues that the Church's evangelizing work is not complete if it does not take into consideration the relationship between the gospel message and concrete situations of human life. The reason for this is that evangelization involves an "explicit message" about the rights and duties of all people, about the life of society, about international relations, and about the Church's concern for justice, peace, and development. Then, recalling that many of the bishops at the 1974 Synod (particularly those from the Third World) spoke of the poverty, injustice in trade relations, and instances of economic and cultural colonialism still endured by their people, he states the Church has a duty to proclaim the complete and integral liberation of all people, to give witness to it, to work toward it, and to ensure that it is realized in the world. Thus, efforts toward temporal liberation should never be seen as "foreign" to the Church's overall mission of evangelization.[20]

Paul VI then continues in this vein by claiming there are "profound links" between Christian evangelization and human development. These links exist not only in the anthropological order because the person to be evangelized is subject to the realities of social and economic life, but they exist also in the theological order because one cannot "dissociate" God's plan of creation from that of redemption. It is precisely through these links in the theological order that one recognizes the primary justification for Church involvement in temporal affairs. Because there is such a profound connection between God's plans of creation and redemption, any notion of salvation must incorporate both the temporal as well as the eternal. Stated differently, salvation must be understood not as "beyond" this world and having no connection with it. Instead, salvation begins with this world and as such the Church must be concerned with the temporal affairs of those to whom it ministers. Then, repeating his own words in the opening address to the 1974 Synod of Bishops, the Pope maintains that true evangelization cannot ignore the temporal problems of liberation and development because to do so would be to disregard the gospel exhortation to love one's neighbor. If the Church wishes to truly evangelize, it must promote justice, peace, and the "authentic advancement" of the entire human race.[21]

Pope Paul VI's explicit link between evangelization and human development in *Evangelii Nuntiandi* had a profound effect on future SECAM statements concerning the Church and the economic future of the African sub-continent.[22] In this next section, I demonstrate how the SECAM bishops drew upon this link in two important pastoral statements from the early 1980s, "Justice and Evangelization in Africa" and "The Church and Human Promotion in Africa Today."

2. SECAM 1981-1984: Justice, Evangelization, and Human Promotion

During the early 1980s, the SECAM bishops published two pastorals that to this day remain perhaps the most influential statements they have ever produced. Following their sixth general assembly at Yaoundé, Cameroon in 1981, they issued "Justice and Evangelization in Africa," a pastoral that focused on the relationship between the Church and human development on the African continent. The bishops introduce this statement by claiming that because of the strong ties between evangelization and human promotion, the "total dimension" of the gospel message must include proclaiming justice in the temporal world.[23] In fact, to emphasize this point they argue that a Church is not fully rooted among its people if it does not seek to establish justice or actively promote the good of those it serves. Then, following a brief summary of how justice is portrayed in both Scripture and Church Tradition,[24] they maintain the African Church must foster within the faithful a greater sense of awareness concerning matters of justice. One must develop the interior virtues of justice, kindness, and dedication to the common good in order to build economic and political structures that are "truly human." Thus, for the bishops, "technical progress" can only foster authentic human development when it is grounded within basic human morality.[25]

The SECAM bishops continue in "Justice and Evangelization in Africa" by describing both the internal and external factors that militate against African economic development. Concerning external factors, they claim the primary problem is the domination that Africans are forced to endure in the international community. As examples, they cite the many "foreign armed interventions" which, while promising freedom and prosperity, have in reality only led to greater instances of dependency, violence, and oppression. They also identify the lack of meaningful dialogue between the North and South, the stranglehold of multinational corporations, the pillage of raw materials from African nations, the continuing deterioration in terms of trade, and ever increasing foreign debts. The bishops maintain that all of these factors in the international arena perpetuate structures of injustice and render true economic and social development next to impossible. Concerning internal factors, the SECAM bishops first identity political leaders who use their "elected" positions to create totalitarian dictatorships for themselves. These leaders suppress freedom of expression, "flout" existing constitutions, and reduce the common good to that which benefits only a small, preferred percentage of the population. The bishops also identify corruption by Africans themselves as a major interior stumbling block to economic development because through embezzling public monies and "buying off [the] consciences" of those who work in the public sector, individuals who engage in corrupt practices both militate against legitimate economic activity and undermine the moral standards of their respective nations. In light of these many injustices, the bishops rhetorically ask whether African Christians realize that their faith calls them to a different kind of behavior, whether they understand that authentic justice is "part and parcel" of the Christian ethic they profess."[26]

After identifying the many injustices facing their people, the SECAM bishops then suggest specific actions the African Catholic Church must undertake in order to "remain at the forefront of justice." First, they claim that in order to be a truly prophetic voice the Church must model justice within its own life. Instead of recalling long-standing animosities and dwelling on the "shortcomings" of others, African Christians must work to overcome both racism and ethnic tribalism, preach mutual love and affection, and also work to manifest the specific talents that each ethnic group brings to the common good of all. As such, all Christians are called to recognize their own sinfulness and commit themselves to greater participation in the Church's temporal work.[27] In terms of finances, the bishops claim the clergy must renounce any lifestyle that is incompatible with the simplicity of the gospel. Practicing evangelical poverty is necessary not only because it sets an example for the faithful, but also because the Church cannot effectively admonish public officials who maintain lifestyles beyond what their nations can reasonably support if clergy members themselves are "seduced" by the lure of material goods. Furthermore, the bishops also deplore the fact that the African Church as a whole is almost completely dependent upon foreign financial assistance for its very survival. While not suggesting that this assistance be curtailed, they state the African Church needs to move toward greater financial autonomy and also assure that any donations be used to benefit the pastoral priorities of the local churches themselves, not the "priorities" of the foreign donors.[28]

In addition to modeling justice in its own activities, the SECAM bishops also speak to the need of educating the faithful for justice. Citing both *Evangelii Nuntiandi* (no. 9) and John Paul II's *Dives in Misericordia* (no.118),[29] they claim the universal Church's social teachings deserve "particular attention" in Africa and that the African Church must revisit them more often, assimilate them more fully, and draw inspiration from them in constructing sermons, catechesis, and religious formation programs. For the bishops, the ultimate purpose of Catholic social teaching is the creation of a just person, one who recognizes the necessity of respecting the freedom, ideas, property, and culture of others, one who appreciates the "general social measures" that bring improvement to people's lives, and one who is able to distribute both "benefits and sanctions" with fairness and impartiality.[30]

Concerning action in the name of justice, the SECAM bishops state that perhaps the African Church's most important function is teaching the faithful that the gospel message extends into every element of their being. In other words, the people need to be taught that the demand to live the gospel message does not end at the doorways of their churches, but reaches into every economic, social, and political aspect of their lives. Because of this, they claim that any pastoral activity must include identifying the responsibilities of those in public life and also encouraging greater participation on all levels (local, regional, and national) from those who are not actively involved in working for justice.[31] However, the bishops also add that while they recognize there are situations where local churches are persecuted and/or not allowed a public voice, in those areas where they are able to speak out they should not do so on their own. They caution that because real change can only occur through joint ecclesial reflection, the "fundamental criterion" of any action for justice is that it be done "in communion with episcopal authority."[32]

The SECAM bishops conclude "Justice and Evangelization in Africa" with a series of resolutions that they propose to all the churches of Africa and Madagascar. Concerning the social teachings of the universal Church, they state: "SECAM is to strive to promote the education of the People of God in Africa, at all levels, in accordance with those principles of the social teaching which is an integral part of the Christian vision of life." Concerning the relationship between justice and authentic human development: "SECAM appeals to all Africans in public office to carry out their responsibilities with justice and impartiality; [it] asks that in public spending, priority be given to meeting the basic needs of the people ... and that public money never be employed [for] extravagant expenses." Concerning politics: "SECAM condemns the rigging of elections, the suppression of freedom of speech, of free association, or of freedom of religion. It also condemns ... the persecution, banning, or arbitrary imprisonment of those who profess political opinions that differ from the official position." Finally, the bishops appeal to Christians and to all people of good will in Africa to help overcome injustice, discrimination, oppression, and the violation of human rights.[33]

The SECAM bishops further emphasized the Church's role in efforts toward authentic human development in their 1984 "The Church and Human Promotion in Africa Today."[34] The bishops begin by reaffirming once again that action on behalf of the poor constitutes an integral aspect of the African Church's overall efforts at evangelization. Their rationale for this claim is that just as Christ's earthly mission was to offer life and offer it to its fullest, so also is this the mission he entrusts to the Church today. They continue by maintaining that because human promotion is a fundamental demand of such a large majority of the world's population, to speak of it is in reality to speak of people's "profound longings," their survival, and both their individual and collective fulfillment. Then, recalling the final declaration from their Kampala assembly (1969), the bishops repeat that if they ignore the injustice and oppression endured by their people they fail in their overall mission as shepherds of the Church.[35]

Following this recommitment of both themselves and the African Church as a whole to active participation in temporal affairs, the SECAM bishops then identify once again the myriad factors working against the development of the African people. Specifically in the economic realm, they cite neo-colonialism, the constant deterioration in terms-of-trade, and the manipulation by both capitalist and communist powers as external factors that trap the continent in a constant state of domination and dependence. As for internal factors, they cite rampant corruption, political instability, the squandering of public funds, and also a sense of atavism or "non-complementary manner ofreferring to the past" characteristic of many Africans that militates against a real and effective desire for development.[36] Echoing the sense of anthropological poverty that underlies African liberation theology, the bishops claim that because of this atavism many Africans are so ashamed of their ancestral heritage that they do not look to it for insights that might help to promote their future development.[37]

The SECAM bishops also speak to the mission of the African Catholic Church. They claim that as Christ continually imparts his Spirit upon the Church, it (the Church) becomes the primordial sacrament that reveals Christ's liberating action in the world today. Because the Church functions as this sacrament of liberation, its evangelizing message must include solidarity with humanity, participation in the struggles for freedom and progress in every domain of human life, and acting as the conscience of society by condemning all "perverted projects" and unjust social structures. However, in addition to working for improvement in their standard of living, the Church also must concentrate its efforts on converting people's hearts as well. Citing Pope John Paul II's opening address at the 1979 conference of Latin American bishops (Puebla, Mexico),[38] the African bishops claim the Church must strive not only to humanize people's work and relationships, but also liberate them from the consequences of sin manifested in unjust social structures, forces of oppression, and alienation of every kind. By announcing liberation and redemption in every aspect of human life, the Church contributes to both the edification and restoration of the entire human community.[39]

Then, recalling the 1971 Synod of Bishops' claim that action on the part of justice and participation in transforming the world are "constitutive" elements of preaching the gospel message, the SECAM bishops maintain that as part of its evangelizing mission the African Catholic Church must unite all people and serve them until they have reached the end of their earthly journeys. As such, the Church's responsibility in finding solutions to the problems of poverty and injustice is not limited to making financial donations or lending materials to the poor, instead it must bring a sense of "Christian inspiration" to all efforts for temporal progress because no material or social plan is "fully human" unless its ultimate end is realized in Jesus Christ. While in the past the African Church had a tendency to consider evangelization and human promotion as two separate projects, today this can no longer be the case. Evangelization and human promotion must never be separated because they are "conditioned in an intimate causality" and together constitute an integral aspect of the Church's overall evangelizing mission.[40]

Further underscoring this link between evangelization and human promotion, the SECAM bishops argue that the Church's credibility is directly proportional to its perceived solidarity with the African people. Concretely, this credibility depends on the responses it offers to the questions, "What role will the Church play in the African situation?" "How does the Church relate Christian thought to the exploitation experienced by the African people?" "What contribution can the Church make to those who for years have faced both oppression and domination because of their race, sex, or social class?" "What can she do about the corruption so rampant in our nations?" Repeating once again Paul VI's teaching in *Evangelii Nuntiandi* that human promotion constitutes an integral aspect of evangelization, the bishops state that the African Church must impress upon the faithful the important roles *they* play both in efforts for human promotion and in educating others for development and self-sufficiency. They claim the ultimate goal of evangelization is not only to convert people's individual and collective consciences, but also to transform both the activities in which they are engaged as well as the economic and socio-political environments in which they live. To assure that the Church remains an authentic sacrament of salvation for the African people, the task of human promotion must remain an integral dimension of its overall evangelizing mission.[41]

As with their 1981 "Justice and Evangelization in Africa," the SECAM bishops conclude "The Church and Human Promotion in Africa Today" with a series of resolutions aimed at guiding the Church's future work on the African continent. Specifically concerning economic development, they hold that human promotion encompasses both development and liberation, and that people must be given the opportunity to "fix their own objectives" and decide for themselves how they will work to improve their own welfare. Thus, they resolve to "establish an organic link" between evangelization and human promotion, claim that true evangelization entails the development of the entire person, and reaffirm that the economic, socio-political, and cultural dimensions of human life must never be separated from the religious. Concerning their priorities, the bishops recommend that any effort at human promotion be directed first and foremost towards those who have been marginalized by society, those living in misery and suffering, and those who do not enjoy basic human rights. Concerning concrete ways of taking action, they maintain the universal Church's social teachings must guide the formation of the African people, that efforts toward human promotion be rooted in traditional African culture and values, and that in both its catechetical formation and its educational institutions the Church improve the ways it teaches charity and relates the Christian faith to the challenges of everyday life.[42]

With these contributions in mind, in the next section of Chapter Four, I shift from SECAM's continent-wide statements on economic development to those of the various African episcopal conferences on both the national and regional levels. There are thirty-three national and nine regional conferences of Catholic bishops on the African continent today and once again simply because of the number of statements they have produced it would be impossible to examine them all in detail. Therefore, I again present a representative sample of statements through which the bishops identify the reasons for their nations' (and regions') economic difficulties and also suggest general reforms to promote the integral development of the African people.

Development and the African Episcopal Conferences

1. Causes of Economic Underdevelopment

During the 1980s and early 1990s, the pastoral letters of the various African episcopal conferences were, even more than those of SECAM, very detailed in identifying the causes for their respective nations' economic difficulties. In their 1988 "Le chrétien et le développment de la nation," the Catholic bishops of Zaïre claim that the primary reason for their nation's economic crisis is the fact that the national economy is structured to produce goods for the West while not providing necessary goods for its own people. This focus on producing a small number of export goods is characteristic of a mono-culture or cash-crop economy which, as described in Chapter One, is one of the primary economic legacies of European colonial rule. The bishops add that because both government policies and international terms of trade favor imports at the expense of exports, and also because the systems of communication and transportation within their nation are in such poor condition, it is easier and often less expensive for the Zaïrian people to purchase products from foreign vendors than from their fellow countrymen. This, in turn, leads to less revenue for local producers, less money being generated for domestic investment, and a further stagnation of the Zaïrian economy. Furthermore, because local producers have no control over prices on the international markets, any wealth generated from the sale of these products disappears within the structures of these markets and the Zaïrian people themselves gain no practical benefit.[43]

However, while its economic structure is an important reason for Zaïre's lack of economic development, it is not the only one. The bishops also identify a number of other factors including unemployment, the ever-increasing cost of living, the declining purchasing power of the Zaïrian currency, the lack of support for local agriculture, and the ever-present national debt. Specifically concerning the debt, they maintain that in addition to its economic consequences, it also carries social and moral consequences because just as an overly-indebted individual loses his dignity and becomes a slave to his creditor, so also a nation that cannot repay its debts loses both its dignity and sovereignty to its creditors. Dignity is lost because creditors regard the debtor nation as irresponsible and incapable of managing its own affairs, sovereignty is lost because these same creditors then impose strict measures (read structural adjustment) to control and manage the debtor nation's economy.[44]

In their 1990 pastoral "Les causes de la crise économique," the bishops of Cameroon argue that not only are there economic factors underlying their nation's economic crisis, but moral factors as well. Cameroon's economic difficulties are primarily the result of structural sin in the economic, political, and cultural orders that "govern" the international community.[45] In other words, the crisis exists because the international economic order is based upon an unbridled quest for profit and is characterized by both egoism and the exploitation of the poor by the rich and powerful. The bishops also argue that speculation has caused the deterioration in price for African raw materials and in turn the economic ruin of those nations who rely on the sale of these raw materials for their very survival. The "magnets" of industry and finance force nations such as Cameroon to overproduce their cash crops (cacao and coffee) thus creating gluts on the international markets. These gluts, in turn, result in lower prices for the West but also less revenue for the Cameroonian people. In response, the bishops argue that because after thirty years of independence their nation has experienced neither true democracy nor any real liberation from colonial economic domination, the time has come to re-examine North-South dialogue and to construct new systems of economic solidarity that are based on "mutual promotion" and the common good of all.[46]

The Cameroonian bishops then state that as a necessary component of realizing true economic development, their nation needs to work in solidarity with the other nations of the world. The reason for this is that the present system of international borrowing does not foster any sense of solidarity nor does it offer the Cameroonian people a viable means of emerging from their poverty. Although structural adjustment was implemented, in part, to help debtor nations emerge from their debts, because it has caused massive unemployment, condemned millions of families to misery, and has allowed lender nations to recoup outstanding loans at exorbitant rates of interest, it is a program that is in desperate need of reform. In fact, the bishops claim that because it does not conform to either the spirit of the gospel or to the social doctrine of the Church, structural adjustment as it is presently practiced is contrary to Christian morality.[47] Appealing to the consciences of those in "rich" nations, the Cameroonian bishops call for the canceling of all foreign debts, the end to structural adjustment, and the creation of a new international marketplace based on solidarity and mutual interdependence.[48]

In terms of structural adjustment and the general economic situation facing the African sub-continent, perhaps the most outspoken and vehement criticisms have come from the Catholic bishops of Zambia. Citing the importance of Catholic social teaching in their 1991 pastoral "You Shall be My Witnesses," the Zambian bishops repeat that a "major challenge" to Christian evangelization is how to demonstrate the "intimate connection" between the gospel message and the realities of everyday African life. They claim that because the rising costs for food and shelter, the reduction of social services (including education and health care), and the deterioration of infrastructure (including roads and systems of communication) all indicate a continually declining standard of living, true evangelization must necessarily incorporate issues of economics, politics, and integral development.[49]

In their July, 1993 "Hear the Cry of the Poor," the Zambian bishops once again speak directly to the devastating effects of their nation's economic situation. Citing statistics from the United Nations' International Fund for Agricultural Development, the World Bank, the University of Zambia, and the Zambian government, they claim that twenty percent of all children in their nation die before the age of five, forty percent of all children under age five are undersized (a sign of malnutrition), eighty percent of the rural and fifty percent of the urban population live below the poverty line, and inflation is increasing at a rate of about 200 percent *per year*. These figures indicate that most Zambians eat only one meager meal per day, there is little or no medical care, many children cannot attend school because their parents cannot afford the fees, and there are increasing numbers of street children and prostitutes. Each of these realities then translates into what the bishops term the "moral problems" facing Zambian life: the ever-widening gap between rich and poor, the escalation of crime in both urban and rural areas, the increase in governmental corruption, and the "get rich quick" mentality whereby people manipulate the prices of necessary commodities for their own good without taking into consideration the effects of their actions on others.[50]

For the Zambian bishops, the primary reason for their nation's economic and social woes is the forced imposition of structural adjustment. While the IMF, World Bank, and representatives of Western donor nations praise Zambia for following restructuring guidelines, the bishops question whether in light of the people's suffering there is really anything to be praised. The government has continually assured that structural adjustment entails "short-term pain but long-term gain," yet while there has been much pain the bishops wonder when the "gain" will be realized and also whether there will be anyone left to enjoy it when it arrives. Specifically, they question the timing, content, and direction of the externally imposed adjustment measures. Concerning timing, they ask why government subsidies for food, health care, and education were removed so quickly, especially in light of the fact that no intermediate programs were introduced to cushion the impact of their removal. Could these subsidies have not been removed more slowly thus allowing the people more time to gradually adjust? Concerning content, they question why human capital improvement (health care and education), job creation programs, small-scale entrepreneurial promotion, and regional cooperation are all missing from the adjustment programs. Are not these elements necessary for true, integral development to take place? Concerning direction, they claim structural adjustment relies on a "trickle down" approach to economic growth because development aid is directed toward the rich and through their spending the economic benefit is eventually supposed to reach the poor. However, what has actually occurred is that the rich have become progressively more wealthy while the poor have waited endlessly to realize this supposed benefit. Speaking then to the "totality" of structural adjustment, the Zambian bishops argue that because it is a "product of theory and practice" it should not be seen as a "fixed law of nature" or a program that is incapable of being modified. As such, structural adjustment must not be "blindly accepted" as the only possible solution to Zambia's economic difficulties, instead it must be continually critiqued both ethically and in terms of sound economic analysis.[51]

Although not offering the same level of analysis as do their Zaïrian, Cameroonian, and Zambian counterparts, other African episcopal conferences on both the regional and national levels speak to the economic difficulties in their respective nations. Meeting for their ninth plenary assembly in 1986, the Association of Member Episcopal Conferences of Eastern Africa (AMECEA) bishops touch upon development issues in their statement "La solidarité avec ceux qui souffrent." Among the causes for "situations of suffering" in East Africa, the bishops cite economic exploitation in that national development programs are oriented toward producing export rather than domestic goods, and that development programs are often controlled by the élite at the expense of the poor.[52] Writing before the fall of the Soviet Union in their 1988 pastoral "Justice et paix en Afrique australe," the Inter-Regional Meeting of Bishops of Southern Africa (IMBISA) point to the lasting effects of neo-colonialism in many southern African nations. During the Cold War many of the newly independent nations were courted (or manipulated) by both the Eastern and Western superpowers through promises of military protection and economic aid. However, in allying itself with a specific superpower, the African nation was also expected to assume the economic and political ideologies of its benefactor. The IMBISA bishops claim this form of neo-colonialism fostered not only economic dependence as a result of both unrestrained speculation and the introduction of foreign economic systems, but also ideological dependence as evidenced by the prevalence of political unrest and civil war.[53]

In their 1990 pastoral "A Society Built on Peace and Love," the bishops of Kenya also cite numerous internal factors that have had disastrous economic consequences for their nation. Because of the ever-increasing cost of living and the fact that the minimum wage is not sufficient to purchase basic necessities, many Kenyans have resorted to corruption simply in order to survive. The bishops maintain that not only does corruption have negative economic consequences for their nation,[54] but because it is accepted within society as a normal part of doing business it is destroying Kenya's moral fiber as well. In addition, the bishops claim the ever-increasing gap between rich and poor signifies that there are actually two forms of tribalism at work in their nation. There is ethnic tribalism whereby members of one tribe discriminate against those of another, but there is also economic tribalism evidenced by the fact that the small percentage of the nation's wealthy has, in many cases, gained its wealth directly at the expense of the poor masses. The bishops conclude by maintaining that although agricultural production amounts to approximately fifty percent of their nation's Gross National Product and employs more than eighty-five percent of the national population, it is also responsible for seventy percent of foreign monies coming into the country. What these figures indicate is the inherent weakness of a modern-day cash-crop economy. The Kenyan agricultural sector is geared towards producing crops for sale on the international markets while not producing the goods that Kenyans themselves need in order to survive.[55]

2. Recommendations for Economic Development

After identifying the many factors working against the economic development of their respective nations, a number of African episcopal conferences offered general recommendations concerning what had to be done to rectify the suffering of their people. The Zambian bishops argue in their 1991 "You Shall be My Witnesses," that African governments, political parties, and even the Church itself must "find guidance" in the basic principles of Catholic social teaching, principles that include economic justice, workers' rights, the "social obligation" of private property, option for the poor, and respect for fundamental human rights and dignity. Then, citing both the United Nations' *Universal Declaration of Human Rights* and the *African Charter on Human and People's Rights*, they claim economic and social rights must never be separated from political and civil rights. The rights to food, clothing, shelter, medical care, just wages, and humane working conditions are just as fundamental as the rights to free speech, free conscience, and free assembly.[56]

Two years later in "Hear the Cry of the Poor" (1993), the same Zambian bishops offer three recommendations as to how their nation can work toward a more prosperous economic future. First, they propose that an independent tribunal be established to monitor both wages and the prices for consumer goods. This tribunal, comprised of consumer, business, and labor union representatives, would negotiate "satisfactory compromises" between both employers and employees and between buyers and sellers in order to hold down the rapidly growing rate of inflation. Second, the bishops call for the establishment of a national task force to oversee the provision of social services. Although the Zambian government does have some social service programs to help cushion the effects of structural adjustment, these programs are not well planned nor well publicized. A national social service task force would better set priorities, ensure effective implementation and monitoring, and coordinate with other agencies doing similar kinds of work. Finally, the bishops call for the convening of a national forum to critically evaluate the effects of structural adjustment. They argue that because in a democracy any program that directly affects the people's well-being must also have their "informed support," the IMF, World Bank, and even the Zambian government itself can no longer ignore the suffering caused by the implementation of these reform measures. In short, because structural adjustment has such a profound effect on millions of Zambians, there needs to be an open and free debate to ensure popular awareness of what these reforms actually entail.[57]

Other African episcopal conferences emphasize education as the primary means to move their nations toward economic development. In their highly controversial 1992 pastoral "Living our Faith,"[58] the Catholic bishops of Malawi comment on the myriad problems facing the Malawian public educational system. First, even though it is widely recognized that illiteracy is one of the main causes of poverty, many Malawians are still unable to read and write. Second, the nation's educational standards are declining due in large measure to overcrowding, a lack of qualified teachers, and shortages in educational materials. Third, there is unequal access to education because the selection criteria used to determine entrance into secondary schools and so called "third-level institutions" is oftentimes based on who the candidates know or how much money their families are willing to spend, not on academic merit. The bishops respond by claiming the only way the educational system can improve is if "mutual trust" and "genuine partnerships" are formed among "interested groups" within society. Included in these interested groups is the Catholic Church which the bishops claim must become a partner with the state to ensure the proper education of all. Because any society that values its future "affords the highest priority" to educating its children, the Malawian bishops argue that open access to comprehensive public education is crucial for the future prosperity of their nation.[59]

The IMBISA Conference and Cameroonian bishops also speak of the important link between education and economic development but focus their attention on the educational function of the Church itself. In their 1988 "Justice et paix en Afrique australe," the IMBISA bishops point to the fact that many African Catholics do not involve themselves in development efforts simply because they are not familiar with the Church's social teachings. As noted in Chapter Three, although for over one hundred years the Catholic Church has developed a comprehensive body of teachings concerning just wages, unemployment, integral development, and workers' rights, these teachings remain largely unknown to a vast majority of African Catholics and as such have not been employed in formulating responses to concrete situations of economic injustice.[60] Citing Pope John XXIII's *Mater et Magistra*, the IMBISA bishops claim that Catholic social teaching must be incorporated into seminary and lay formation programs, and that it also be taught through homilies and in the curriculum of religious schools.[61] The bishops also suggest that more diocesan Justice and Peace Commissions be established to educate the faithful in Church doctrine. The commissions would work to form people's consciences in the evangelical understandings of justice and peace and also alert them to the suffering that exists as a result of racism, tribalism, and differences of both ideology and religion.[62]

Although somewhat less directly, the bishops of Cameroon also speak to the role of the Church in the educational process in their 1990 "Les causes de la crise économique." They state that in order for their nation to prosper, Cameroon's number one priority must be to find people of integrity: those who have been "formed" not only in the professional sense but also in the moral sense. Their point is that Cameroon does not lack technicians and other professionals who *could* help the nation emerge from its economic difficulties, however it does lack individuals who possess moral integrity and who are willing to form their fellow countrymen in a spirit of authentic human development. Thus, although they do not specifically state it, the implication of the bishops' message is that the Church has an important role to play in the moral formation of those who will assume leadership positions within Cameroonian society.[63]

As a final example of an episcopal conference offering recommendations in the economic realm, the Zaïrian bishops speak to both the laity and the Church itself in their 1988 "Le chrétien et le développment de la nation." Concerning the laity, the bishops cite the Second Vatican Council's *Ad Gentes* and maintain that it is primarily through the faithful that the Church as a whole participates in development-related activities.[64] Then, claiming that Third World stagnation exists, in part, because people lack the ability to recognize the internal causes for underdevelopment, that peace will not be achieved until nations "harmonize" their relationships (including economic relationships) in a spirit of truth and active solidarity, and that foreign aid should be offered in a way that allows recipient nations to maintain their dignity and remain the "principal artisans" of their own development, the bishops unequivocally state that Christians must participate *as Christians* in constructing a new international order. In other words, because they both manifest Christ's love-for-others as well as the Church's presence in the world, the lay faithful have a mandate to change any economic structure that causes dependence and allows the rich to exploit the poor. The bishops further state that all Christians must work to rebuild the nature of human relationships so as to construct a world that is characterized by truth, justice, and love.[65]

Concerning the Church itself, the Zaïrian bishops begin by claiming it must do whatever it can to become financially autonomous. They make this claim, in part, through the recognition that the Church cannot study the economic challenges facing its people while at the same time disregarding its own economic situation. In other words, by being conscious of its own poverty, the Church can better participate in the struggle to liberate the Zaïrian people from inhumane living conditions and all forms of servitude. In terms of concrete action, the bishops maintain the Church must fight for greater social justice on both the national and international levels, work to introduce appropriate methods of savings and development, and support educational programs that favor and encourage local production. Finally, the Church must also continue its participation in "micro-realization" programs where it actively supports the Zaïrian people in planning and executing small development projects.

3. Politics and Development

In Chapter One, I demonstrated that economic factors are not the sole reason for sub-Saharan Africa's lack of development. An equal, if not greater, reason concerns the actions of its political leaders. As with the economic factors, the African bishops are acutely aware of this problem and speak to it in various pastoral letters. The Cameroonian bishops claim that just as structural sin is present in the international order, it is present within African political life as well. As examples, they identify the purchase and selling of arms, the frenetic waste of "megalomaniac tyrants," and the embezzlement of public funds as internal causes for ever-increasing national debts. They also speak out against "pseudo-investments" of prestige such as presidential palaces, uncompleted skyscrapers, and other "phony" projects that both drain state banks of millions of francs (the Cameroonian currency) and further increase the misery of those who are condemned to repay foreign debts.[66]

In two pastorals from the early 1990s, the Kenyan bishops identify generalized corruption and their country's single-party political system as root causes for their nation's lack of economic development. Corruption is rooted in the fact that there is a lack of transparency and accountability at all levels of government so people view public office as a means to private gain.[67] Because it undermines societal standards and drains funds from those most in need, corruption is a moral evil that must be eradicated in order to bring about a more just political order. Concerning the single-party political system, the bishops maintain that it is not in Kenya's best economic (or other) interests to give unchecked and practically unlimited power to one political organization. Reasons for this include that uncontrolled power almost always leads to corruption, any criticism of the state is taken as a threat to national security, and, citing John Paul II's *Sollicitudo Rei Socialis*, absolute political authority tends to destroy popular subjectivity and reduce the masses to being "objects" through which the good of the few is realized.[68]

Other episcopal conferences speak to the psychological effects that corrupt political systems have had on the common person. The Tanzanian bishops claim that because their nation's political system is affected by hypocrisy, double standards of justice, and the placement of unqualified individuals into high-ranking political positions, many Tanzanians have lost faith in their government and now wallow in a dual sense of outrage and confusion.[69] The Malawian bishops argue that as the strength of any society rests in the ability of its people to employ their gifts for the benefit of the community, people are only "honored as humans" if they are free to voice their opinions and serve the community through associations of their own choosing. In this light, they decry the lack of academic freedom in their nation, the censorship that prevents people's true beliefs from being known, and the restricting of access to hospitals, markets, and other public places to those who hold party membership cards. For the Malawian bishops, each of these factors helps to create an atmosphere of resentment among the people, a resentment that breeds fear, mistrust, and suspicion while at the same time not allowing the individual's talents to bear fruit.[70] The bishops of Nigeria also speak to the psychological effects of corrupt political systems by claiming that for many years Church leaders, university professors, and representatives of human rights groups have warned about the growing sense of despair in Nigeria as a direct result of the unstable and undemocratic governments. Citing Amos 6:1-7, they claim it is both immoral and an "abomination in God's eyes" that a small number of rich live amid so much poverty, and in fact this gross inequality between rich and poor constitutes a great danger to the nation's peace and stability. In response, the bishops call on their people to help bring about political reform by more faithfully participating in the electoral process. They urge people to resist accepting money for their votes, to not vote for a candidate based solely on the candidate's ethnic background, and to empower themselves as individuals by defending the nation's fledgling democratic institutions.[71]

In addition to simply speaking out against repressive political systems, in some African nations the Catholic Church has been instrumental in bringing about political change. During the 1970s in Rhodesia, the Catholic bishops' Justice and Peace Commission was instrumental in both pressuring and eventually achieving the defeat of Ian Smith's racist and repressive government. The commission involved many Rhodesians in the struggle for freedom by opening greater dialogue with people from rural areas, offering legal support and providing people with a voice in their cries against the atrocities perpetrated by the Rhodesian Security Forces, and also informing the world about the injustices of Ian Smith's "Internal Settlement" (a proposal that would have retained the privileges of the white settlers).[72] In large measure because of this commission, in 1979 Britain called a meeting of all political factions in Rhodesia and out of this meeting a new constitution was drafted. In the ensuing 1980 elections, Ian

Smith's government was defeated and the nation of Zimbabwe was born.[73]

The Catholic Church has also been instrumental in helping to bring about multi-party elections in a number of other African nations. In Benin, Burkina Faso, Gabon, Congo (Brazzaville), and Zaïre, national conferences assembled to prepare for the transition from single-party to multi-party political systems elected Roman Catholic bishops as their chairs. One of the primary reasons for these bishops' elections was that in the face of rampant governmental corruption, the Catholic Church was the only moral authority on which the people could realistically rely.[74] Also in Zambia, the Catholic Church's vocal opposition to former President David Kenneth Kaunda has been cited as a key factor in undermining his credibility and ultimately forcing him from office. With the Zambian economy in serious crisis and Kaunda not allowing for multi-party elections, in February of 1987 the Zambian bishops issued "Christian Liberation, Justice, and Development: The Church's Concern for Human Development in Zambia." In this pastoral, the bishops first identify the Kaunda regime's inefficiency and misuse of public resources and then they attack the nation's single-party political system claiming the people have a right to participate in the decision-making processes concerning issues that directly affect them.[75] Three years later, the Zambian bishops issued "Economics, Politics, and Justice" in which they identify both lack of democratic participation and lack of governmental accountability as root causes for their nation's economic difficulties.[76] Finally, in their 1991 "You Shall Be My Witnesses," the bishops call upon all Zambians to heed the Church's social teachings concerning political participation, accountability, the state's duty to promote the common good, and fundamental respect for both the dignity and rights of all people.[77] While it was certainly not the only organization that pressured the Kaunda government, the Zambian Catholic Church has been hailed as an important reason for Kaunda's landslide defeat in the November, 1991 national elections.[78]

While the SECAM statements concerning economic development were offered by representatives of the various African episcopal conferences, and statements from both the national and regional conferences were made by the bishops of those specific nations or regions, it was not until the 1994 Synod for Africa that the African bishops were able to speak to the development issue with a unified voice. In the third section of this chapter I explain what a regional synod is and why one was convened for the African Church, and then examine the African Synod's contributions to the issue of economic development through both its preparatory and assembly stages.

Development and the Synod for Africa

1. What is a Synod?

From the Greek "syn-hodos" or "path together," synods of bishops were established as a permanent institution by Pope Paul VI in his September, 1965 "Motu proprio, Apostolica sollicitudo."[79] As defined by Canon Law, there are three types of synod: ordinary, extraordinary, and special session. An ordinary synod is called to deal with matters that "directly concern the good of the Church" and consists of bishops who are called from around the world. An extraordinary synod is very similar to an ordinary synod except that it is convened when the issue(s) in question "requires a speedy solution." A regional or special session synod of bishops is convened to deal with issues facing the Church in a specific area of the world.[80] The 1994 African Synod falls into this third category and thus is oftentimes referred to as the "Synod of Bishops Special Assembly for Africa."[81]

While it is questionable whether the present papal magisterium considers synods to be authoritative teaching bodies in themselves, they do play an important function within the Church. Oftentimes it is from the declarations and/or recommendations of a synod that a Pope will issue an authoritative encyclical letter. As examples, following the 1974 Synod on Evangelization, Pope Paul VI promulgated *Evangelii Nuntiandi*, the 1980 Synod concerning the Christian family was followed by John Paul II's *Familiaris Consortio*, and in terms of this study, the 1994 Synod for Africa was followed by John Paul II's *Ecclesia in Africa*.[82] It should be noted, however, that although questions remain as to whether synods are authoritative in themselves, their teachings are regarded as more than just the "common opinion" of an assembly of bishops. John Paul II himself maintains that synod bishops "attest to the faith" through their concern for the universal Church and if their vote concerning a declaration or recommendation is "morally unanimous," it carries with it "a qualitative ecclesial weight which surpasses the merely formal aspect of the consultative vote."[83]

2. Synod or Council?

Before examining the issue of economic development within the African Synod, it is important to note the controversy surrounding the question of whether the African bishops' assembly should have been a synod or a council. According to Canon Law, a plenary or particular council is a meeting of all the particular churches belonging to a specific conference of bishops and, although requiring papal approval, it differs from a synod because it is authoritative in itself:

> A particular council sees to it that provision is made for the pastoral needs of the people of God in its own territory, and it possesses the power of governance, especially legislative power, so that with due regard always for the universal law of the Church *it can decree what seems appropriate* for increasing faith, organizing common pastoral activity, directing morals and preserving, promoting, and protecting common ecclesiastical discipline."[84]

Because of pressing issues including the inculturation of the Christian faith, the nature and practice of marriage, and relations with the Church of Rome (along with other issues described in Chapter Two), numerous African bishops and theologians have repeatedly called for the convening of a council so that the African Church could authoritatively respond to these issues and thus more intimately relate the Christian faith to the everyday lives of African Catholics.

Requests for an African council date back over twenty-five years before the Synod for Africa was convened in 1994. At the first SECAM assembly in 1969, President Paul Cardinal Zoungrana called for the creation of a pan-African episcopal entity by stating, "Our very being must not be conferred upon us from outside; the gospel is a germ of life and the Church of Africa must develop itself and build itself up ... according to its own objectives and apostolic priorities."[85] At the 1972 SECAM assembly, Senegalese Alioune Diop proposed the convening of an African council to discuss the topic "Black Civilization and the Catholic Church," and in 1977 he organized a colloquium on this subject in Abidjan, Ivory Coast, under the sponsorship of the Société Africaine de Culture. In their final recommendations, the participants at the 1977 colloquium stated that in order for the African Church to "identify itself with its own projects" and for Africans to become "missionaries for themselves," a council was urgently needed.[86]

In the 1980s, calls for an African council were further echoed by both the Zaïrian bishops' conference and by SECAM itself. The Zaïrian bishops actively proposed the convening of a council during John Paul II's papal visit to Zaïre in 1980 and also during their own "ad limina" visit to Rome in 1983. In his 1983 allocution to the Pope, Joseph Cardinal Malula, Chair of the Zaïrian Bishops' Conference, explained the necessity of a council by arguing it would allow the local African churches to ascertain better their own situations and also help to establish "adequate bases" for the future evangelization of the African continent.[87] At their 1984 plenary in Kinshasa, Zaïre , the SECAM bishops officially proposed the convening of a particular council for Africa that would have full deliberative and legislative powers subject to papal ratification. The intent was that the council would work towards "integral evangelization" by allowing the African Church to set its own priorities concerning appropriate rites and structures, and also make its own decisions regarding the "duty of inculturation" in the areas of ecumenism, ministry, justice, evangelization, sacraments, canon law, and relations with the universal church. To assuage the fears of those who believed they were overstepping their bounds, the SECAM bishops were careful to stress that the proposed council would only be convened "with Peter and under Peter."[88]

However, these particular calls for an African council were not met with continent-wide support. During the 1970s and early 1980s the convening of a council was supported mainly by those in francophone Africa; anglophone Africans claimed they knew very little about it and in fact were very suspicious of any proposal arising from the French-speaking countries (particularly Zaïre and Cameroon).[89] The SECAM bishops had resolved at their 1984 assembly (Kinshasa) that every African episcopal conference should study the possibility of convening a council, yet by their 1987 assembly (Lagos, Nigeria) it was clear that support for the proposal had sharply waned. After the 1984 assembly, surveys to measure the perceived need for a council were sent out by both SECAM and the Vatican's Congregation for the Evangelization of

Peoples. While the results of the SECAM survey were not made public, the Holy See's survey revealed that although most African bishops desired some form of assembly, less than twenty percent of the over three hundred respondents offered unqualified support for the convening of a council.[90]

Not finding overwhelming support for a council within Africa itself, on December 6, 1988, Pope John Paul II met with the SECAM President and Vice President, the presidents of the nine regional episcopal conferences, the prefect of the Congregation for the Evangelization of Peoples, and the General Secretary of the Synod of Bishops to discuss the future of the proposed African assembly. One month later on the Feast of the Epiphany (January 6, 1989), the Pope announced the convening of the "Special Assembly for Africa of the Synod of Bishops."[91]

3. Development and the Synod's Preparatory Documents

Immediately following John Paul II's announcement of the Synod for Africa, preparations began in earnest. At its meetings in June and December of 1989, the synod's General Secretariat established five sub-committees (one for each of the five proposed topic areas) and then prepared the "Lineamenta" or "Outline" of the synod which was released on July 25, 1990 at the SECAM General Assembly in Lomé, Togo.[92] In the first part of the "Lineamenta," the General Secretariat presents a brief survey of the Catholic Church's missionary history in Africa and then speaks to various dimensions of evangelization and their relationship to the African continent. The second part discusses in five detailed chapters the main topic areas of the upcoming synod: Proclamation of the Good News (referred to simply as Evangelization), Inculturation, Dialogue, Justice and Peace, and Social Communication. The General Secretariat concludes the "Lineamenta" with a series of eighty-one questions covering specific issues within the five topic areas, questions sent to the individual African dioceses in order to gain concrete responses from the local churches.[93]

In terms of this study, the most important section of the "Lineamenta" is its chapter on Justice and Peace. The drafting sub-committee begins by citing specific biblical passages that identify how evangelization and concern for humanity are intimately intertwined within Christ's earthly mission. As examples, Jesus initiates his public ministry by quoting the prophet Isaiah's "The Spirit of the Lord is upon me because he has anointed me to bring glad tidings to the poor..." (LK 4:18-19); he repeatedly demonstrates his concern for the suffering through his ministry to the sick, paralyzed, and those in mourning; and he ultimately teaches that the Kingdom of Heaven will be opened to those who feed the hungry, give drink to the poor, and visit the sick and imprisoned (MT 25:31-46). The sub-committee then states that Christ shatters long-standing societal prejudices by relating to his followers the parable of the Good Samaritan (LK 10:29-37), commending the faith of the Roman centurion (Mt. 8:5-13), and in many ways engaging both tax collectors and women. Finally, it maintains that Jesus teaches his disciples to devote themselves to serving others (John 13:1-20) and in fact places the commandment to love one another "on a par with" the commandment to love God (Mt. 22:34-40). Through each of these examples, Jesus demonstrates that both the gospel message and the coming of God's Kingdom "are manifested and put into action" through love of one's neighbor and "concern given to the poorest of the poor."[94]

The sub-committee then speaks to the temporal mission of the African Church itself. Citing *Gaudium et Spes* (no. 38), *Populorum Progressio* (no. 21), and *Evangelii Nuntiandi* (nos. 29-30), it claims that as a "commitment on behalf of humanity" is intimately related to the Church's overall evangelizing mission, the Church must be "primarily concerned" that both individuals and communities "become more human." It then reaffirms the intimate link between evangelization and human promotion by stating the Church's overriding mission is to transform the African continent through its preaching of the gospel message. Finally, after once again identifying both the internal and external factors underlying Africa's lack of economic development, the sub-committee underscores the need for greater lay participation by claiming that "total and integrated promotion" will not be possible without the common effort of all.[95]

The "Lineamenta" as a whole concludes with a series of questions aimed at fostering both discussion and responses from the local African churches. The questions from the chapter on justice and peace are as follows:

1) Describe the awareness of the Church in Africa – particular, regional, and continental – to the vital link between the church's mission of evangelization and action on behalf of human promotion. What programs of formation exist in this regard, particularly toward the lay faithful's active participation in civil life and politics?
2) There are many papal documents, and those of national, regional, and continental episcopal bodies, which express the appeal of the church in this area. How well is the Church's message known and put into practice at the various levels of African society? How can it be improved?
3) What is the present situation in your diocese, region, or country concerning: a) Human promotion [which concerns] health, education, social structures, respect for the human person, the situation of prisoners, torture, etc.? b) Justice [which concerns] violations of human rights, recognition of political rights, the right of association and free expression, etc.? c) Peace [which concerns] relations between ethnic, racial, religious and ideological groups, situations of armed conflict and war, refugees, etc.?
4) What are the root causes of situations in various disorders in the area of the promotion of human dignity, justice, and peace?
5) What are the main efforts aimed at changing these situations, which have been already undertaken in your country or region by Churches or ecclesial communities? the State or other groups?
6) How can the Church at her various levels contribute to help improve these situations through a renewed effort in evangelization?[96]

In March of 1992, the General Secretariat met in Rome to examine the responses from the "Lineamenta" questions and to begin work on the "Instrumentum Laboris" or "Working Document" for the synod. The "Instrumentum Laboris" is in reality the preparatory agenda for a synod because based on the responses from the "Lineamenta" questions, it both demonstrates the specific issues raised by the local churches and provides a framework for discussion within the synod itself.[97] In June of 1992, the General Secretariat met at Luanda, Angola, to finalize the second draft of the "Instrumentum Laboris" which was then given to the final editing committee. This editing committee approved the final text in September of 1992 and on February 9, 1993 in Kampala, Uganda, Pope John Paul II presented the completed "Instrumentum Laboris" to the African Church. It was during this presentation of the "Instrumentum Laboris" that the Pope announced the "Synod of Bishops Special Assembly for Africa" would convene on April 10, 1994 and would take place at the Vatican.[98]

Similar to the "Lineamenta," the "Instrumentum Laboris" is comprised of two parts. In the first part, the General Secretariat presents the theological framework for the synod's overall theme of evangelization and demonstrates how the five topic areas relate to it. Specifically concerning "Justice and Peace," the General Secretariat cites John Paul II's *Redemptoris Missio*[99] and claims that any commitment to justice and human promotion can be considered a witness to the gospel message so long as it is "a sign of concern for persons and is directed toward integral human development." The General secretariat also cites *Evangelii Nuntiandi* (no. 31) and maintains that in speaking of evangelization one cannot ignore the many factors militating against justice and authentic development because to do so would be to ignore the gospel teaching to aid one's neighbor in need.[100]

In Part Two of the "Instrumentum Laboris," the five sub-themes are systematically addressed based upon the responses received from the "Lineamenta" questions. The "Justice and Peace" sub-committee begins its chapter by reaffirming the "vital link" between the Church's evangelizing mission and the socioeconomic and political concerns of the African continent. In fact, it states that the African Church must never neglect its duty to work for justice and human promotion because "to separate the works of development from the love which prompts them ... is to deny the profound unity of Christian involvement."[101] Then, after repeating a number of the same biblical citations it employed in the "Lineamenta" to demonstrate Christ's concern for earthly life,[102] the sub-committee maintains that in proclaiming Christ's Good News the Church aims to transform people so they may live in "renewed relationships" with one another. As such, it suggests that the upcoming synod be an opportunity for Christians to commit themselves not only to transforming external structures, but also to transforming their own hearts as well.[103]

The Justice and Peace sub-committee continues in the "Instrumentum Laboris" by speaking to the importance of educating Africans in the principles of Catholic social teaching. Once again it claims that although there are numerous documents concerning economic development from both the universal magisterium and the African Church itself, these teachings remain unknown to a vast majority of the African faithful. Reasons for this lack of knowledge include that the documents are not translated into the people's native languages and also that their circulation is limited almost exclusively to academics. In light of this, the sub-committee states that these teachings must become more accessible so that the people may be inspired by them to act for greater development, justice, and peace.[104]

The sub-committee then identifies once again the many challenges to Africa's economic development. Concerning politics, it claims that self-serving political systems function to the detriment of the poor and that the corruption, exploitation, and immorality characteristic of many African governments actually "devalues" the common person and causes problems on the "psychological-religious level." It also points to dependence upon foreign aid, a lack of respect for both human rights and popular participation in the political process, and declines in education, health care, and other social service programs. Concerning specific economic issues, it claims that "disorganization in monetary matters" renders the poor defenseless because simply in order to survive they are forced to submit themselves to the exploitation of the rich and powerful. Also, the gap between the rich and poor is steadily widening as a direct result of both the unequal distribution of national resources and the constant misappropriation of public funds.[105]

The Justice and Peace sub-committee concludes its contribution to the "Instrumentum Laboris" by speaking directly to the role of the African Church. While admitting that in the past the Church may not have spoken out as strongly as it could have or in some cases may have actually collaborated with exploitative regimes, it states that this must no longer be the case. Pastoral letters from the national, regional, and continent-wide episcopal conferences need to speak out against both sinful social structures and the violation of human rights, and the upcoming synod offers the bishops a unique opportunity both to re-evaluate the Church's role in African society and also chart its course for the future. On the theoretical level, it claims that because development, justice, and peace are not "supplementary elements" to evangelization but an "integral part of pastoral work as a whole," the Church must continue to hold the necessary link between evangelization and human promotion. On the practical level, it claims that the Church must model justice and human promotion within its own activities, work more closely with "professional schools" that teach basic job skills, offer greater follow-up after the publication of pastoral letters, and assure that its social teachings be included in the formation curriculum of seminaries and other religious institutions.[106]

4. Development and the Synod Assembly

On April 10, 1994, the "Synod of Bishops Special Assembly for Africa" convened at the Vatican. Overall, the synod was attended by more than three-hundred people. Most attendees were "members" of the synod and included the fourteen African Cardinals, the Patriarch of Alexandria, the Presidents of the nine regional and thirty-three national episcopal conferences, the president and vice President of SECAM, four heads of Roman Dicasteries, and the General Secretary of the Synod of Bishops. Other members included the one-hundred thirty representatives elected by the national episcopal conferences (each national conference was allotted one synod member for every four bishops), the eight representatives elected by the Union of Superiors General of Religious Institutes of Men, and thirty-seven representatives appointed by John Paul II from various areas around the world. In addition to the synod members, the Pope also appointed seventy-three "participants" including twenty experts from various fields, forty-six observers or "auditors" (twenty men and twenty-six women), and seven delegates from other Christian communities.[107]

Specifically in terms of economic development, the synod's "Propositions" and its final message "Synod of Resurrection for the Family of God" offer similar recommendations concerning the internal and external challenges facing the African sub-continent. The synod states in Proposition 45 that as integral development implies a respect for human dignity, true development cannot be achieved without a prior commitment to justice and peace. Because of this, it condemns the many African civil wars caused by tribalism, racism, intolerance, and the thirst for unbridled power. The synod also claims that for its part, the Church must take on a greater prophetic role by condemning "foreign manipulations" that pillage national resources, pleading for an end to embargoes that cause undue suffering, and calling upon political leaders to guarantee freedom and the authentic development of their people.[108] Similarly, in "Synod of Resurrection for the Family of God," the assembly appeals to political leaders to adopt an attitude of service, implores those in public office to restore both human dignity and a true sense of brotherhood in their communities, and "emphatically condemns" those who seek political office through a self-serving "lust for power." The synod also speaks to the perceived dichotomy between politics and Christian faith by exhorting the African laity to "educate themselves for democracy" and also to become more actively engaged in public life.[109]

Concerning economic relations in the international community, the synod introduces Proposition 49 by asking the IMF, World Bank, and all other creditors to alleviate the massive and unpayable foreign debts owed by African nations.[110] It then asks that foreign nations stop selling arms to Africa and that the African governments take the money used to purchase arms and reinvest it into programs that promote the health, education, and integral well-being of their people. Then, after stating the need for greater Church/state dialogue concerning issues of justice and peace, the synod exhorts all the African episcopal conferences (both national and regional) to better educate the faithful in the principles of Catholic social teaching.[111] In Proposition 54, the synod further calls upon industrialized nations to pay fair and stable prices for African raw materials and upon African governments to adopt "appropriate economic policies" to foster increased growth, productivity, and job creation. It then condemns all forms of corruption (particularly capital flight) and requests that "people of integrity" from both within the continent and abroad search for ways to return all "stolen" monies to the people of Africa.[112]

The synod assembly also speaks to international economic relations in "Synod of Resurrection for the Family of God." As a result of external debt and the "structured inequality" of unjust pricing systems imposed by the West, it claims many African nations are rendered "insignificant" and are thus burdened with a "regrettable sense of inferiority and indigence" that militates against true development. In light of this, the synod fathers appeal to their Christian brothers and sisters around the world to intervene in the economic and political affairs of their own nations in order to find just solutions for Africa's economic woes. They call upon Christians in industrialized nations to help stop the sale of arms to Africa, end reform measures (structural adjustment) that are contrary to human dignity, resolve the debt issue (either through a reduction or complete elimination of it), and create a more just economic order where African nations can participate as full partners within the world community.[113]

At the beginning of this chapter I stated that simply because of sheer volume, I am not able to examine all of the African bishops' statements concerning economic development. Nevertheless, I believe the representative sample of statements chosen accurately reflects the general theological position of most (if not all) African episcopal conferences concerning the Church's role in economic affairs. Therefore, in the final section of this chapter I synthesize the bishops' teachings to demonstrate how they contribute to the articulation of a theology of African economic development.

Toward an African Theology of Development

In terms of formulating a theology of economic development for sub-Saharan Africa, I maintain that the African Catholic bishops make two important contributions. The first and perhaps more important contribution is that they focus on the moral questions underlying economic policy, questions that must be addressed in order to construct an economic order that benefits all people. This focus on morality, or what might be better termed economic ethics, is most evident in their repeated calls for the re-evaluation of structural adjustment programs. The Cameroonian bishops (1990) argue that structural adjustment is antithetical to Christian morality because it causes massive unemployment which, in turn, causes increasingly greater hardship for those who can no longer support themselves. The Zambian bishops (1993) question the "short-term pain, long-term gain" mentality of these reform measures by demonstrating how the quick removal of government subsidies for food, health care, and education has left millions of Africans with no viable means to provide for their basic welfare. Also, the Synod for Africa (1994) calls upon the international community to reexamine structural adjustment because in many instances its effects contradict the universal Church's teachings on basic human dignity. I must note, however, that in making these claims no bishops' conference nor individual bishop ever disputes the need for serious internal economic and political reforms to take place. Sub-Saharan Africa faces many economic challenges and in order for these challenges to be met difficult decisions will have to be made. Nevertheless, although reform may be necessary, the means by which structural adjustment has been imposed and the consequences it has brought to the African people raise serious ethical questions for both the Church and the international community as a whole.

Similar moral/ethical questions also surround the issue of compelling African nations to repay foreign debts. The SECAM bishops (1981) offer a moral critique of forced repayment by identifying it as one of the primary sources of domination that Africans face in the world community. Regardless of how the debts were incurred, they question the morality of an international financial system whose structures do not allow African nations to emerge from their debts and thus take responsibility for their own economic futures. The Zaïrian bishops (1988) call for the remission of foreign debts by claiming the dignity of the African person is undermined through the forced acceptance of creditors' repayment conditions and structural reform measures. The 1994 Synod for Africa also employs ethical arguments in calling for the alleviation of foreign debt by claiming it (the debt) has a "crushing" effect on the overall welfare of African society, and that it "humiliates" African nations and imposes a sense of inferiority on their people. As with structural adjustment, the African bishops carefully maintain that there is nothing intrinsically wrong with borrowing money on the international markets or that African nations should refuse to repay debts that were contracted "in good faith." However, when the poorest of the poor are forced to bear the greatest burden of repaying debts that they neither contracted nor from which they have ever gained any real benefit, and also when debt principal increases exponentially as a result of interest rate increases in the international financial markets (increases completely out of the control of the African people), the bishops are correct to point out how forced repayment again poses serious ethical questions for all parties involved.

While structural adjustment and foreign debt are perhaps the most visible examples of how the African bishops critique prevailing economic policy, they are certainly not the only ones. The SECAM bishops (1969) decry the "conditionalities" attached to foreign aid programs that they claim contradict both human dignity and the traditional values of African society. The AMECEA (1986), Cameroonian (1990), Kenyan (1990), and Zaïrian bishops (1993) each question the morality of cash-crop economic systems whereby African nations are compelled to produce goods for export while at the same time neglecting the basic needs of their own people. The SECAM bishops (1981), Kenyan bishops (1990), and Zambian bishops (1993) speak to ethical issues concerning corruption by claiming its prevalence throughout African society not only undermines economic growth, but also destroys societal moral standards as well. Finally, the Cameroonian bishops (1990) underscore all of these shortcomings by claiming the egoism, exploitation, and unbridled quest for profit characteristic of the West demonstrates the prevalence of social sin in the international economic order.

In terms of what these claims bring to the construction of a theology of development, the African bishops clearly demonstrate the Catholic Church has a duty to continually evaluate secular economic policy in light of fundamental principles of human morality, principles that are articulated, in part, within Catholic social teaching. The overarching question concerning foreign debt, structural adjustment, cash-crop economies, etc., is how do the specific policies embedded within these programs conform to the fundamental demand of human dignity? Is basic human dignity respected in forcing Africannations to repay debts, accept externally imposed reform measures, or produce export goods exclusively for the benefit of the West? If the answer is no, then radical changes need to be made. Similar questions can also be asked concerning the various other principles of Catholic social teaching. Do debt-repayment, structural adjustment, and cash-crop policies promote the common good, encourage popular participation, respect local initiative, and adequately take into consideration their effects on the poor? Once again if the answer is no then radical changes must be made.[114]

In making this claim I should also note that, although the African bishops strongly critique secular economic policies, they never propose specific "solutions" to their respective nations' economic difficulties. In other words, apart from calling upon secular leaders to embrace the principles of justice, cooperation, human dignity, and dedication to the common good, the bishops recognize that economists, political scientists, and governmental officials maintain the primary task of determining how African economies are to function and also how reform is to take place. For their part, the bishops recognize it is their (and by extension the Church's) role to critique these policies to assure that the temporal welfare of the African people always remains paramount within them. Thus, the African bishops do not *make* economic policy, but they demonstrate the responsibility of the Church to understand it, to suggest general goals, and to assure that it always conforms to the dignity, rights, and general well-being of all God's children.[115]

A second important contribution the African bishops make to the formulation of a theology of economic development concerns their effort to maintain continuity with the teachings of the universal Church. This continuity is vital because as the universal Church holds the principles of its social teaching (human dignity, common good, preferential option for the poor, etc.) to be "normative," any discussion regarding the relationship between economics and Catholic morality must take them into consideration.[116] The African bishops clearly recognize this fact and as a result they seek to ground their teachings on economic affairs within those of the Church as a whole. One recognizes this effort first and foremost in the bishops' claim that they must educate the faithful in the basic principles of Catholic social teaching. In 1981, the SECAM bishops explicitly state that in order to create a "just person" the African Church must draw upon, assimilate, and educate all Africans in the principles of Catholic social teaching, a claim they repeat three years later in the final declaration from their 1984 plenary assembly. Both the IMBISA bishops (1989) and the "Instrumentum Laboris" from the 1994 African Synod maintain that as most African Catholics are ignorant of the Church's social teachings, these teachings need to be better integrated into both homilies and formation programs so as to educate the faithful on the roles *they* can play in the development of their respective nations. Within each of these statements is, once again, the explicit recognition that the principles underlying any authentic development program exist within the universal Church's social teachings and that it is from these teachings that the African Church must draw its guidance. Thus, instead of looking toward government officials, so-called "development experts," or even the international community for guidance as to how to construct economies that service basic human welfare, the bishops seek to educate African Catholics that this guidance already exists within the teachings of their own faith tradition.

Continuity with universal Church teachings is also evident in the bishops' emphasis on the intimate link between evangelization and efforts toward human development. Even before Pope Paul VI made this link explicit in *Evangelii Nuntiandi*, the SECAM bishops (1969) recognized that to ignore poverty, hunger, and oppression is to fail in their mission as shepherds of the Church. The African delegation to the 1974 International Synod on evangelization upholds this teaching by claiming Church participation in development efforts is not only integral to proclaiming the gospel message, but also that its prophetic message is in fact meaningless if not coupled with practical action in the real world. Following the publication of *Evangelii Nuntiandi*, the SECAM bishops again emphasize this link by claiming the Church is not "fully rooted" among its people if it does not promote their temporal good (1981), and also by stating that its overall credibility within African society depends in large measure on how it responds to the temporal economic (and other) challenges facing the African people (1984).

This intimate link between evangelization and human development is also evident twenty years later in the preparatory documents for the 1994 African Synod. In the "Lineamenta," the justice and peace sub-committee speaks to the Church's role in temporal affairs by citing specific biblical passages that demonstrate how Christ ministered to the needs of his followers, and also passages from *Evangelii Nuntiandi* and the final statements from both the 1969 and 1984 SECAM assemblies that claim the Church must actively participate in efforts that directly affect human welfare. The "Instrumentum Laboris" echoes these teachings by claiming there are "vital links" between evangelization and socioeconomic (among other) concerns and also that the African Church must never neglect to work for both justice and human promotion in the temporal realm. Overall, emphasizing the link between evangelization and human development is central because it offers the African bishops a theological foundation within Church Tradition on which to base their call for involvement in temporal economic affairs. In other words, as acting in the name of justice is a "constitutive" element of the Church's overall evangelizing mission, the bishops' emphasis on this link provides the African Church with both a theological justification and a theological mandate for active participation in efforts to transform unjust societal structures.

A third way the African bishops maintain continuity with the teachings of the universal Church is through their call for greater popular participation in public life. Because sub-Saharan Africa's lack of economic development is as much a function of politics as economics, the bishops recognize the need for the African people to become more actively involved in their respective nations' political systems. The SECAM bishops (1981) state that because the gospel message encompasses both the economic and political realms of temporal existence, Christians are called to actively participate in public life and to commit themselves to remedying all instances of injustice, discrimination, and violation of human rights. The Zaïrian bishops (1988) hold that because the lay faithful are mandated to bring the Church's vision of integral development to fruition in the world, they (the laity) must participate *as Christians* in the creation of a new economic order. Reaffirming these two earlier statements, the African Synod bishops exhort the faithful to transcend the dichotomy between their faith and the world by becoming more actively involved in public life. Within each of these calls for greater participation is the bishops' implicit recognition that the African people have both a right and a duty to take responsibility for their own temporal welfare. Because corrupt government officials and single-party political systems militate against the economic well-being of the African continent as a whole, true development will never occur until the people are afforded the opportunity to both influence and construct public policy in light of the common good. Thus, it is only through greater participation in both local and national decision-making processes that the African people will be able to chart their own economic futures, take responsibility for their own destinies, and ultimately be afforded the opportunity to fulfill themselves as human persons.[117]

One final way the African bishops maintain continuity with universal Church teachings is by claiming that any notion of liberation in the economic realm must incorporate liberation from sin. The SECAM bishops (1981) claim that in order for the Church to maintain its prophetic voice in African society, the faithful must be taught not only to overcome sentiments of ethnic tribalism and/or racism, but also to liberate themselves from their own sinfulness. The "Instrumentum Laboris" from the 1994 African Synod also maintains that as the Church's temporal aim in preaching the gospel message is to help people live in "renewed relationship" with one another, the synod itself presents a unique opportunity for the African faithful to transform not only sinful societal structures, but also their own hearts as well. Overall, this emphasis on liberation from sin is highly relevant to the issue of economic development because in reality human sinfulness is the root cause of economic injustice. The African bishops recognize this fact and rightly point out that any effort to overcome the ethical challenges presented by the African economic reality must also focus on the interior hearts and consciences of individual people.

Notes

[1] Terrence McGoldrick, "Episcopal Conferences Worldwide on Catholic Social Teaching," *Theological Studies* 59 (1998), 28-31. McGoldrick also points out that in terms of frequency, the African bishops' pastorals focus most often on education, followed by human rights, corruption, poverty, family, and finally economic development. The reason for this is that because poverty is so prevalent on the continent and people do not need to be reminded of it, the African bishops focus their attention on the need to educate people for development and also on both human rights and corruption in order to combat the effects of ethnic tribalism.

[2] All of these statements are catalogued in Roger Berthouzoz et. al.'s comprehensive study concerning worldwide Catholic episcopal conference documents on development and economics. See Berthouzoz et. al. (eds.), *Economie et développement: Répertoire des documents épiscopaux des cinq continents: 1891-1991* (Fribourg: Editions Universitaires, 1997). Terrence McGoldrick (note 1) participated in this research and his essay is a synopsis of the Berthouzoz study.

[3] Although I can only present a sample of statements within this chapter, they are representative of the bishops' contributions as a whole because almost all episcopal conference statements concerning development employ similar theological foundations and reach the same conclusions.

[4] The nine regional conferences are as follows: 1) Association of Member Episcopal Conferences in Eastern Africa (AMECEA) which includes Eritrea, Ethiopia, Kenya, Malawi, Sudan, Tanzania, Uganda, and Zambia; 2) Association of Episcopal Conferences of Anglophone Africa (AECAWA) which includes Gambia, Ghana, Liberia, Nigeria, and Sierra Leone; 3) Inter Regional Meeting of Bishops of Southern Africa (IMBISA) which includes Angola, Botswana, Lesotho, Mozambique, Namibia, South Africa, Swaziland, Zimbabwe, Sáo Tome, and Principe; 4) Association of Episcopal Conferences of Central Africa (ACEAC) which includes Rwanda, Burundi, and the Democratic Republic of Congo (formerly Zaïre); 5) Association des Conférence Episcopale Régionale de l'Afrique Centrale (ACERAC) which includes Congo, the Central African Republic, Cameroon, Chad , Gabon, and Equatorial Guinea; 6) Conférence Episcopale Régionale de l'Afrique de l'Ouest (CERAO) which includes Benin, Burkina Faso, Ivory Coast, Guinea,

Mali, Mauritania, Niger, Senegal, Togo, Cape Verde, and Guinea Bissau; 7) Conférence Episcopale de Madagascar (CEM) which includes Madagascar, Seychelles, Mauritius, Comores, and Reunion; 8) Conférence Episcopale Régionale du Nord d'Afrique (CERNA) which includes Algeria, Libya, Morocco, and Tunisia; and 9) the Catholic Hierarchy of Egypt (AHCE) which includes Egypt and the Oriental Churches of Northern Africa.

The bishops of most African countries meet in national conferences as well. Notable exceptions include the bishops of South Africa, Botswana, Namibia and Swaziland who meet as one "national" conference as do the bishops of Libya, Algeria, Morocco, and Tunisia. For further information concerning the history, collegiality, and overall function of African episcopal conferences, see Bernard Munono Muyembe's *Eglise, évangélization et promotion humaine: Le discours social des évêques africains* (Fribourg: Editions Universitaires, 1995), 48-60.

5 See SECAM's statement of self-definition at the beginning of its "Justice and Evangelization in Africa," in *Seeking Gospel Justice in Africa: Spearhead 69* (Eldoret, Kenya: AMECEA Gaba Publications, 1981), 4; Charles Valy Tuho's "L'Afrique," in *Ethique, économie et développement: L'enseignement des évêques des cinq continents* (1891-1991), ed Roger Berthouzoz and Roberto Papini (Fribourg, Switzerland: Editions Universitaires, 1995), 101-125 at 102; and also Munono Muyembe, 76-78.

6 The SECAM bishops use the term "Third World" in this document.

7 SECAM, "Le Symposium des évêques d'Afrique: Déclarations finales du symposium," *La Documentation Catholique* 1548 (1969), 862-863.

8 Second Vatican Council, "Gaudium et Spes: Pastoral Constitution on the Church in the Modern World," in *Catholic Social Thought: The Documentary Heritage*, eds. David J. O'Brien & Thomas A. Shannon (Maryknoll, NY: Orbis Books, 1995). 166-237 at no. 42.2.

9 Pope Paul VI, "Populorum Progressio: On the Development of Peoples," in *Catholic Social Thought: The Documentary Heritage*, 240-262 at no. 13.

10 *Gaudium et Spes*, no. 85.2. While recognizing the need for reform in economic and social structures, the Vatican II bishops also warn that African nations must beware of technological innovations that are "immaturely

proposed," particularly those that, while offering material advantage, actually militate against one's spiritual nature (no. 86d).

[11] Pope Paul VI, "Africae Terrarum: To the Peoples of Africa: Message of Pope Paul VI (October 29, 1967)," in *The Gospel of Peace and Justice: Catholic Social Teaching Since Pope John*, ed. Joseph Gremillion (Maryknoll, NY: Orbis Books, 1976), 417-426 at nos. 20-22. In this document, Paul VI also claims that urgent needs facing the African continent include basic education for children (especially literacy training), technical training programs that are geared toward meeting the actual needs of the continent (especially the needs of those in the rural areas), and that the methods and "ways of thinking" about agricultural production need to updated to meet the demands of the African population. John XXIII's *Pacem in Terris* can be found in *Catholic Social Teaching: The Documentary Heritage*, 131-162.

[12] *Populorum Progressio*, nos. 57-61.

[13] An international episcopal synod is a gathering of bishops called by the Pope to discuss and offer recommendations on specific issues facing the Church. The nature and function of synods will be discussed more thoroughly in part three of this chapter which deals with the development question at the 1994 Synod for Africa. In addition to justice and peace, the 1971 synod also focused on questions concerning the priesthood.

[14] Synod of Bishops, 1971, "Justice in the World," in *Catholic Social Thought: The Documentary Heritage*, 287-300 at no. 6. According to Donal Door, the use of the term "constitutive" in this passage was very controversial. For those who believed the Church should work more actively in temporal affairs, the choice of the term was seen as a justification for their position. In fact, for those seeking to gain Church support in their efforts to challenge oppressive political, social, and economic structures it became a sort of "manifesto." However, the use of "constitutive" also came under great criticism from those who believed the evangelizing mission of the Church was primarily spiritual and that social issues should remain secondary. These people sought to replace "constitutive" with "integral" in order to demonstrate that working for temporal justice was, as Door maintains, "not absolutely essential to the life of the Church but pertains rather to its fullness." Not surprisingly, those most opposed to this term were also the ones most critical of Latin American liberation theology. They did not want "constitutive" to force the Church to become more involved in efforts to gain political liberation. See

Dorr's *Option for the Poor: A Hundred Years of Catholic Social Teaching*, Revised Edition (Maryknoll, NY: Orbis Press, 1992), 238-240.

[15] "Justice in the World," nos. 34 and 36.

[16] Episcopal Conferences of-All Africa, "Report on the Experiences of the Church in the Work of Evangelization in Africa," in *Modern Missionary Documents and Africa*, ed. Raymond Hickey, OSA (Dublin: Dominican Publications, 1982), 209-245 at 225-226.

[17] "The Spirit of the Lord is upon me, because he has anointed me to bring glad tidings to the poor. He has sent me to proclaim liberty to captives and recovery of sight to the blind, to let the oppressed go free, and to proclaim a year acceptable to the Lord."

[18] Concerning this emphasis on liberation, Donal Door claims that by the early 1970s many in Latin America had begun to equate the term "development" with a model of economic growth that simply led to greater exploitation and further widened the gap between rich and poor. Instead of speaking of development, these people spoke of "liberation." However, in other parts of the Third World, especially in the newly independent nations of Africa, development was still seen as a positive term in that political as well as church leaders believed the primary way to alleviate poverty was through authentic development programs. In order to take into account both points of view, the bishops at the 1971 synod coined the term "liberation through development" in speaking of the need to overcome social structures that trap the poor in poverty (see "Justice in the World," no. 16). Employing "liberation through development" was in reality a means for the bishops to maintain a middle ground. They could recognize that economic policy alone was inadequate to free people from poverty but at the same time not endorse the political understanding of liberation proposed by many Latin American liberation theologians. This "middle ground" understanding of liberation continues here in "Evangelization of the Modern World." See Door's *Option for the Poor*, 183-184, 229-230. For more on the relationship between liberation and development, see the chapter entitled "Development as Liberation" in Charles Elliott's *The Development Debate* (New York: Friendship Press, 1971).

[19] Synod of Bishops, 1974, "Evangelization of the Modern World," in *The Gospel of Peace and Justice*, 593-598 at 597. It should be noted, however, that

in making this claim the bishops are very careful to uphold the primary function of the Church's liberating mandate. While this mandate does include freeing people from any and all forms of temporal oppression, its primary function is to free humanity from sin (both individual and collective) and lead people to full communion with God.

[20] Pope Paul VI, "Evangelii Nuntiandi: Evangelization in the Modern World," in *Catholic Social Thought: The Documentary Heritage*, 303-345 at nos. 9, 29-30.

[21] *Evangelii Nuntiandi*, no. 31.

[22] Paul VI's *Evangelii Nuntiandi* also influenced two further SECAM statements concerning economic development during the 1970s. Reuniting in 1977 at Accra, Ghana, the SECAM bishops issued "Conscience chrétienne et violation des droits de l'homme en Afrique," a brief communiqué concerning the violation of human rights in Africa. Speaking specifically of economic development, they claim that a process of recolonization is in progress in many African nations; a recolonization that is based in ideology, pursues both commercial and military objectives, and prevents Africans from employing their own means to bring about a better future for themselves and for the continent as a whole. Then, citing Paul VI in union with the bishops of the 1974 synod, they reaffirm that because each human person reflects the image and likeness of God, everyone must be afforded proper dignity and as such enjoy the fundamental right to justice, freedom, and autonomous development. See SECAM's "Conscience chrétienne et violation des droits de l'homme en Afrique," *La Documentation Catholique* 1722 (1977), 572-573. In "Justice et paix en Afrique," the final statement from their 1978 general assembly in Nairobi, Kenya, the SECAM bishops briefly touch upon the "intimate connection" between liberation and development by claiming that as Christ came to save humanity from every form of oppression, his liberating function impacts not only the interior or spiritual order but also concrete human life in both its individual and collective dimensions. Precisely because Christ's liberating work impacts all aspects of human life, any understanding of liberation must include decolonization, development, social justice, and a respect for the individual's fundamental rights and liberties. See "Justice et paix en Afrique," *La Documentation Catholique* 1751 (1978), 927-929.

[23] Here they cite Paul VI's *Evangelii Nuntiandi*, no. 31.

[24] Concerning Tradition, the SECAM bishops cite St. Ambrose's *De Officiis*, I, 24, 115; St. Augustine's *De Libero Arbitrio*, I, 13, 27 and *De Diversis Quaestionibus*, 83, 1; St. Gregory's *Moral.* II, 49, 76; and St. Thomas Aquinas' *Summa Contra Gentiles*, II, 130.

[25] SECAM, "Justice and Evangelization in Africa," in *Seeking Gospel Justice in Africa*, 5-28 at nos. 3-8. In speaking of the need to develop the "virtues" necessary for true progress to occur, the SECAM bishops cite *Gaudium et Spes*, nos. 35 and 73.

[26] "Justice and Evangelization in Africa," nos. 10-12.

[27] Interestingly, the SECAM bishops relate this call for "in-depth" conversion to the claims of so-called "best experts in economic and social development" who state that without both a change of heart and a mobilization of conscience even the best development plans are doomed to failure. Unfortunately, the bishops never identify who these "best experts" are.

[28] "Justice and Evangelization in Africa," nos. 15-17.

[29] "The Church shares with people of our time this profound and ardent desire which is just in every respect, nor does she fail to examine the various aspects of the sort of justice that the life of people and society demands. This is confirmed by the field of Catholic social doctrine, greatly developed in the course of the last century. On the lines of this teaching proceed the education and formation of human consciences in the spirit of justice, and also individual undertakings, especially in the sphere of the apostolate of the laity, which are developing in precisely this spirit." Pope John Paul II, "Dives in Misericordia," in *The Papal Encyclicals: 1958-1981*, ed. Claudia Carlen, IHM, 275-298 (Raleigh, NC: McGrath, 1981), no. 118.

[30] "Justice and Evangelization in Africa," nos. 19-20.

[31] The bishops cite Pope Paul VI's *Africae Terrarum*: "As regards community life- which in African tradition was family life writ large- we note that participation in the life of the community, whether in the circle of one's kinfolk or in public life, is considered a precise duty and the right of all. But the exercise of this right is conceded only after progressive preparation through a series of initiations whose aim is to form the character of the young

candidates and instruct them in the traditions, rules, and customs of society" (no. 12).

[32] "Justice and Evangelization in Africa," nos. 26-30.

[33] SECAM, "Resolutions on Justice," in *Seeking Gospel Justice in Africa,* 29-30 at nos. 1, 5-8.

[34] In this study I am using the French version of this text, "L'Eglise et la promotion humaine en Afrique aujourd'hui" in *La Documentation Catholique* 1913 (1986), 260-272. This pastoral was published following SECAM's 1984 plenary assembly in Kinshasa, Zaïre.

[35] "L'Eglise et la promotion humaine en Afrique aujourd'hui," nos. 1-5.

[36] Webster's New Collegiate Dictionary defines atavism as "recurrence in an organism ... of a form typical of ancestors more remote than the parents usually due to genetic recombination."

[37] Ibid., nos. 18-29.

[38] Pope John Paul II, "Discours pour l'ouverture de la troisième conférence de l'Episcopat latino-américain," *La Documentation Catholique* 1758 (1979), 169.

[39] "L'Eglise et la promotion humaine en Afrique aujourd'hui," nos. 37-47. Concerning the importance of liberating people from sin, one year earlier at the 1983 Synod of Bishops in Rome (which itself focused on the importance of reconciliation) the African delegation took the opportunity to issue a brief statement in which it linked specific challenges of development with the need for authentic repentance. In its "Appel à la réconciliation et à la pénitance en Afrique" (Appeal for Reconciliation and Penance in Africa), the bishops first affirm that because the Church functions as the sign, agent, and locus of both fraternity and reconciliation among people, it has an important role to play in contemporary (1983) African life. Then, identifying specific challenges such as corruption, the unilateral fixing of prices for African goods, and the sale or donation of products that harm peoples' health, the bishops once again cite *Evangelii Nuntiandi* (no. 30) and claim the Church must safeguard fundamental human rights and human dignity, combat all that condemns people to remaining on the margins of life, and proclaim the complete and integral liberation of all

people. However, the bishops also recognize that none of this will be possible unless people begin to hear God's Spirit and renounce evil in their hearts. Citing Jesus' teachings about forgiveness in the gospel Beatitudes (Matt 5:23-24 and 43-47), they maintain that individuals must not be guided by hate but by love, forgiveness, and reconciliation. In short, one cannot be an "artisan of peace" if one does not fight with the "arms of peace," one cannot liberate others if one has not first liberated oneself. See the African Delegation to the Synod of Bishops (1983) statement "Appel à la réconciliation et à la pénitance en Afrique," *La Documentation Catholique* 1864 (1983), 1182-1183.

[40] "L'Eglise et la promotion humaine en Afrique aujourd'hui," nos. 48-51.

[41] Ibid., nos. 77-91.

[42] SECAM, "Seventh General Assembly of SECAM: Final Communique, Resolutions and Recommendations," *African Ecclesial Review* 26 (1984), 376-381. Many of these same recommendations were made in the final communiqué of the 1988 Pan African Justice and Peace Seminar held in Roma, Lesotho from May 29 to June 3. This seminar, which was sponsored by SECAM, brought together bishops, priests, and both religious and lay men and women from throughout the continent to discuss pressing issues of justice and peace. For more on this seminar, see Jaime Goncalves' (SECAM Vice-President) and P. Obinna Aguh's (SECAM Acting Secretary), "Pan African Conference on Justice and Peace," *African Ecclesial Review* 30 (1988), 218-225.

[43] Catholic Bishops' Conference of Zaïre, "Le chrétien et le développment de la nation," *La Documentation Catholique* 1992 (1988), nos. 54-59. It is interesting to note that in the introductory paragraphs of this statement, the Zaïrian bishops justify the publication of their pastoral by claiming its purpose was to evaluate the first two decades of the so-called "project for Zaïrian society" as defined by the 1967 "Manifeste de la N'Sele." According to this Manifeste, Zaïrian society was to become independent, all fundamental liberties were to be guaranteed, and the methods of both agricultural and industrial production were supposed to be altered to allow for greater popular participation. More specifically in the economic realm, this Manifeste also proposed that Zaïrian society would be "inspired" by a sense of communitarian humanism where all people shared in the "fruits of the common effort," and where the economy would be constructed so that it profited the nation as a whole and not just the ruling élite. As one might guess, the grand promises of

the "Manifeste de la N'Sele" were never realized and the bishops used its twentieth anniversary as an occasion to present their critique (nos. 1-10).

[44] "Le chrétien et le développment de la nation," nos. 68-82.

[45] In making this claim, the Cameroonian bishops cite John Paul II's teachings on social sin in both "Redemptor Hominis" and "Sollicitudo Rei Socialis." See John Paul II's "Redemptor Hominis" in *The Papal Encyclicals: 1958-1981*, 245-273 at no. 55; and "Sollicitudo Rei Socialis" in *Catholic Social Teaching: The Documentary Heritage*, 395-436 at no. 36.

[46] Catholic Bishops' Conference of Cameroon, "Les causes de la crise économique," *La Documentation Catholique* 2010 (1990), nos. 2, 5-7, 24-25.

[47] In making this claim, the bishops cite the Pontifical Commission for Justice and Peace's "An Ethical Approach to the International Debt Question:" "Debtor countries, in fact, find themselves caught in a vicious circle. In order to pay back their debts, they are obliged to transfer ever greater amounts of money outside of the country. These are resources which should have been available for internal purposes and investment and therefore their own development ... When credit agencies consider the situation solely from the economic and monetary angle, they often impose on debtor countries terms, in exchange for accrued credit, that can contribute, at least in the short term, to unemployment, recession, and a drastic reduction in the standard of living. This causes suffering, first of all, for the poorest as well as for certain sectors of the middle class. In brief, it is a situation that is intolerable and, in the medium term, disastrous for the creditors themselves. Debt servicing cannot be met at the price of the asphyxiation of a country's economy, and no government can morally demand of its people privations incompatible with human dignity." See the Pontifical Commission for Justice and Peace's "An Ethical Approach to the International Debt Question," *Origins* 16 (February 5, 1987), 603.

[48] "Les causes de la crise économique," nos. 8-10.

[49] Catholic Bishops of Zambia, "You Shall be My Witnesses: A Second Century of Evangelization in Zambia," *Catholic International* 2 (October, 1991), nos. 26-28. This pastoral was written to commemorate one hundred years of Christian evangelization in Zambia.

[50] Catholic Bishops' Conference of Zambia, "Hear the Cry of the Poor: A Pastoral Letter on the Current Suffering of the People in Zambia," *Catholic International* 4 (October, 1993), 474-475.

[51] "Hear the Cry of the Poor," 476. Peter Henriot, SJ, of the Jesuit Center for Theological Reflection (Lusaka, Zambia) offers both an ethical and economic critique of structural adjustment in his essay "Development in Light of the African Synod: An Alternative to the Structural Adjustment Program," *Catholic International* 7 (June/July, 1996), 285-294.

[52] Association of Member Episcopal Conferences in Eastern Africa (AMECEA), "La solidarité avec ceux qui souffrent," *La Documentation Catholique* 1928 (1986), 1059-1060.

[53] Inter-Regional Meeting of the Bishops of Southern Africa (IMBISA), "Justice et paix en Afrique australe," *La Documentation Catholique* 1980 (1989), nos. 28-30.

[54] See Chapter One at notes 37-41 for an explanation of the various causes and consequences of corruption.

[55] Catholic Bishops of Kenya, "A Society Built on Peace and Love," *Catholic International* 1 (October, 1990), nos. 10, 12-13.

[56] Catholic Bishops of Zambia, "You Shall be My Witnesses," nos. 28-30. See also Articles 23 and 25 of the United Nations' "Universal Declaration of Human Rights," in *Freedom's Charter: The Universal Declaration of Human Rights*, no. 76 (New York: Foreign Policy Association, 1949), 55-62; and Articles 14-17 of the "African Charter on Human and People's Rights" (also known as the "Banjul Charter") in *Catholic International* 2 (1991), 631-632.

[57] Catholic Bishops of Zambia, "Hear the Cry of the Poor," 477-478.

[58] This pastoral letter was read in all Malawian Catholic Churches on the first Sunday of Lent (March 8) of 1992. Two days later, all seven bishops who signed the letter were detained, questioned, and repeatedly accused of sedition by the Malawian police. All known copies of the statement were destroyed and Malawian radio claimed that anyone holding a copy would be arrested and charged with a criminal offense.

[59] Catholic Bishops of Malawi, "Living our Faith: Lenten Pastoral Letter of the Catholic Bishops of Malawi," *Catholic International* 3 (May, 1992), nos. 5-6.

[60] See Chapter Three, note 76.

[61] "Above all, we affirm that the social teachings proclaimed by the Catholic Church cannot be separated from her traditional teaching regarding man's life. Wherefore, it is our earnest wish that more and more attention be given to this branch of learning. First of all, we urge that attention be given to such studies at Catholic schools at all levels, and especially in the seminaries, although we are not unaware that in some of these latter institutions this is already being done admirably. Moreover, we desire that social study of this sort be included in all religious materials used to instruct or inspire the lay apostolate, either in parishes or associations." Pope John XXIII, "Mater et Magistra: Christianity and Social Progress," in *Catholic Social Teaching: The Documentary Heritage*, 84-128 at nos. 222-223.

[62] IMBISA, "Justice et paix en Afrique australe," nos. 80-83.

[63] Catholic Bishops' Conference of Cameroon, "Les causes de la crise économique," nos. 29, 31.

[64] "...the laity, that is Christians who have been incorporated into Christ and live in the world, are of primary importance and worthy of special care. It is for them, imbued with the Spirit of Christ, to be a leaven animating and directing the temporal order from within, so that everything is always carried out in accordance with the will of Christ." Second Vatican Council, "Ad Gentes: Decree on the Church's Missionary Activity," in *Vatican II: The Conciliar and Post Conciliar Documents*, ed. Austin Flannery, O.P (Dublin: Dominican Publications, 1992), 813-856 at no. 15.

[65] Catholic Bishops' Conference of Zaïre, "Le chrétien et le développment de la nation," nos. 151-152, 183-189. The IMBISA bishops make a similar claim concerning the laity in their "Justice et paix en Afrique australe." According to the IMBISA bishops, Christians cannot divorce faith from everyday life but instead must seek to manifest this faith in every aspect of their lives. For this reason, all Christians, but in particular the laity, have a duty to participate in public life to assure that political parties and governments adhere to the principles of justice, liberty, and human rights. While the Church acts as

the conscience of society, it is only through the commitment of the laity that true change can take place (nos. 86-89).

[66] Catholic Bishops' Conference of Cameroon, "Les causes de la crise économique," no. 11.

[67] In fact, the bishops claim this lack of transparency and accountability at higher governmental levels is an "implicit invitation" to corruption at lower levels.

[68] See the Catholic Bishops of Kenya's "A Society Built on Peace and Love," nos. 7-8; their "Kenya 1992: Looking Toward the Future With Hope," *Catholic International* 3 (April, 1992), nos. 4, 10-11; and also Pope John Paul II's "Sollicitudo Rei Socialis: On Social Concern," in *Catholic Social Teaching: The Documentary Heritage*, 395-436 at no. 15. Furthermore, as they were writing in anticipation of their nation's 1992 Parliamentary elections, the Kenyan bishops conclude "Looking Toward the Future With Hope" by exhorting the faithful to vote for those candidates who see themselves as accountable to God and the people, who will remain in touch with their constituencies, who will respect the rights and property of others, who will promote the common good and not use their positions for personal gain, who will promote partnerships between government, religious bodies and parents in all areas of development (especially in education), and who respect religious beliefs, the rights of the unborn, and the importance of the family. In sum, the bishops exhort the people to vote for candidates who demonstrate genuine integrity, moral courage, and the competence to perform the functions for which they are elected.

[69] Catholic Bishops' Conference of Tanzania, "The Truth Will Make You Free: Solidarity in Truth," *Catholic International* 4 (December, 1993), 577.

[70] Catholic Bishops of Malawi, "Living our Faith," no. 10-13. In claiming that people must be free to use their individual gifts, the Malawian bishops cite Ephesians 4:7-16 and 1Peter 4:10-11.

[71] Catholic Bishops' Conference of Nigeria, "The People's Responsibility-To Themselves," *Catholic International* 3 (December, 1992), nos. 3-9.

[72] The Commission's rationale for these actions was Pope Paul VI's call in *Octogesima Adveniens* for Christians to make a greater commitment to

working for justice in the world. See Paul VI's "Octogesima Adveniens," in *Catholic Social Teaching: The Documentary Heritage*, 265-286 at nos. 48-49.

[73] John Baur, *2000 Years of Christianity in Africa: An African Church History* (Nairobi, Kenya: Paulines Publications Africa, 1994), 317-318.

[74] Ibid., 488. Baur's claim about the Church's moral leadership is echoed by Julius Ihonvbere, an Associate Professor of Political Science (University of Texas at Austin). Ihonvbere states that because of the political situations in many sub-Saharan nations, the people oftentimes take more comfort in their ethnic and religious organizations than they do in their governments. See Ihonvbere's "Pan-Africanism: Agenda for African Unity in the 1990's?" in *Issues and Trends in Contemporary African Politics: Stability, Development and Democratization*, ed. George Akeya Agbango (New York: Peter Lang, 1997), 337-366 at 356.

[75] Catholic Bishops of Zambia, "Christian Liberation, Justice, and Development: The Church's Concern for Human Development in Zambia," cited in Austin Cheyeka's "The Distinctive Contribution of the Catholic Church to the Struggle for Justice in Kaunda's Zambia," *African Christian Studies*, vol. 15 number 3 (September, 1999), 28-29.

[76] Catholic Bishops of Zambia, "Economics, Politics, and Justice," *African Ecclesial Review* 32 (1990), 314-321.

[77] Catholic Bishops of Zambia, "You Shall be My Witnesses," nos. 29, 34.

[78] For further information on the Church's role in Zambian politics, see Austin Cheyeka's "The Distinctive Contribution of the Catholic Church to the Struggle for Justice in Kaunda's Zambia," 19-34.

[79] Pope Paul VI, "Moto Proprio Datae: Synodus Episcoporum pro universa Ecclesia constituitur," *Acta Apostolicae Sedis* 57 (1965), 775-780. For more on the importance of synods in the life of the Church see the Second Vatican Council's "Christus Dominus: Decree on the Pastoral Office of Bishops in the Church" in *Vatican Council II: The Conciliar and Post Conciliar Documents*, 564-590 at no. 37.

[80] See Canons 345 and 346 of the Code of Canon Law. Canon Law also states that synods are to be convened by the pope and their purpose is three-

fold: 1) to discuss and make recommendations concerning specific temporal issues facing the Church, 2) to assist the Pope in safeguarding the faith and preserving ecclesial discipline, and 3) to foster a greater sense of collegiality between the Pope and bishops and also amongst the bishops themselves (Canon 342). The role of the Pope is clearly defined in Canon 344. "The synod of bishops is directly under the authority of the Roman Pontiff whose role it is to: 1) convoke a synod as often as he deems it opportune and to designate where the sessions are to be held; 2) ratify the election of those members who are to be elected in accord with the norm of special law and to designate and name its other members; 3) determine the topics for discussion at a suitable time before the celebration of the synod in accord with the norm of special law; 4) determine the agenda; 5) preside over the synod in person or through others; and 6) conclude, transfer, suspend, and dissolve the synod." See the *Code of Canon Law*, Latin-English Edition (Washington DC: Canon Law Society of America, 1983).

[81] From 1967 to 1994 there were fourteen synods: nine ordinary, two extraordinary, and three special sessions for specific regions. For a brief overview of these fourteen synods see Gilbert Kazingufu, SCA, "Synods in the Life of the Church and in Particular the African Synod," in *What Happened at the African Synod?*, ed. Cecil McGarry, SJ (Nairobi, Kenya: Paulines Publications Africa, 1995), 12-32 at 14-15.

[82] Pope John Paul II, *Familiaris Consortio: On the Family* (Washington DC: United States Catholic Conference, 1982); and "Ecclesia in Africa" in *The African Synod: Documents, Reflections, Perspectives*, ed. Africa Faith and Justice Network (Maryknoll, NY: Orbis Books, 1996), 233-283.

[83] Pope John Paul II, "The Synod of Bishops: A Service to Unity of the Church," *L'Osservatore Romano*, Weekly English Edition (May 23, 1983), 9. In this address to the General Secretariat of the Synod of Bishops, John Paul II adds that a synod is "a particularly faithful expression and the very valuable instrument of episcopal collegiality," a collegiality that "serves the communion of bishops and faithful and, finally, the ever deeper and more organic unity of the Church." In concluding this address, he states: "For my part, you may be assured of my highest consideration for the function of the synod of bishops in the Church and of the complete confidence I place in its activity at the service of the universal Church."

For further information concerning the general topic areas of past synods and the papal encyclicals that followed from them, see the table "Synods of Bishops" in *Catholic International* 6 (1995), 120; and Kazingufu, 15-17.

[84] Canons 439 and 445; my emphasis.

[85] Paul Cardinal Zoungrana, "Opening Address at the First Assembly of SECAM," *La Documentation Catholique* 1548 (1969), 860. Interestingly, many Africans justify their call for a council by citing Pope Paul VI's address to this same SECAM assembly where he calls upon Africans to be missionaries to themselves: "'Missionaries to yourselves': in other words, you Africans must now continue, upon this continent, the building up of the Church." Further on in this address, the Pope also states the need for a uniquely African expression of the Christian faith: "The expression, that is, the language and mode of manifesting this one [Christian] faith, may be manifold. Hence, it may be original, suited to the tongue, the style, the character, the genius, and the culture of the one who professes this one faith. From this point of view, a certain pluralism is not only legitimate but desirable. An adaptation of the Christian life in the fields of pastoral, ritual, didactic, and spiritual activities is not only possible, it is even favored by the Church. The liturgical renewal is a living example of this. And in this sense you may, and you must, have an African Christianity." See Pope Paul VI's "An African Christianity: Address of Pope Paul VI at the closing of the Symposium of African Bishops, July 31, 1969," in *Modern Missionary Documents and Africa*, 200-205 at 201-204.

[86] "Such a Council, capable of mobilizing the African peoples' initiative, would have to give itself the task of looking for the necessary structures and means of bringing African Catholicity into a state of permanent reconciliation, enabling it to assume the tasks of an endogenous African mission in the spiritual, intellectual, political, and economic dimensions." See the Société Africaine de Culture's "Recommendations," in *Civilization noire et Église catholique: Colloque d'Abidjan, 1977* (Paris: Présence Africaine, 1978), 371-374 at 373. More specifically, the colloquium maintained the proposed council should 1) set up an information service that offers both individuals and communities a means to mutual understanding and self-education, 2) become, along with other Christian bodies, a moral authority that can speak and act in the name of the African people in times of violence and arbitrary decision making, 3) establish an African Catholic University to help foster evangelization, 4) set up institutions for teaching African spirituality along with individual and collective responsibility, and 5) organize both an autonomous

financial body and, in the meantime, an inter-African organization to consolidate Christian assistance (373-374). Prominent African theologians attending the Abidjan colloquium included Jean-Marc Éla, Engelbert Mveng, SJ, and Fabien Eboussi Boulaga. It was also at this colloquium that Boulaga offered his often-quoted proposal for an African council: "I propose that a Council of the Catholic Church in Africa should be convened [because] the spiritual changes in the continent, the enormous and unheard problems which must be faced, suggest it is necessary and at this time favorable..." See Eboussi Boulaga's "Pour une catholicité africaine" in *Civilization noire et Église catholique*, 342-347.

[87] Joseph Cardinal Malula, "Allocution du Cardinal Malula," *La Documentaion Catholique* 1852 (1983), 513.

[88] See Aylward Shorter's *The African Synod: A Personal Response to the Outline Document* (Nairobi, Kenya: St. Paul Publications-Africa, 1991), 16. Engelbert Mveng adds that topics considered for the proposed council included taking stock of Christianity's current state in Africa, creating conditions so that the Christian faith could take deeper root in African society, and exploring the future of Christianity in the areas of theology, doctrine, liturgy, spirituality, pastoral options and orientations, and the role of the Church in African society. See Mveng's "The Historical Background of the African Synod," in *The African Synod: Documents, Reflections, Perspectives*, 20-31 at 23. An earlier version of Mveng's essay was published under the title "The African Synod: Prolegomena for an African Council?" in *Toward the African Synod: Concilium, 1992/1*, ed. Giuseppe Alberigo & Alphone Ngindu Muchete (London: SCM Press, 1992), 112-128.

[89] This is the claim of René Luneau in his "The Expectations of the Catholic Church," in *Toward the African Synod*, 83-87 at 85.

[90] Kazingufu, 19. In addition to these survey results, Aylward Shorter claims that over one-third of the episcopal conferences attending the Lagos assembly offered no opinion at all as to whether SECAM should continue to pursue the idea of a council. The remaining conferences were evenly divided among those who thought the project should continue, those who thought it should be abandoned, and those who did not think it was an opportune time to convene a council. See Shorter's *The African Synod: A Personal Response to the Outline Document*, 17.

[91] For more on the question of "synod or council?" as well as preparations for the synod as a whole, see Juvénal Ilunga Muya's "La réception du Synode des évêques pour l'Afrique," *Nouvelle revue de science missionnaire* 54 (1998), 277-278; "Repères chronologiques," in *Le Synode africain: Histoire et textes*, ed. Maurice Cheza (Paris: Karthala, 1996), 21-24; Joseph Oladejo Faniran's "The Council or Synod for Africa: The Overlooked Aspect," *African Ecclesial Review* 36 (1994), 59-67; Peter Lwaminda's "The African Background to the African Synod," *Catholic International* 2 (December, 1991), 1074-1076; Bernard Agré's "My Involvement in the Preparatory Work for the African Synod," translated by John Bowden, in *Toward the African Synod* 99-103; Guiseppe Alberigo's "A Historic Occasion or Bureaucratization?" translated by Mortimer Bear, in *Toward the African Synod*, 147-155; Justin S. Ukpong's "A Critical Review of the Lineamenta on the Special African Synod," in *The African Synod: Documents, Reflections, Perspectives*, 32-42; and Nicholas I. Mbogu's "The Church in Africa on the Eve of the First African Synod," *African Ecclesial Review* 31 (1991), 298-304.

[92] The General secretariat consisted of SECAM President Bishop Gabriel Ganaka and Vice-President Christian Cardinal Tumi, Bishops John Amissah of AECAWA, Henri Tessier of CERNA, Jamie Goncalves of IMBISA, Bernard Agré of CERAO, Faustus Ngabu of ACEAC, Dennis De Jong of AMECEA, and His Beatitude Stéphanos II Ghattas of AHCE. Further members included Cardinal Tomko, Prefect of the Congregation for the Evangelization of Peoples; Archbishop Jan Schotte, General Secretary of the Synod of Bishops; Francis Cardinal Arinze, President of the Pontifical Council for Interreligious Dialogue; Archbishop Albert Tsiahoana, President of the Episcopal Conference of Madagascar; Archbishops Paul Verdzekov of Cameroon, Stephen Naidoo of South Africa, Anthony Mayala of Tanzania, and Laurant Monsengwo of Zaïre; and Bishops Joseph Willigers of Uganda and John Onaiyekan of Nigeria

[93] For further information on the work of the General Secretariat, see Paulos Cardinal Tzadua, et. al., "The Road to the Synod for Africa," *Catholic International* 5 (1994), 159-160; Chukwuma Okoye, "The Synod of Bishops/Special Assembly for Africa: Is this Another Roman Programme for Africa?" *African Ecclesial Review* 34 (1992), 208-210; and Kazingufu, 20-21.

[94] Synod of Bishops Special Assembly for Africa, "Lineamenta," *African Ecclesial Review* 33 (1991), nos. 79-80. The full text of the "Lineamenta" can be found in this issue on pages 1-100.

[95] "Lineamenta," nos. 82-85. These internal and external factors include corruption, tribalism, misappropriation of public funds, unilateral fixing of prices for raw materials, lack of North-South dialogue, and conformity to foreign political ideology.

[96] For these and the seventy five other "Lineamenta" questions, see the *African Ecclesial Review* 32 (1990), 322-329.

[97] It should be noted, however, that the "Instrumentum Laboris" is not meant to be restrictive because during a synod the participants are free to deviate from it and raise other issues. Jan Schott, General Secretary of the Synod of Bishops, states of the "Instrumentum Laboris," "[It] should not be seen as in any way anticipating the conclusion of the synod assembly, although the consensus that emerges with regard to certain points in the answers to the "Lineamenta" will be reflected in the results of the synod." See Schotte's "Preface" to the "Instrumentum Laboris" in *Origins* 22 (1993), 655.

[98] Kazingufu, 21-23; Paulos Cardinal Tzadua, 160; and Chukwuma Okoye, "The Special Assembly for Africa of the Synod of Bishops-The Instrumentum Laboris," *African Ecclesial Review* 35 (1993), 172-173.

I must note that while the "Lineamenta" and "Instrumentum Laboris" did set the foundation for the African synod, criticisms were raised almost immediately following their respective publications. Perhaps the most important criticism concerning the synod as a whole was the question, "What is this synod all about?" Bishop Bernard Agré, a member of the original Ante-Preparatory committee, claimed that because Pope John Paul II effectively ended debate concerning whether there should be a synod or council, many in Africa wondered whether he (or some other Vatican official) would "hijack" the synod by declaring "off limits" those issues most pressing to the African Church. Giuseppe Alberigo underscored this claim by stating that the announcement of the Synod for Africa caused perplexity both for those who wanted to convene an African council and for those who were opposed to it. Those who wanted the council saw the synod as the "choking off" or end to any possibility of a council while those who opposed the council saw the synod as the first step toward making it a reality. Questions were also raised concerning the sheer scope of issues the synod proposed to discuss. In four short weeks could the African bishops realistically expect to discuss evangelization, inculturation, dialogue, justice and peace, and social communication in a comprehensive manner? Furthermore, the synod was criticized because of the lack of lay participation in its preparatory process. If the synod was supposed to be of and for the African Church as a whole, why were its preparations being carried out almost exclusively by the clergy? See Bernard Agré's "My Involvement in the Preparatory Work for the African Synod," in *Toward the African Synod,* 99-103 at 102-103; and Giuseppe Alberigo's "A Historic Occasion or Bureaucratization?" in *Toward the African Synod,* 147-155 at 150-151. For more on the issue of lay participation, see Peter Damien Akpunonu, Barthélémy Nyom, and Buetubela Balembo's "Declaration by the Catholic Institutes of Higher Education," *Catholic International* 3 (1992), 416-417.

[99] Pope John Paul II, *Redemptoris Missio: On the Permanent Validity of the Church's Missionary Mandate* (Washington, DC: United States Catholic Conference, 1990), nos. 14, 42.

[100] Synod of Bishops Special Assembly for Africa, "Instrumentum Laboris: Evangelizing Mission of the Church in Africa," *Origins* 22 (1993), no. 19.

[101] "Instrumentum Laboris," nos. 112-113. In making this claim the "Instrumentum Laboris" cites SECAM's "L'Eglise et la promotion humaine en Afrique aujourd'hui;" John Paul II's *Redemptor Hominis,* no. 14; and the Second Vatican Council's *Gaudium et Spes*, nos. 23-32.

[102] "The Spirit of the Lord is upon me... (Luke 4:18-19 and Is. 61:1-2), teaching his disciples to be servants (John 13:1-20), and placing the command to love one's neighbor "on an equal footing" with the command to love God (Mt. 22:34-40).

[103] "Instrumentum Laboris," no. 112.

[104] Ibid., no. 114.

[105] Ibid., nos. 115-121

[106] Ibid., nos. 122-125.

[107] See Kazingufu, 25-30. Following the opening liturgy, the first two weeks of the synod were devoted primarily to the presentations or interventions of the synod members. Limited to eight minutes apiece, these oral presentations offered each member an opportunity to speak on the subject of his choice. Interestingly, of all the spoken interventions, the general topic area

most frequently discussed was justice and peace followed respectively by inculturation, proclamation/evangelization, dialogue, and social communication (all of the synod interventions are available on-line at *http://www.afrikaworld.net/synod/themes.htm*. In the third week, the participants divided into twelve working groups (five English-speaking, five French, one Portuguese, and one Italian) to discuss the oral interventions and then present a summary of their findings to the synod as a whole. In the fourth week, the working groups met once again to formulate the formal synodal propositions to be presented to the Pope. The initial proposals from each group were submitted to the synod secretariat which consolidated them, sent them back to the groups for further revision, and then prepared a final list for ratification by the entire synod assembly. In the end, sixty-four propositions were proposed and the vote in favor of accepting them was almost unanimous. In its final acts, the synod approved (after some revision) the text of its final message "Synod of Resurrection for the Family of God" and also elected nine members (one from each of the regional conferences) to aid the Pope in preparing his post-synodal Apostolic Exhortation. The "Synod of Bishops Special Assembly for Africa" concluded on May 8, 1994, with a Mass of thanksgiving at St. Peter's Basilica.

[108] Synod of Bishops Special Assembly for Africa, "Propositions," in *The African Synod: Documents, Reflections, Perspectives*, 87-108 at 102.

[109] Synod of Bishops Special Assembly for Africa, "Synod of Resurrection for the Family of God: Final Message of the Synod for Africa," *Catholic International* 5 (1994), nos. 33, 35-36.

[110] In addition to speaking of foreign debt in this proposition, during the synod thirty-seven African bishops drafted the letter "Forgive Us our Debts" which they addressed to their fellow bishops in Europe and North America. In part, the letter reads as follows: "The bishops of Africa taking part in the African Synod pledge ourselves to uncompromising solidarity with the poor and make their cry known: Forgive us our debts ... The right of the Church to intervene in political and economic affairs is limited in any part of the Church. Yet the social teaching of the Church is part of her mandate to go and teach all nations. These are times when justice compels us to speak publicly on these matters. If we remain silent and inactive, whether in Africa or in the countries of the North, we may appear as cowards and accomplices rather than as champions of justice. We have the right and duty to enlighten the consciences of the decision-makers. The question of African debt offers the opportunity for

the bishops of Africa to work in partnership with their fellow bishops in Europe and America to seek a just and speedy way of resolving it ... For our part in Africa we pledge ourselves to address the internal factors that contribute to the debt crisis. The Church in Africa has always been a fearless champion of human rights and democracy; we reaffirm our resolve to continue to use non-violent ways to overcome corruption, oppression, and economic mismanagement among our government officials, military, and ruling elite. We ask our sister churches in Europe and America to help bring about a swift and just resolution of our problem of unpayable debts. This is inextricably linked with unjust conditions of world trade where the price of our commodities has collapsed to an all-time low. It is also related to the urgent need for reform in the structural adjustment programs which cause great suffering among the poor."

For the full text of this letter and a complete list of signatories, see the bishops', "Forgive Us Our Debts: An Open Letter to Our Brother Bishops in Europe and North America," in *The African Synod: Documents, Reflections, Perspectives*, 114-116.

[111] Further concerning education, in Proposition 46 the assembly also asks that all African episcopal conferences establish Justice and Peace Commissions in order to educate the faithful as to their "evangelical responsibilities" concerning human rights.

[112] Synod of Bishops Special Assembly for Africa, "Propositions," 103-106.

[113] Synod of Bishops Special Assembly for Africa, "Synod of Resurrection for the Family of God," nos. 32, 40-41. It is important to note that while the Synod for Africa was convening at the Vatican, another assembly was also meeting in Rome made up of African (including Jean-Marc Éla and Engelbert Mveng) and Africanist theologians who were not invited to participate in the synod itself. Sponsored by SEDOS, the Servizio di Documenatzione et Studi, this assembly issued its own message following the conclusion of the synod entitled "Syn-Hodos: Africans Working and Walking Together." Specifically concerning economics and development-related issues, these theologians claim the African Church must work to overcome material, cultural, and spiritual (i.e. anthropological) poverty because the misery experienced by so many Africans is not only a crime against humanity, but it is also a negation of Christ's gospel. According to the SEDOS conference:

"The Church's ministry will have to go into two directions: one the one side, in our own nations we will have to call to accountability dictators and exploiters of their own people, the choking regime of widespread corruption and incompetence, the criminal exclusion of competent African experts, [and] the denial of democratic participation in civic, social, and political life ... On the other side we challenge the theologians in the opulent states of the North to take more seriously the crime against humanity perpetrated in the form of unjust and immoral trade and monetary mechanisms. Following the lead of the synodal fathers, we call on our sister churches in the North to join us in condemning Structural Adjustment Programs which do not take into account the human and social costs which have to be paid by the poorest, and which are imposed on our nations by the international financial powers. The present structures of the World Bank and the International Monetary Fund exclude authentic representation and need radical restructuring. Their present policies and programmes cause misery and death in Africa as well as in other parts of the world. The spiral of debt service is self-defeating and takes away any hope of improvement. This calls for immediate action by groups and organizations fighting for international justice and peace, in order to cancel the foreign debt of the countries of the South ... The all too often used slogan 'option for the poor' must get a less exhortative connotation and be filled with more practical, political, and ethical content." See the Post-Synod Africa Network's "Syn-Hodos: Africans Working and Walking Together," *Catholic International* 5 (1994), 375-376.

For further reactions to the synod, see Jean-Marc Éla's "Rencontrer Dieu sur les chemins de notre histoire," in *Le Synod Africain: Histoire et textes*, 7-18; Juvénal Ilunga Muya's "La réception du Synode des évêques pour l'Afrique," 287-294; the Africa Faith and Justice Network's *The African Synod: Documents, Reflections, Perspectives*, 119-226; and Cecil McGarry, ed., *What Happened at the African Synod*?

[114] Here, the African bishops respond (although unknowingly) to one of Bernard Lambert, OP's general conclusions following the 1969 SODEPAX (a joint Roman Catholic/World Council of Churches committee on Society, Development, and Peace) consultation concerning the construction of a theology of development. According to Lambert: "What we hope for and regard as necessary is a constant synchronization of theological thought with changes in the world, enabling the Church to act as a constantly probing and detecting head which as well as following the evolution of the world is also a social and therefore an anticipating guide at the heart of development." See Bernard Lambert, OP, "A Personal Report on the Consultation," in *In Search of*

a Theology of Development: A SODEPAX Report (Lausanne, Switzerland: Imprimerie La Concorde, 1969), 36-50 at 46.

[115] To clarify, I believe the bishops have an important role to play in their respective nations' economic lives, however they are *not* the ones charged with creating or implementing economic policy. The bishops have a duty to speak out on economic issues and can even suggest specific goals such as canceling debt, reforming structural adjustment, and allowing for greater African participation in the global marketplace. However, the "nuts and bolts" details of how these suggestions are to be realized must always remain in the hands of experts in the field.

[116] Recall in Chapter Three that Jean-Marc Éla, and Laurenti Magesa each spoke to these principles (although indirectly) in their calls for economic liberation.

[117] By claiming greater participation will allow Africans to "chart their own economic futures, take responsibility for their own destinies, and ultimately be afforded the opportunity to fulfill themselves as human persons," the bishops implicitly uphold the Catholic social principle of subsidiarity.

Chapter Five

Toward a Theology of Economic Development in Sub-Saharan Africa: Synthesis, Criticism, and A Look To the Future

At the outset of this fifth and final chapter, I wish to state once again that it is not my intention in this study to articulate a *comprehensive* theology of economic development for sub-Saharan Africa or to claim that Christian theological reflection can provide all of the answers to Africa's economic woes. Instead, I simply argue that together the contributions of the African Catholic bishops and theologians offer a specifically Catholic perspective to the overall question of African development theology. In this final chapter, I begin by synthesizing the similarities in the bishops' and theologians' teachings, similarities that I believe form the basis for this specifically Catholic contribution. In my second section, I critique both the bishops' and theologians' contributions by asking some pointed questions. Admittedly, up to this point in the study I have presented the bishops' and theologians' contributions in a positive light. However there are a number of shortcomings in their works that I believe must be addressed so that their theological contributions can take on greater relevance. Finally, I conclude my study by looking toward the future, by briefly identifying some of the non-Catholic sources whose contributions need to be included in any comprehensive development theology, and also by stating what I believe to be the future role of the African Catholic Church.

Synthesis of the Bishops' and Theologians' Statements

Based on the conclusions drawn from Chapters Three and Four, I maintain that together the African Catholic bishops and theologians make an important contribution to the articulation of a sub-Saharan theology of economic development. My primary reason for making this claim is that there are very close connections in the economics-related teachings of the two groups. Primarily, these connections can be seen in how each group relates the principles of Catholic social teaching to the African situation. For the bishops, the relationship is overt because they claim that the Church not only must teach these principles to the faithful, but also must commit itself to applying these principles more forcefully to the African economic reality. This overt linkage is understandable given the fact that the bishops are mandated to uphold and teach the overall tradition of the Church. However, while certainly not as overt as the bishops, Engelbert Mveng, SJ, Jean-Marc Éla, and Laurenti Magesa all allude to the importance of Catholic social teaching insofar as they each implicitly (or in the case of Magesa, explicitly) maintain that these teachings provide a means to address both anthropological and material poverty. Thus, in terms of articulating a theology of economic development, both the bishops and theologians demonstrate that the principles of human dignity, community, solidarity, subsidiarity, participation, common good, and preferential option for the poor act as a moral "blueprint" for creating economic structures that serve humanity as a whole.

This joint focus on the principles of Catholic social teaching is also important because it demonstrates a means to link the Church's universal teachings to the particular challenges facing the African people. In Chapter One, I stated that because of the differing economic, political, and social conditions in various areas of the world, one of the "limitations" to articulating any theology of economic development is that this theology always remains contextual.[1] While not claiming that the bishops and theologians completely overcome this limitation, I believe their joint recourse to the principles of Catholic social teaching is a positive step in this direction. In speaking of the relationship between theology and economics, the two groups ground their theological reflection in two different starting points. The bishops' primary starting point is the social teachings of the universal Church whereas the theologians start with the reality of their people's concrete existence. However, despite these different starting points, the end result of both group's theological reflection is similar. In order to develop and move toward economic self-sufficiency, the African people must be afforded the dignity, freedom, and opportunity articulated within the principles of Catholic social teaching. Thus, what the bishops and theologians together demonstrate is that any theological reflection on the existing African economic order must take into consideration *both* continuity with Church Tradition and those theological insights arising from the concrete realities of people's everyday lives. In other words, any proposed theology of development must maintain both a "top-down" and "bottom-up" approach in order to be accepted by those mandated to preserve the faith while at the same time remaining relevant for those at the grassroots level.

Similarities between the bishops' and theologians' teachings also exist concerning the role of Christian theology in the world and the importance of liberation from sin. The bishops demonstrate the importance of theology's temporal role by critiquing present-day economic policies on moral grounds (particularly debt repayment and structural adjustment) and also by affirming the intimate link between Christian evangelization and efforts toward human development. The theologians echo this by maintaining that in order for Christian theology to remain relevant, the theology must have a practical effect in the lives of the faithful. Interestingly, economist Charles Elliott[2] has argued that Christian theology is vitally important to the issue of economic development because although theology does not respond to the practical question, "What should I do about situations of injustice in the world?" it does speak to the normative question, "What *ought to be* my response to situations of injustice in the world?" For Elliott, these normative or "ought" questions are at the foundation of the Christian experience because in reality they are questions about God. For example, the question, "Ought I to feed the hungry?" is in reality, "Is it God's will that I feed the hungry?" Thus, Christian theology offers a particular perspective about the *kinds* of questions that individuals should be asking and it also questions whether a given economic policy is consistent with what we believe God's will seeks to accomplish in the world.[3] I believe that responding to these normative or "ought" questions is exactly what the bishops and theologians are doing when they speak to the economic development (or lack thereof) of the African sub-continent. No theologian, individual bishop, or episcopal conference identified in my study ever claims to have the final word on any secular economic issue. Instead, by identifying the many challenges to development in their specific regions and suggesting general economic goals, they respond to the question, "What *ought* we to do?" In other words, as I first noted in Chapter Four (note 116), both the bishops and the theologians have important roles to play in formulating their respective nations' economic policies. They have a moral mandate to speak out on the ethical issues underlying economic policy and can even suggest specific goals such as canceling debt, reforming structural adjustment, and allowing for greater African participation in the global marketplace. However, even with this mandate, the bishops and theologians are *not* the ones charged with creating or implementing the specific policies that will lead to the desired economic ends. Exactly how economic policies are to be formulated and implemented, the so-called "nuts and bolts," must always remain in the hands of experts in the field.

Concerning liberation, the bishops and theologians also emphasize the importance of "overcoming" human sinfulness in order to create a more just and equitable economic order. As the root cause of any form of injustice is (human) sin and because no theology of development can ignore humanity's "enduring potential to destroy as well as create,"[4] both the bishops and theologians maintain that the Church must help individuals to recognize their own sinfulness as the first step in creating a society where people can meet basic needs and fulfill themselves as human persons. However, in addition to personal sin, they also claim that liberation must include overcoming the greed, exploitation, and unrestrained quest for power that for so many characterizes the present-day economic order. In this sense, they are speaking of social sin, the systemic sinfulness ingrained within the economic, political, and other social structures of human society.[5] Thus, through their identification of both personal and social sin, the African bishops and theologians recognize that any notion of liberation in the economic realm must begin with an examination of conscience. Political leaders, international development "experts," and even western consumers must always ask what effect their individual and collective decisions are having on the lives of the African people.

Before concluding this section, I note that the African bishops and theologians examined in this study also avoid two of the limitations concerning development theology that I identified in Chapter One. First, although they employ biblical citations to justify both individual Christian and Church participation in development-related efforts, neither group ever claims that Scripture speaks directly to the development question or that it offers a concrete model for Christian action in the world. Stated differently, although they employ the liberating message of Exodus, the prophet Isaiah's "The Spirit of the Lord is upon me ...," the "spirituality of liberation" within the gospel Beatitudes, and Jesus' dual commands, "Your sins are forgiven" and "Get up and walk," neither group views the Bible as an unambiguous "guidebook" for temporal action. Second, neither bishops nor theologians resort to any secular ideologies in their calls for Christians to take active roles in transforming unjust social structures. In Chapter Three I demonstrated how the three liberation theologians conspicuously distance themselves from the Marxist tendencies of their Latin American counterparts and even claim that Marxist ideology as a whole is irrelevant for the African situation. While not as overtly as the theologians, the African bishops carefully avoid references to secular ideologies in their statements concerning the Church and economic development. Aware of both Pope John Paul II's and the Congregation for the Doctrine of the Faith's "responses" to certain proponents of Latin American theologies of liberation, the African bishops barely mention Marxism but instead make a concerted effort to keep their teachings firmly grounded within the Tradition of the Church.

In sum, while I do not claim that the African bishops and theologians offer a *comprehensively stated* theology of economic development for sub-Saharan Africa, I am convinced that their contributions would have to be included in the articulation of any proposed development theology. In other words, the articulation of any proposed Roman Catholic theology of development would have to include how the basic principles of the Church's social teachings can be applied to the many economic difficulties facing the African sub-continent.[6] This theology would have to balance the Church's universal teachings with the theological insights arising from the people's historical contexts. It would have to maintain the role of Christian theology in the world and continually demonstrate to the African people (and to the wider world) that faith can play an important role in their everyday lives. Finally, the articulation of this theology would have to address the realities of human sinfulness and help people to recognize that poverty exists as a result of both the individual and collective decisions that people make within the economic, political, and other realms of human society. Because each of these elements is present within their respective teachings and because they neither employ the Bible to justify temporal action nor rely on secular ideology in order to further their claims, I argue that *together* the African Catholic bishops and theologians examined in this study make an invaluable and specifically Catholic contribution to the articulation of a theology of economic development for sub-Saharan Africa.

Criticisms of the African Bishops and Theologians

In my introduction to this chapter I admitted that up to this point in the study I have not been critical of either the African bishops or theologians. The reason for this lack of criticism is that I have been trying to demonstrate the important contributions they have made to the issue of African economic development. Nevertheless, while I claim that they make some valuable contributions, I have a number of criticisms for them as well. In the first part of my second section I address these criticisms to the three liberation theologians. In the second part I address them to the bishops.

1. Critique of African Liberation Theology

The first questions or criticisms that I pose to Engelbert Mveng, Jean-Marc Éla, and Laurenti Magesa are 1) how exactly do they propose that liberation will take place in sub-Saharan Africa and 2) what will be their theology's function if and when true liberation is ever achieved? One of the major criticisms of Latin American liberation theology is that as a whole it offers little in the way of demonstrating how societal institutions should be constructed to serve the common good. Michael Novak, arguably one of the most well-known North American critics of Latin American liberation theology, makes this point in his book *Will It Liberate? Questions about Liberation Theology* (1986). Novak maintains that although Latin American theologians "uphold" the preferential option for the poor and seek to reduce both repression and the abuse of human rights, there is in fact a clear and stable standard that their theology must meet, "Does it liberate?" Novak argues that the main problem with many of these theologians is that although they aim to help the poor emerge from poverty and also overcome violence and oppression, in practical terms they never actually state *how* their theologies will accomplish these goals. More specifically he asks, how exactly do these theologians propose to bring about the economic growth necessary to improve their people's standards of living? How exactly do they propose that human rights be both protected and promoted within society, and what specific societal structures do they believe are necessary in order to assure that these rights will be respected?[7]

Regardless of the fact that they distance themselves from their Latin American counterparts, similar questions may also be posed to Mveng, Éla, and Magesa. In a general way, how do these three theologians see their expressions of liberation actually "freeing" people from the oppression they face in the various economic, political, and cultural spheres of African life? In more specific ways, how do they propose that liberation actually take place on the African sub-continent? Who will begin the process and upon what societal institutions will the liberation movement primarily focus its attention? Then, supposing liberation from oppressive economic and political structures were to occur, how then do they view a "just" ordering of societal institutions? Unfortunately, Mveng, Éla, and Magesa offer few, if any, concrete responses to these and other related questions. Perhaps the problem lies with how they balance the theoretical with the practical. While these three theologians are on firm theological ground in speaking of the need for temporal liberation, they are not clear in how they envision a liberation ethic. Stated differently, I donot believe they have sufficiently "translated" their theoretical notion of liberation into practical actions that will help to bring about real change for the African people. African liberation theology (as well as liberation theology as a whole) only becomes "authentic" when it helps to effect real, positive change in the lives of those for whom it claims to speak. Thus, in order for their theologies to become more relevant and also realize a greater reception within the wider world community, Mveng, Éla, and Magesa need to formulate more comprehensive and practical responses to Novak's overall question, "Does it liberate?"[8]

My second question for Mveng, Éla, and Magesa concerns how they understand the relationship between the temporal and the eternal. While in Chapter Three I argued that each of these theologians avoids the trap of "sacralizing" the temporal order, I nevertheless wonder how they understand the ultimate fulfillment of their respective notions of liberation. Perhaps the best way to pose the question is, "What is the ultimate end of a theology of liberation and what do these three theologians believe the implications of working for temporal liberation are on God's Kingdom to come?" One could make the argument that striving to help "liberate" people from their sinfulness carries with it eternal consequences as does freeing them to fulfill themselves as individuals in accord with God's design. The problem is that Mveng, Éla, and Magesa rarely, if ever, make any of these claims nor do they make clear, explicit connections between what might be termed the temporal and eternal ends of liberation. If theology is the study of God's revelation to humanity, it would seem that any form of theological inquiry should seek to realize its fulfillment in God, in the eternal. Unfortunately, while Mveng, Éla, and Magesa would almost certainly maintain that there is in fact an eternal "end" to their theological reflection, the precise relationship between these temporal and eternal ends needs to be further clarified.

A third question for Mveng, Éla, and Magesa concerns the ability of their theologies to dialogue with other contextual theologies and with Church doctrine as a whole. Frank Chikane, a former President of the South African Council of Churches, states that liberation theology as a whole has been criticized for its contextual nature because in different areas of the world certain theologians have assumed (incorrectly of course) that their own expressions of liberation are the "most authentic." He further maintains that in order to avoid the twin dangers of assuming an arrogant "universality" (a charge for which Western theology has been roundly denounced) and being reduced to a simple "ghetto theology," any contextual theology must be able to actively dialogue with other contextual theologies from around the world.[9] While Mveng, Éla, and Magesa's expressions of African liberation theology may or may not be guilty of Chikane's first two charges,[10] one could certainly question whether the foundations they employ threaten the possibility for true, fruitful dialogue with other theologies be they contextual or not. For example, a foundational issue for both Magesa and Éla is their insistence that in order to be authentic the African Catholic Church must free itself from the domination of

"Vatican rule." In the 1970s, Magesa argued that in order for the African Church to become more self-reliant and self-propagating, there needed to be a moratorium on its dependence on Rome. This proposed moratorium included the suspension of financial assistance, a reduction in the number of foreign missionaries, and a curtailing of both the "theological treatises" and "ecclesial orders" that were continually being sent to Africa from abroad.[11] In more recent years, he claimed that although it must remain in communion with the other Catholic churches, a "truly African Church" is one whose "being" is not determined by outside forces. Instead, the African Church's theology, ministry, and forms of worship must be drawn from the "longings and questions" of those at the local level and they must also be shaped by the African people's dialogue with others.[12] Éla echoes Magesa by claiming that because ecclesial regulations concerning liturgy, the sacraments, forms of marriage, and clerical celibacy (among other issues) do not take into consideration African cultural realities and are in fact imposed upon Africa from Rome, they actually function as a form of alienation and militate against the birth of an "authentically" African Church. He further maintains that because "Catholic" does not mean "Roman," local churches "have a right to be different" and therefore must gain a true sense of autonomy in directing their own affairs.[13]

While I recognize that the primary focus of this study is the African Catholic Church's role in sub-Saharan economic development, ecclesial autonomy is an issue that cannot be ignored. The question here is how do Éla and Magesa propose that the local African churches balance their longing for autonomy with their desire to remain in communion with the Church of Rome? This question becomes all the more difficult to answer when confronted with the variety of issues that the African Church must face. What about clerical celibacy, ancestor veneration, and the overall inculturation of the Christian faith? Specifically concerning the Church and economic development, what about clerical dependency on foreign donations and both the formation and focus of African priests as described in Chapter Two? Further complicating the issue is Éla's understanding of Church Tradition. When asked why he relies almost exclusively on the Bible and not on Tradition to advance his theological arguments, he answers that Church

Tradition was formed through a reading of the Bible that was void of any African consciousness and one that for many Africans was neither definitive nor unique. Therefore, what is normative for the Church as a whole is the Bible, not Tradition.[14]

In Éla's defense, when speaking about Church Tradition, he is speaking of how divine revelation is mediated to humanity and not specifically about the relationship between the local and universal Church. Nevertheless, both his and Magesa's comments concerning ecclesial autonomy raise some serious questions. How specifically do they propose that a balance be maintained between autonomy and communion? Which subjects should be open to "experimentation" and which should remain "off-limits?" If at some point in the future the African churches do gain some measure of autonomy, how do they avoid moving further and further away from the Church of Rome? Then, specifically for Éla, does Church Tradition have nothing to say to the African reality? What about Catholic social teaching and in particular those teachings concerning economic development? Should this aspect of the Church's Tradition be abandoned in Africa even though, as previously demonstrated, Éla implicitly holds that many of its basic tenets are particularly relevant for the African situation? Again, I pose these questions not because I believe these theologians are necessarily wrong or because I think the African Church should silently conform to every "norm" that emanates from the Vatican. Instead, I believe that on this foundational point both Éla and Magesa need to temper the rhetoric of their calls for autonomy with a more nuanced description of what they believe authentic communion actually entails.

One final critique for Mveng, Éla, and Magesa concerns their overall understanding of ecclesiology. In short, how do their three expressions of African liberation theology understand what it means to be Church – and in particular an African Catholic Church? Other than Éla's brief claim that the Church functions as Christ's sacrament of liberation in the temporal world and Magesa's equally brief claim that it functions as the "agent and articulator" of Christ's liberation, we really have very little idea. Borrowing from the models proposed by Avery Dulles, SJ, how do these theologians view, for example, the Church as institution, as a mystical community of believers, as herald of God's message, as servant, as community of disciples, or as the sacrament of Christ in the world?[15] I grant that Éla and Magesa speak in some measure to Dulles' model of the Church being Christ's sacrament in the world, however I question how they would reconcile his other models with their own especially in light of their calls for ecclesial autonomy? Also, what do these three theologians believe it means for an individual to claim membership within the African Catholic Church? From their collected works, one gets the impression that working for temporal liberation is the primary function of one who claims to be a Catholic (or a Christian). Furthermore, what about those members of the faith community who are not poor, what is their role within the Church? By placing such an emphasis on liberating the marginalized of society, these three theologians not only run the risk of transforming the *preferential* option for the poor into an *exclusive* option for the poor, but they also fail to offer any comprehensive understanding of what it means for a diverse community of believers to live and worship *as Church.* Overall, the question that Mveng, Éla, and Magesa need to more comprehensively address is, "What is liberation ecclesiology?"

2. Critique of the African Catholic Bishops

As with the three liberation theologians, I also have a number of critical points to make concerning the contributions of the African Catholic bishops. Charles Valy Tuho, Ivory Coast's Ambassador to both the BENELUX countries (Belgium, the Netherlands, and Luxembourg) and the European Union, claims that although the Symposium of Episcopal Conferences of Africa and Madagascar (SECAM) is correct in stating that Africa's economic difficulties have resulted from decreases in prices for African goods, a continual deterioration in terms-of-trade, and the effects of foreign debt, its economic statements reveal a certain "ambiguity" in terms of both economic doctrine and "instruments of analysis." In terms of doctrine, he claims that the economic theory to which the bishops refer is not explicit. Sometimes they refer to a classical or neo-classical school of economic thought while at other times they refer to a Keynesian or neo-Keynesian school. In terms of analysis, more embarrassing ambiguities concern the fact that the bishops often speak of "capitalism" but not "capital," they do not distinguish "labor" from "laborers," and they also fail to recognize the interrelationships among money, salaries, and prices as well as among profit, production, and employment.[16] In short, Valy Tuho believes the African bishops need to better educate themselves in economic "complexities" in order to establish a solid foundation on which to construct their social message.

Valy Tuho's criticism is important to note because it demonstrates the difficulties that arise when the African bishops (both individually and collectively) speak to issues outside their areas of expertise. Based on my own research, I am quite certain that there are few African bishops (either native or foreign born) who have had any formal economic training and therefore when they speak to economics-related issues they are not "experts in the field." Now, despite this lack of formal training I am not suggesting that the bishops refrain from speaking out on economic issues. As I stated in both the conclusion to Chapter Four and in the first section of this chapter, the African bishops are justified in critiquing secular economic policy on moral grounds primarily because of the devastating effects these policies have had on their people. Nevertheless, the bishops' critiques must be tempered by the recognition that when they engage specific economic policies they are in fact speaking "outside the boundaries" of their own "expertise." Obviously this critique can be extended to Mveng, Éla, and Magesa as well. Although Éla's training as a sociologist may afford his works some added weight, the contributions of these three theologians would also benefit from a more comprehensively stated examination of the economic reality to which they speak.

A second criticism of the African bishops concerns the function of SECAM as an ecclesial body. Returning to Chapter Four and the question of whether there should have been a synod or council for the African Church, Engelbert Mveng, SJ, states that supporters of a council cited Canon 439.1 of the *Code of Canon Law* and claimed that a council could be convened by the SECAM President with the approval of Rome. However, Mveng points out that while Canon 439.1 states that a particular council must be convened by an episcopal conference, because SECAM is in reality a symposium with no power or true legal/canonical existence (he in fact describes it as a "friendly meeting over drinks") it does not fulfill the requirements of actually being an episcopal conference. In other words, regardless of the perceived need for an African council, under Canon Law SECAM simply did not possess the authority to convene it. Mveng continues by claiming that SECAM's "legal void" is no accident, but exists as the result of a lack of consensus that has continually plagued the symposium since its inception. Although it has existed since 1969, SECAM members have never reached a consensus as to the organization's true function or role within African society, and their efforts often have been undermined by differences of both language and theological orientation.[17]

Mveng's critique is underscored by what I perceive to be a sharp decline in both the quantity and quality of SECAM statements in the 1990s. While it is understandable that in the late 1980s and early 1990s the SECAM bishops would have been preoccupied with preparations for the 1994 African Synod and thus not issue any major new statements, in the years following the synod its statements have been very brief and have done little to advance the teachings from "Justice and Evangelization in Africa" (1981) and "The Church and Human Promotion in Africa Today" (1984).[18] What are the reasons for these declines in SECAM statements? Perhaps the member bishops are just too busy with other projects in their own dioceses or regions. Perhaps they fear offending either Rome or their financial benefactors. Perhaps they fear angering government officials and thus jeopardizing their own safety.[19] Whatever the reasons for their collective silence, I believe the SECAM bishops must find a way to regain the voice they had in the early 1980s and once again lend this voice to those who are unable to speak for themselves.

In terms of more theological criticisms, I have a question for the African bishops concerning the emphasis they place on the link between evangelization and efforts toward human promotion (or development). While not intending to undermine the link between the two, I question what the bishops intend as the ultimate end of their development work within the context of the Church's overall evangelizing mission. In other words, what do the bishops expect to gain in terms of evangelization when they promote development-related activities in the temporal world? If evangelization and development are as closely related as the bishops maintain they are, then one could argue that there should be at least some proselytizing dimension to the Church's development work. Supposing then that this proselytizing dimension does exist, exactly how do those offering aid in the name of the Church both inform recipients of the rationale for this aid and then invite them, albeit gently, to more deeply explore the teachings of the Catholic Church? However, supposing this proselytizing dimension does not exist, what then becomes of the "intimate link" between evangelization and efforts at human promotion? These questions are very relevant for the sub-Saharan Church especially in light of the growing Islamic influence from the north as well as the ever-increasing numbers of evangelical Christian denominations and independent churches in the south. Should the Catholic Church make a greater commitment to preaching the Gospel message within its development programs in order to maintain its presence on the African sub-continent? Is it even appropriate to do so? I do not know the answers to these questions nor do I hold that the Church should commit itself to making a greater proselytizing effort, however the sub-Saharan bishops need to explain more clearly how they view both the intended end of this link and the ramifications it entails within their own specific communities.

I also find it problematic that the African bishops as a whole (SECAM as well as the national and regional conferences) ground their many statements on economic development almost exclusively within Catholic social teaching. Now there is obviously nothing wrong with the bishops basing their own teachings on those of the universal Church (in fact, I have already argued that this is one of their strengths), however I wonder if their contributions would not become more relevant for the African faithful if the bishops wereto open themselves to gaining insights from other theological sources. For example, Mveng, Éla, and Magesa each to varying degrees reflect the basic principles of Catholic social teaching in their work, yet the common starting point for each of them is the theological "truths" learned from within the contexts of those whom they served. The question for the bishops then becomes what theological truths can they learn from the poor and oppressed whom they are entrusted to serve? This question is posed particularly in light of how Catholic theology has been imposed upon the African people. As demonstrated in Chapter Two, one the biggest challenges facing the African Church today is what Magesa terms "dual religious consciousness," or the tension felt by many Africans who strive to practice Christianity without completely abandoning their traditional religious customs.[20] Because this "dual religious consciousness" (or syncretism) is a fact for many African Catholics, the bishops should make a greater effort both to understand and apply the theological insights of traditional African society and/or religion, particularly those insights that are compatible with the principles of Catholic social teaching.[21] Perhaps a better way to state this is that because Christian theology was formulated primarily within the Western philosophical context, the bishops need to be in active dialogue with traditional African beliefs in order to make the Church's teachings more comprehensible and thus more relevant for the African people.[22]

Another area of concern for the African bishops is their statements on justice and peace from both the preparatory and final documents of the 1994 Synod for Africa. Nigerian Justin Ukpong, CSSp., charges that while the "Lineamenta" upholds justice and peace as constitutive elements of evangelization and thus part of the Church's overall mission in Africa, it does not adequately demonstrate how Jesus' own methods of evangelizing constitute the paradigm for the African Church today.[23] Rogrigo Mejia also criticizes the "Lineamenta" because it barely acknowledges the plight of political refugees even though at the time of the synod's preparation there were approximately five million of them on the African continent. For Mejia, it is particularly unfortunate that the refugee issue was not better articulated in the "Lineamenta" because it would have greatly enriched the chapter on justice and peace which was, in his opinion, "the shortest and poorest section of the questionnaire."[24] In an open letter to Pope John Paul II, Renato Sesana criticizes the synod's "Instrumentum Laboris" by claiming that it ignores (among other issues) civil wars, AIDS, the malnutrition of children, movements for democracy, and the African woman. Also, because the local churches' responses to the "Lineamenta" questions had to be funneled through both the local bishop and the episcopal conference to which that bishop was a member, by the time they reached the Synod General Secretariat they had lost much of their original "richness." As a result, he claims that a "seeing/judging/acting" methodology did not "enjoy the preference" of those preparing the "Instrumentum Laboris" and that the upcoming synod (his letter was published in 1993) would in all likelihood become an exercise in familiarizing the African bishops with Church documents rather than an opportunity for a true discernment of the realities faced by the local communities.[25]

While I agree with these three criticisms, my main question for the synod bishops is did they actually advance any of the teachings on development from previous SECAM or other episcopal conference statements? The preparatory and final documents did an admirable job of both restating the economic challenges facing Africa and reaffirming earlier episcopal conference teachings, but apart from the letter "Forgive Us Our Debts" I do not believe the synod bishops actually stated anything that was substantially new. This lack of advancement causes me to wonder whether the issue of economic development received adequate attention during the synod's four-plus year preparatory process. Were no new insights gained through this process? Did any of the bishops come to the synod specifically prepared to discuss development issues from a theological perspective? In the bishops' defense, they probably did not have enough time to adequately discuss development-related questions given the sheer volume of topics on the synod agenda, the time restrictions for both interventions and deliberation, and the relatively short duration (four weeks) of the synod itself.[26] Nevertheless, on an issue that concerns so many in Africa (both Catholics and non-Catholics alike), it would seem that the synod bishops should have drafted a statement that, building upon previous SECAM and episcopal conference teachings, more clearly addressed the economic needs of so many of the world's poor.

My two final criticisms are more general and are addressed to both the bishops and theologians as a whole. First, in reading the various episcopal conference statements and contributions of the three liberation theologians, I get the impression that many of them believe Western capitalism is the primary economic "evil" facing Africa. This belief is especially prevalent in the Cameroonian bishops' "Les causes de la crise économique"[27] and in both Jean-Marc Éla's *My Faith as an African* and *African Cry*[28] because in each of these works the authors specifically claim that Western capitalism is characterized by greed, exploitation, and an unrestrained quest for profit. My question is what exactly do these people consider immoral about the capitalist economic system? Is it the system itself that is immoral or is it the individual and collective decisions/actions of human beings within the system that are immoral? I have difficulty with the claim that capitalism itself is inherently immoral for the simple reason that any economic system (socialism included) is in fact a human creation. In other words, I do not necessarily believe that the ethical difficulties associated with capitalism (including those concerning debt reduction and structural adjustment programs) exist because of the system itself; ethical difficulties exist as a result of the decisions and actions of human beings. Thus, my question for the African bishops and theologians is really one of clarification. Where exactly do they see the root of economic immorality? Do they believe it lies with individuals working within the capitalist system or does it lie within the system itself?

Second, I question whether the African Church's past colonial legacy and its present-day financial dependency actually work to undermine its calls for authentic economic development. In Chapter Two, I demonstrated how Christian missionaries often worked hand-in-hand with secular colonial powers to instill a sense of inferiority within the native African people and also how the sub-Saharan Church today is almost completely dependent upon foreign financial assistance for its very survival. Briefly, how can a Church that in so many ways helped to establish economic *de*pendence now be expected to help bring about economic *in*dependence? Then, in a reflection of the overall economic problem facing the sub-continent as a whole, how can the African Church effectively demand justice, preach self-sufficiency, and criticize both domestic and international policies when its own economic dependence actually renders it subservient to its own foreign benefactors?

In concluding this section, I repeat that I raise these criticisms not to negate or otherwise undermine the overall message of the African bishops and theologians, I am simply asking questions that need to be more fully addressed. In the final section of this study, I look to the future by offering suggestions for further study and for the practical role the Roman Catholic Church can play in the ongoing development of the African sub-continent.

Toward the Future: Suggestions for Further Study and the Role of the Church Today

Throughout this study my purpose has been to demonstrate the contributions that specific members of the African Catholic Church have made to the articulation of a sub-Saharan theology of economic development. While I believe these contributions constitute an invaluable resource for any proposed development theology, I also recognize that they are not the "final word" but that there are numerous other religious traditions on the African sub-continent whose theological contributions must also be taken into consideration. In this final section, I first briefly identify three "other" theological sources whose teachings both complement and expand upon those already examined. I then conclude by commenting on the significance of the study's title and offering my own reflections as to the Church's future role in the economic development of sub-Saharan Africa.

1. "Other" Christian Sources for a Theology of Economic Development

The first "non-Catholic" source that needs to be taken into consideration is the work of theologians who write from other Christian traditions. As first noted in Chapter Two, there are many mainstream and independent Christian churches at work on the African sub-continent and theologians from many of these traditions have offered their own insights to the question of economic development. For instance, in his essay "Ethics of the Economic Principles: Church and Secular Investments," South African Methodist Itumeleng Mosala claims that in response to the greed and overall injustice that pervades programs of economic development, the people of South Africa (and by extension one might claim Africa as a whole) must return to more traditional understandings of community and economic production. According to Mosala, traditional African society understood ownership to be communal in that all people maintained access to the basic necessities of life. Because of this understanding, economic production was viewed as a function of use in that the only goods produced were those that would be used directly by a specific household or community. Because it was based on meeting actual human needs and its ultimate end was the well-being of the community as a whole,

Mosala argues that this "needs-only" approach to production was in itself inherently moral. Contrast this with the greed, inequality, and corruption characteristic of Western development programs and one begins to realize that this traditional notion of production has something to contribute to present-day development policy. Mosala concludes by claiming that because any notion of economic morality implies that a nation's resources (both natural and human) be used for productive purposes, that every family have equal access to necessary basic goods, and that being able to live without fear is a fundamental criteria of any just economy, South Africa must revisit the traditional "needs-only" approach to economic production in an effort to counter the devastating effects of Western-imposed development programs.[29]

Writing from the feminist perspective in her *Daughters of Anowa: African Women and Patriarchy*, Methodist theologian Mercy Amba Oduyoye argues that women have played, and continue to play, important economic roles in both traditional and modern-day African society. African women contribute to the economic well-being of their communities through both farming and trading, and in fact the survival of many African children today is dependent upon women because in many cases it is they (the women) who function as the breadwinners in society. However, even in light of their important economic roles, Oduyoye claims that for many reasons African women have not been able to gain any real political power. Specifically concerning economics, one reason for this lack of political power can be traced directly to the colonial Christian missionaries whose goal was to create "kept women" (or housewives) and thus remove them from participating in the marketplace. Stated differently, the indigenous women who were "Westernized" by missionaries were allowed to learn a hobby or "make themselves useful as helpmates," but following the model of the pastor's wife they were barred from participating in the economic life of their communities. A second reason for this lack of political power concerns the present-day modernization in many sectors of the traditional African marketplace. Modernization has increasingly marginalized women's roles in the economy because large-scale agricultural programs have seized lands traditionally farmed by women and there has also been a sharp increase in the numbers of mass production companies and supermarkets whose goods "compete" against those traditionally produced by women. Further factors concerning modernization include that when Gross National Product (GNP) of an African economy is calculated, women exist as consumers and not producers; when educational policies are being debated, women are oftentimes considered "unskilled" or "unlettered;" and when policies aimed at closing the gap between rich and poor are being implemented, African women are never consulted and thus find themselves participating in programs that actually lead to their further exploitation. Oduyoye is careful to note that although both the missionaries and modernization have undermined the status of women in the economic realm, one cannot lay all of the blame upon them. One must also look closely at patriarchy or the "prevailing ideology of sexism" in African society which has done more to deny women their God-given rights than any other factor. However, in the economic realm she argues that the Western idea of the "maintained" woman, one that does not reward familial or domestic work with a paycheck, one whose logic justifies unequal pay for equal work, and one that reserves certain jobs for men, is one of the primary reasons for the feminization of poverty in Africa.[30]

As a final point concerning the contributions of non-Catholic Christian sources, in my own presentation "SODEPAX: An Ecumenical Model for Contemporary Social Ethics" I argued that questions of economic injustice offer the different Christian denominations both a means and an opportunity for ecumenical collaboration.[31] In brief, I maintained that although there are theological differences between the Roman Catholic Church and the World Council of Churches on variety of different issues, the question of economic development provides the two organizations with a "common opponent" against which they can express theological critiques and, more importantly, work together for the common good of humanity. Similarly, I believe the injustices characteristic of structural adjustment, debt-repayment, and other present-day development programs provide this same "opponent" for the many Christian denominations on the African sub-continent. These traditions may disagree on a number of different theological issues, however concerning the question of economic development many of them are saying almost exactly the same thing. Because of these similarities, perhaps the various Christian traditions should look toward the development question as a potential means for joint ecumenical reflection and practical cooperation in order to help alleviate the suffering of so many in sub-Saharan Africa.

2. African Traditional Worldview

A second "other" source of theological reflection that can contribute to the articulation of a sub-Saharan theology of economic development is traditional African religion. Numerous African theologians (including Itumeleng Mosala above) have demonstrated commonalities between the ethical principles of traditional African religion and those of Christian social teaching concerning economic affairs. From the Catholic perspective, Rev. Dr. Juvenalis Baitu, professor of moral theology at the Catholic University of East Africa (Nairobi, Kenya), claims that one of the "basic foundations" of African ethics is the principle of "communality," or the traditional belief that individual acts are a means to strengthen the "integral life" of each member of a community. For Baitu, the principle of "communality" is very similar to the Christian principle of solidarity because with communality clan members recognize their societal obligation to contribute to the common good and to the self-actualization of all community members. He also states that because clan leaders are mandated to assure that the community's political and socio-economic systems facilitate the self-actualization of all, traditional African society also reflects the Christian principle of subsidiarity.[32]

Baitu further claims that the traditional African understanding of property ownership also reflects similar Christian teachings concerning the universal destination of goods. Within many expressions of Christian social teaching (including Catholic social teaching), individuals maintain a right to own private property, however this right is limited in the sense that one is morally bound to share one's property with others in times of dire need.[33] In traditional African society, the understanding of property ownership was very similar. Individuals did not "own" earthly goods in the sense that they could use them in any way they chose, instead people were viewed as "administrators" of goods and thus were bound to use them for the good of the community as a whole. According to Baitu, the rationale for this understanding of ownership was that any earthly good had "consequences" for the life of the entire community, a reality evidenced by the fact that in many cases the individual could not dispose of property without the expressed permission of either family or clan.[34]

Other African Catholic theologians also speak to this traditional understanding of how property should be used. Zaïrean Bénézet Bujo claims that because the primary focus of traditional African religion is life, any ethical principle derived from it must uphold both the preservation of human life and the good of the human person. Specifically in terms of ownership, he states that the right to private property was recognized within traditional African society because through gaining property a man demonstrated his independence, security, and fitness for marriage. However, similar to Baitu, he also claims that the communal dimension of ownership was always stressed because in cases of emergency one's property was always made available for use by the community as a whole.[35] Laurenti Magesa also maintains that the right to private ownership was understood by traditional African religion as a "joint or public right of access" to the basic goods necessary for human life, a balance between public and private ownership that existed in order to assure a measure of economic equality within the community. Magesa then adds that because in traditional African society one could never separate economics from the other "spheres of life," the underlying principle of economic organization in traditional African society was always community. In other words, the key economic concepts (particularly those concerning production and distribution) of the traditional African community actually expressed kinship obligations, tribal affiliation, and both religious and moral duty.[36]

3. Islam

In addition to including the theological insights from non-Catholic Christian denominations and from traditional African religion, any proposed theology of sub-Saharan economic development must also take into consideration the contributions of Islam.[37] Islam is the predominant religion in northern Africa and, similar to many independent Christian churches, it is actively recruiting new members and gaining increasing influence south of the Sahara as well. Speaking from the Islamic perspective, Maulana Muhammad Ali[38] argues that lasting world peace will not be realized until the economic question is "settled," and in fact that the social order established by Islam is the means by which this peace can be achieved. According to Ali, Islam teaches that although individuals must work in order to gain necessary material goods, they must also recognize the "higher value" to which any economic interest is always subject, namely God or Allah. In other words, Islam maintains that people may be justified in pursuing temporal wealth, however this pursuit of wealth must always remain secondary to their duties toward God. Ali also claims that because Islam teaches that the social order is an expression of divine will, Muslims should always strive for the economic equality of all people. Now this movement toward equality should not happen by forcibly taking possessions from the wealthy and giving them to the poor. Instead, equality will occur when the social order is constructed so that the poor are offered the opportunity to "raise" themselves to the level of the rich, when they are provided with the means and conditions by which they can better their lot in life.[39] Through these two teachings one recognizes a similarity between Islam and Christianity, a similarity that must be reflected in any proposed theology of development. Both traditions recognize that 1) even when speaking of economics the individual's primary duty is to serve God, and 2) that society as a whole has an obligation to provide the conditions through which individuals may grow and prosper using the talents and abilities granted to them by their Creator.

Islam also contributes to the articulation of a sub-Saharan theology of development through the practice of Zakat, the religion's compulsory system of charity. Zakat is in effect a two-and-a half-percent tithe on the Islamic person's savings (the money is given to the state to be used to help those in material need) and it is viewed by the people as both a form of charity and a tax. According to Ali, the rationale for Zakat is that it functions as a means of purification. Because "love of wealth" can potentially turn an individual's heart away from God, Islam maintains there is a degree of "uncleanness" associated with accumulating material possessions. Zakat is therefore understood as a means to "wash away" the uncleanness of money and also to remind individuals of their primary duties toward God. Ali further claims that Zakat not only facilitates a redistribution of wealth within society, but it also functions as a means to "uplift" the entire Islamic nation because it cultivates the "higher sentiments" of love and sympathy for one's neighbor.[40] Once again, through Zakat one recognizes similarities between Islamic and Christian teaching. Although there is no physical compulsion forcing one to donate money to the poor, Islam echoes Christianity[41] by maintaining that individuals have a moral mandate to share their excess wealth with those in need, a mandate that in some form must be included in any proposed theology of economic development.

From these brief examples it is clear that there are certain commonalities between the African Catholic Church's teachings on economic issues and those of other religious traditions. While it is beyond the scope of this study to examine these commonalities in further detail, I do believe that any comprehensive theology of sub-Saharan development would have to take them into careful consideration. The Roman Catholic Church is certainly not the "be all and end all" of theological reflection concerning African economic development, these other sources provide insights that Catholic theologians must take to heart in order to formulate a theology that speaks to the entirety of the African reality.

Concluding Remarks: The Future Role of the African Catholic Church

In concluding this study I return to where I began, to the title "Voices Yet Unheard in a Listening World." I stated in my introduction that if the African Catholic bishops and theologians are to succeed in contributing to the articulation of sub-Saharan theology of economic development, they have two separate but closely related mandates. First, they must listen to Catholic social teaching, to the voices of the African people, and to each other in order to determine how the Church as a whole can empower the faithful to assume responsibility for their own economic well-being. Second, they must also speak out to the international community concerning which development policies and programs are, in their judgment, in the best economic interests of the African people. They must speak to those who view sub-Saharan Africa in terms of dependency and inferiority, and also to those who wait impatiently for the emergence of a truly

African voice. My study has focused primarily on the first mandate, however the true challenge facing the African Church of the future lies with the second. No one can doubt that Africa does not receive the attention it should. Debt-reduction and structural adjustment programs are imposed by Western financial powers to serve Western economic interests, Africans are depicted by the world media as being destitute and otherwise incapable of providing for their own needs, and the only familiarity that many Americans have about Africa is that in 1998 two United States embassies (in Nairobi, Kenya, and Dar es Salaam, Tanzania) were bombed by radical Islamic fundamentalists. In response to this ever-growing sense of "non-existence,"[42] the African bishops and theologians need to find a way to forcefully say to the international community, "We matter," "We are important," and, specifically concerning economic development, "We must be given the opportunity to participate freely and fully in the global economy in order to work toward self-sufficiency."

It is precisely within this second mandate that I view the importance of this study's title: "Voices Yet Unheard in a Listening World." The various books, articles, pastoral letters, and other statements cited in this study constitute the "Voices Yet Unheard." For over thirty years, the African bishops and theologians have critiqued colonial economic policies as well as the lasting effects these policies have had even to this very day. They have criticized African governments for their clientelism, corruption, and outright disregard of those they are entrusted to serve. They have criticized Western development and economic reform programs because these programs are either irrelevant for the African situation or their effects actually harm those they are intended to help. Finally, the bishops and theologians have also suggested specific principles, principles articulated within Catholic social teaching, that they maintain must be included within any just African economic system.

Unfortunately, although the African Catholic bishops and theologians have written much concerning economic development, their contributions remain largely unknown in the Western world, particularly in the United States. They are the "Voices Yet Unheard." In light of this situation, the questions to ask are: "If the African Church is speaking out on these issues why is no one listening?" "Why does hardly anyone in America seem to care about the plight of the African people?" "What can the African Church do about this sense of apathy?" I suggest that any possible response to these questions has to begin with education. In the classroom, when as a teacher I discuss the ethical implications of the colonial legacy, the actions of corrupt government officials, the forced repayment of foreign debts, and the devastating effects of structural adjustment, my students' almost unanimous reaction is, "Why don't these people just rise up and overthrow their governments?" I admit this reaction is somewhat naïve. However it does demonstrate that once North American students have actually learned what is happening in Africa they exhibit both a degree of concern for the plight of the people and also a willingness to hear from those who speak for the suffering. In this sense, my students have become the "Listening World." My point is that if Americans were to become more broadly educated about the economic (and other) realities facing the sub-Saharan people, I believe they would not only recognize the need for serious economic and political reform, but would also recognize the profound ethical questions underlying the entire development issue. Thus, concerning economic development, the future challenge facing the African bishops and theologians is two-fold. They must first educate the world community about the realities of everyday life in Africa, and then they must challenge all people (both Africans and non-Africans) to pressure their own governments and financial institutions to help bring about real economic change.

Now the question becomes, "how is this to be done?" How exactly should the African Church work to educate the American faithful, not to mention American society as a whole? Perhaps what is needed in effect is a reverse-mission. High-ranking African Church leaders (cardinals and archbishops) need to come to the United States not to beg for money or boast about the number of Africans being baptized in a given year, but come to American parishes, seminaries, and universities to teach people in unambiguous terms the reasons *why* poverty and injustice exist in Africa, including those reasons directly attributable to U.S. foreign policy. Similarly, African theologians must make a greater effort to speak in the United States or otherwise make their message known both in American theological circles and in American public life. In short, it is not sufficient for either the theologians' or the bishops' contributions to remain "hidden" in relatively obscure theological, liturgical, or other church publications. In order to have any effect here in the United States and in their own countries, they must bring their message to the public in the most widely accessible way possible. Once again, when people are educated about the effects of the economic policies (both domestic and foreign) imposed upon the African people, when they are educated about the realities of racism, and nationalism so prevalent both on the African continent and in international relations, and when they are educated about the need for conversion and solidarity with their brothers and sisters from around the world, I suspect that on some level there would be calls for change.

A second practical example of how the African Catholic Church can better speak to the international community is through closer cooperation with other religious traditions and with the secular social sciences. As demonstrated earlier in this chapter, there are many other religious traditions (both Christian and non-Christian) on the African sub-continent and representatives from some of these traditions speak directly to the issue of economic development. Perhaps the African Catholic Church should make a more concerted effort to work with these other communities not only in helping to provide for temporal material needs, but also in formulating theological and practical responses to the foundational development questions facing the African people.[43] Similar cooperation could also be extended to the secular social sciences. In Chapter One, I presented an overview of the sub-Saharan economic situation by drawing upon the contributions from numerous secular economists and political scientists. Although I emphasized earlier in this chapter that as a whole the African bishops and theologians are not experts in the social sciences, their theological writings can dialogue with them because, as stated by the well-known Kenyan theologian John Mbiti (Anglican), "religion is part and parcel of the African heritage" and it has also strongly influenced the shaping of African culture, political organization, and economic activity.[44] In other words, because within African culture one can never completely separate the sacred from the secular, the Church must be ready and willing to work with anyone "of good will" in order to promote the common economic good of all African people. Recalling the conclusion from Chapter Two, if the African Catholic Church wishes to remain relevant in the lives of its people and to participate in the future development of the African sub-continent, then it must commit itself to active dialogue with other religious traditions and with the secular social sciences in order to formulate authentic and credible responses to each and every form of economic injustice.

Finally, the African Catholic Church can help to bring about economic development by continually pressuring African governments to respect the freedom, dignity, and God given rights of all people. It is widely acknowledged that true economic development cannot happen without sweeping reform in the political structures of most African nations. The Church must take an active role in this process by continually pressuring African governments to allow this reform to take place. In making this claim, however, I recognize that in many ways the local African churches are in a precarious position because if they speak too loudly in favor of political reform they risk reprisals at the hands of government officials. In fact, when I first began this study I had planned to be much more critical of African church officials (especially the bishops) because I did not see the Church doing much to overcome the injustices (economic or otherwise) perpetrated by African political leaders. However, after spending time in Kenya, I realized that this was not a valid criticism. In the face of corrupt, militarized regimes controlled by a small number of individuals who view the state as a means to personal wealth, what can the Church really do? How outspoken can I realistically expect Church leaders to be when any criticism of the state is seen as a threat to national security and in fact is punishable by death? Nevertheless, even though the danger of reprisal exists, the Church has a mandate to demand justice, equality, and democratic participation for all people. Exactly how this mandate can be accomplished is a complicated and open-ended question, one that is open to different interpretations and one for which I do not have comprehensive answers. However, no matter what the situation, the local church in every African nation, region, and village has a duty to uphold unwaveringly the freedom, dignity, and rights of each human person.

In closing, I have stated a number of times in this study that my purpose has not been to propose a *comprehensive* theology of sub-

Saharan economic development but instead to demonstrate the particular contribution that the African Catholic Church has made to the articulation of any *proposed* development theology. While the issues may be complex and the struggle may seem insurmountable, through their efforts the African bishops and theologians are in reality responding to Jesus' message in Matthew 25:31-46, the story of the Last Judgment. In this story, Christ teaches that the ones who will be saved on the last day are those who feed their brothers and sisters when they are hungry, give them drink when they are thirsty, clothe them when they are naked, welcome them when they are strangers, care for them when they are ill, and visit them when they are in prison. Through their many books, essays, and pastoral statements, the bishops and theologians are not only themselves acting upon Christ's words but they are also challenging each of us to do the same. Working for the temporal development of the African people is not only a mandate of Catholic social teaching, it is also a concrete response to Christ's own teaching that our eternal salvation is dependent, in part, on how we aid our brothers and sisters in need.

Notes

[1] See Chapter One at notes 77 and 78.

[2] Recall from Chapter One (note 75) that in addition to his work as an economist, Elliott also served as the Assistant Secretary to SODEPAX, the joint Roman Catholic/World Council of Churches Commission on Society, Development, and Peace.

[3] Charles Elliott, *The Development Debate* (New York: Friendship Press, 1971), 73-74.

[4] Quotation taken from Philip Land, SJ, and Paul Abrecht's "Common Christian Convictions about Development," in *World Development: Challenge to the Churches*, ed. Denys Munby (Washington DC: Corpus Books, 1968), 137-146 at 140.

[5] Pope John Paul II defines social sin in his 1987 *Sollicitudo Rei Socialis.* He argues that the structures of sin "are rooted in personal sin, and thus always linked to the *concrete acts* of individuals who introduce these structures, consolidate them and make them difficult to remove." As such, these structures "grow stronger, spread, and become the source of other sins, and so influence people's behavior." See John Paul II's "Sollicitudo Rei Socialis: On Social Concern" in *Catholic Social Teaching: The Documentary Heritage*, eds. David J. O'Brien & Thomas A. Shannon (Maryknoll, NY: Orbis Books, 1995), no. 36b.

[6] I must note that the principles of Catholic social teaching (human dignity, community, solidarity, subsidiarity, participation, common good, and preferential option for the poor) are not unique to the Catholic Church. Through various expressions, these principles are recognized by other Christian and non-Christian traditions.

[7] See Michael Novak's *Will It Liberate? Questions about Liberation Theology* (New York: Paulist Press, 1986), 34-35.

[8] In making this statement I recognize that the three African theologians are in fact theologians and not ethicists. As such, my criticism is tempered by

this fact. I also recognize that because Mveng is no longer alive he would not be able to respond to Novak's question.

[9] See Chikane's "EATWOT and Third World Theologies: An Evaluation of the Past and Present," in *Third World Theologies: Commonalities and Divergences,* ed. K.C. Abraham (Maryknoll, NY: Orbis Books, 1990), 147-160 at 150. Engelbert Mveng, SJ, made similar claims concerning Latin American liberation theology in *Théologie, libération et cultures africaines.* See Chapter Three, note 22.

[10] Joseph McKenna, SJ, claims that despite the fact that African liberation theology is grounded in the lives of the African people, its proponents respect the contributions of other liberation theologians and never claim that the African understanding of liberation should be "exported" to other parts of the world. In other words, no African theology of liberation sees itself as a "model theology" for the rest of the Third World as many believe Latin American liberation theology purports itself to be. See McKenna's *Finding a Social Voice: The Church and Marxism in Africa* (New York: Fordham University Press, 1997), 68.

[11] Magesa, *The Church and Liberation in Africa: Spearhead #44* (Eldoret, Kenya: AMECEA Gaba Publications, 1976), 28-35.

[12] Magesa, "The Church in Eastern Africa: Retrospect and Prospect," in *How Local is the Local Church? Small Christian Communities and Church in Eastern Africa,* ed. Agatha Radoli, SOM (Eldoret, Kenya: AMECEA Gaba Publications, 1993), 3-35 at 24-25.

[13] See Éla's *African Cry* (Maryknoll, NY: Orbis Books, 1986), 105-120 and *My Faith as an African* (Maryknoll, NY: Orbis Books, 1988), 55-64 and 137-143. I should note, however, that Éla never advocates the local African churches breaking away from Rome as did the African independent churches. In fact, he specifically states they should not. In *African Cry,* he affirms his desire to maintain communion with Rome by stating "local church cannot be divorced from the center charged with the ministry of unity" (109) and "a church retains its being only in virtue of its communion with other churches" (112). Nevertheless, he does holds that in order to meet the pastoral needs of those to whom it purports to minister, the African Catholic Church must be free to form itself within the context of its own cultural reality.

[14] See Éla's interview with Philip Gibbs in Gibbs' *The Word in the Third World: Divine Revelation in the Theology of Jean-Marc Éla, Aloysius Pieris, and Gustavo Gutiérrez* (Rome: Pontifical Gregorian University, 1996), 353. Éla further claims that any biblical interpretation that helped to form Tradition was done in light of specific historical events within the Western Church, a Church that until a century ago was hardly aware that Africa even existed and in more recent years continues to pretend that it does not.

[15] See Avery Dulles' *Models of Church*, 2nd rev. ed. (New York: Doubleday, 1987).

[16] Charles Valy Tuho, "L'Afrique" in *Ethique, économie et développement: L'enseignement des évêques des cinq continents* (1891-1991), ed Roger Berthouzoz and Roberto Papini (Fribourg, Switzerland: Editions Universitaires, 1995), 101-125 at 120-122.

[17] Mveng, "The Historical Background of the African Synod," in *The African Synod: Documents, Reflections, Perspectives*, ed. Africa Faith and Justice Network (Maryknoll, NY: Orbis Books, 1996), 20-31 at 27-28. Paul Gifford adds that in comparison to its Latin American counterpart CELAM (the association of episcopal conferences of Latin America), the African symposium maintains a very low profile, does not attempt to do much, and is remarkably ineffective. One of the reasons for this is that SECAM has seen what happens when a continental episcopal assembly does speak out. Because of its controversial statements, CELAM (which does have legal/canonical status) has been in conflict with Rome and the SECAM bishops fear the same thing happening with them. See Paul Gifford's *African Christianity: Its Public Role* (London: Hurst & Co., 1998), 310.

[18] As examples, see SECAM's message from its eleventh plenary assembly "Church as Family of God and Hope for Africa," *African Ecclesial Review* 39 (1997), 278-285 and "Africa Will Rise," *Catholic International* 8 (1997), 355-359. In contrast, the development issue has continued to receive attention from episcopal conferences on both the national and regional levels. The AMECEA (Association of Member Episcopal Conferences in Eastern Africa) bishops dedicated their entire 1995 Plenary Assembly (Malawi) to the theme "The Role of the Church in Development in Light of the African Synod." In their "Resolutions on Development," they suggest the East African Church make development education part of seminary formation, focus on small Christian communities as the locus for development efforts, and seek

greater cooperation with other groups involved in similar work. See the AMECEA bishops' "The Twelfth AMECEA Plenary Resolutions on Development." *African Ecclesial Review* 37 (1995), 353-359. During their 1998 Plenary Assembly in Ghana, the AECAWA (Association of Episcopal Conferences of Anglophone West Africa) bishops called upon the world community to "address the inequalities" of economic globalization, allow for greater African participation in world markets, reevaluate structural adjustment, and insist that ethics and morality govern the international economic order. See the AECAWA's *A Self-Reliant Church* (Kumasi, Ghana: AECAWA, 1998), 48-49. Finally, in 1999, the government of Zambia invited the nation's Catholic Commission for Justice and Peace to submit its own contribution to the debate concerning the national budget. In the ensuing document, the commission recommended that a greater percentage of the national budget be used for education, small farmers be allowed greater access to international markets, and government address shortcomings in both the nation's health care system and efforts at reducing foreign debt. See the Zambian Catholic Commission for Justice and Peace's "1999 Budget Revisions, Priorities, and Parliamentary Responsibilities," *Catholic International* 10 (1999), 290-296.

[19] Recall that Engelbert Mveng, SJ, was murdered most likely as a result of his criticizing the government of Cameroon.

[20] See Chapter Two at notes 30-32.

[21] I demonstrate some of the similarities between traditional African and present-day Christian ethics in the next section of this chapter.

[22] One of the reasons the African bishops do not sufficiently take into consideration the theological insights arising from the people is that in many cases they have separated themselves from those they are mandated to serve. Again from Chapter Two, many of the African faithful view the clergy (including the bishops) as "not one of the them" because they (the clergy) live in modern homes, drive fancy cars, travel to far-away places, and enjoy benefits that are simply unattainable for the common person. So long as the bishops remain "apart" from the common person, the theological insights arising from the *sensus fidei* will remain largely absent from any episcopal statements.

[23] Justin S. Ukpong, "A Critical Review of the Lineamenta on the Special African Synod," in *The African Synod: Documents, Reflections, Perspectives,*

ed. Africa Faith and Justice Network (Maryknoll, NY: Orbis Books, 1996), 32-42 at 38-40. At the time this article was written, Ukpong was a professor and deputy rector of the Catholic Institute of West Africa (Port Harcourt, Nigeria). Interestingly, he concludes his critique of the synod's preparatory process by stating: "The Synod will not fulfill that promise (to create a new future for the Church in Africa) unless it is seen as an occasion for African Christians to give voice to their daily struggle to clarify for themselves what it means to be church; unless that voice is given a hearing; and unless there is critical awareness of this in the African church itself. It must be noted that Christianity will never take root in the hearts of Africans unless there is a struggle by African Christians themselves to understand the Christian faith and unless that struggle is encouraged" (41).

[24] Rodrigo Mejia, "Presence of the Lay Christians in the Preparation for the Synod of Bishops on Africa," *African Ecclesial Review* 33 (1991), 174. Mejia is a lecturer at Hekima College in Nairobi.

[25] Renato Kizito Sesana, MCCJ, "An African Synod Without Africa?" *African Ecclesial Review* 35 (1993), 136-139. Sesana is the editor of *New People Magazine* (New People Media Centre, Nairobi, Kenya). Sesana also criticizes the "Instrumentum Laboris" claiming the African churches had been hardly consulted in the synod's preparatory process. As evidence, he cites the fact that of the 171 quotations in the document itself, a majority come from the "general" encyclicals and exhortations of John Paul II (although not once is there a quotation from any of his African journeys), followed respectively by the documents and statements of the Second Vatican Council, Pope Paul VI (although almost exclusively from *Evangelii Nuntiandi*), various papal congregations and commissions, and finally SECAM itself with just five quotations. Because of this focus on universal statements, Sesana claims that although there are over five hundred bishops on the continent and numerous episcopal conferences, the "Instrumentum Laboris" gives the impression that there is no teaching authority within the local African churches.

[26] Some might argue that each of these built-in "restrictions" was the Vatican's way of preventing the African bishops from discussing issues that it (the Vatican) was not willing to discuss.

[27] See Chapter Four at notes 45-48.

[28] See Chapter Three at notes 42-43.

[29] Itumeleng Mosala, "Ethics of the Economic Principles: Church and Secular Investments," in *Hammering Swords into Ploughshares*, eds. Buti Tlhagale and Itumeleng Mosala (Grand Rapids, MI: Eerdmans, 1986), 121-127. As with the African Catholic bishops and theologians, I would like to see Mosala better clarify his understanding of economic morality.

[30] Mercy Amba Oduyoye, *Daughters of Anowa: African Women and Patriarchy* (Maryknoll, NY: Orbis Books, 1995), 99-101, 104-105, 159-160.

[31] "SODEPAX: An Ecumenical Model for Contemporary Social Ethics." Paper presented in the Ethics Section at the November, 1999 Annual Convention of the American Academy of Religion (Boston, MA).

[32] Juvenalis Baitu, "Christian Ethical Principles and Societal Problems in Sub-Saharan Africa," *African Christian Studies* 15 (1999), 2-7. Anglican John Mbiti underscores this communal notion by claiming that because "a basic African view is that the individual exists only because others exist," traditional African morals tend to emphasize social conduct. See Mbiti's *Introduction to African Religion*, Second Edition (Oxford: Heinemann, 1991), 174.

[33] Catholic social teaching bases this understanding of the "right use of property" on St Thomas Aquinas' *Summa Theologia*, II-II, 67.

[34] Baitu, 13-15. Baitu also speaks to similarities between traditional African and present-day Christian social ethics in the areas of integral justice and love, human rights, and preferential option for the poor.

[35] Bénézet Bujo, *African Theology in its Social Context*, translated by John O'Donohue, (Maryknoll, NY: Orbis Books, 1992), 34-36. In another work, Bujo argues that this communal understanding of property ownership was in fact an expression of solidarity because possessions were gained through the joint effort of the community and the claim to their use was always secondary to the notion of hospitality. See Bujo's *The Ethical Dimension of Community: The African Model and Dialogue Between North and South* (Nairobi, Kenya: Paulines Publications Africa, 1998), 162.

[36] Laurenti Magesa. *African Religion: The Moral Traditions of Abundant Life* (Maryknoll, NY: Orbis Books, 1997), 277-282.

[37] Particularly in light of the events of September 11, 2001, I recognize that this treatment of Islam in Africa is incomplete. What I am attempting to demonstrate here is that Islam can make a contribution to a proposed theology of sub-Saharan economic development. Nevertheless, a much more exhaustive examination of Islam is needed, an examination that takes into consideration Islam's political, social, and cultural influences as well.

[38] Ali (d. 1951), a staunch defender of Islam, was a prolific writer with the Ahmadiyya Society for the Propagation of Islam (Lahore, Pakistan). He authored an English-language translation of the *Quran* with commentary (1917), *The Religion of Islam* (1936), *Living Thoughts of the Holy Prophet Muhammad* (1947), and a revised English-language edition of the *Quran* (1951).

[39] Maulana Muhammad Ali, *The New World Order* (St. Lambert, Quebec, Canada: Payette & Simms Inc., 1989), 40-43. From the Quran itself: "Glorifying [God] therein, day and night – are people who are not distracted by business or trade from commemorating God...." (24:36-37). See *Quran: The Final Testament*, translated by Rashad Khalifa (Tucson, AZ: Islamic Productions, 1989).

[40] Ibid, 44-47. From the Quran: "Righteous are those who believe in God, the Last Day, the angels, the scripture, and the prophets; and they give money, despite loving it, to the relatives, the orphans, the needy ... and they observe the contact prayers (Salat) and give the obligatory charity (Zakat)" (2:177); and "Surely, those who believe and lead a righteous life, and observe the contact prayers and give the obligatory charity, will receive their recompense from the Lord; they have nothing to fear, nor will they grieve" (2:277). See also Ali's *Islam: The Religion of Humanity* (Columbus, OH: Ahmadiyya Anjuman Isha'at Islam Lahore-USA, 1995), 32-33.

[41] Laurenti Magesa makes a similar claim in Chapter Three at note 70.

[42] Recall that Jean-Marc Éla identified this problem in Chapter Three at note 52.

[43] Speaking to the issue of inter-faith or inter-religious cooperation, Laurenti Magesa states: "The responsibility of Christians extends much further than the boundaries of one's own denomination or one's religion. The necessities for a decent human life are not restricted to the adherents of a

particular faith or religion. Human needs are the elements that show the divine in all persons. They unite them as men and women and as children of God. The responsibility to see that they are satisfied is a general one, without discrimination or distinction as to one's way or religious belief ... What does this imply for Christian discipleship in Africa in the coming century? Doesn't it demand of Christians to be ecumenical in the order of doing good? It seems incontestable that the Gospel requires Christians to join hands with anyone, of whatever faith or religion, who is ready, interested and willing to promote the integrity and wholeness of life." See Laurenti Magesa's "Christian Discipleship in Africa in the 21st Century," *African Ecclesial Review* 36 (1994), 295-296.

[44] Mbiti, *Introduction to African Religion*, 10, 13.

Bibliography

Primary Sources

African Liberation Theologians:

Éla, Jean-Marc:

________. "Le droit à la différence ou l'enjeu actuel des églises locales en Afrique noire." In *Civilization noire et Église catholique: Colloque d'Abidjan 12-17 Septembre, 1977*, 204-217. Paris: Presence Africaine, 1978.

________. *Le cri de l'homme africain: Questions aux chrétiens et aux églises d'Afrique*. Paris: L'Harmattan, 1980.

________. *Ma foi d'Africain*. Paris: Karthala, 1985.

________. *African Cry*. Translated by Robert R. Barr. Maryknoll, NY: Orbis Books, 1986.

________. *My Faith as an African*. Translated by John Brown and Susan Perry. Maryknoll, NY: Orbis Books, 1988.

________. "Église-sacrement de libération." *In Africa, the Kairos of a Synod: SEDOS Symposium on Africa*, ed. Walter von Holzen, SVD and Seán Fagan, SM, 105-116. Rome: SEDOS, 1994.

________. "Christianity and Liberation in Africa." Translated by Robert R. Barr. In *Paths of African Theology*, ed. Rosino Gibellini, 136-153. Maryknoll, NY: Orbis Books, 1994.

________. *Afrique: L'irruption des pauvres: Société contre ingérence, pouvoir et argent*. Paris: Éditions L'Harmattan, 1994.

________. "The Church-Sacrament of Liberation." In *The African Synod: Documents, Reflections, Perspectives*, ed. Africa Faith and Justice Network, 131-138. Maryknoll, NY: Orbis Books, 1996.

________. "Rencontrer Dieu sur les chemins de notre histoire." In *Le Synode africain: Histoire et textes*, ed. Maurice Cheza, 7-18. Paris: Karthala, 1996.

________. "Globalization et paupérisation: Un défi à la théologie africaine." In *Liberation Theologies on Shifting Grounds: A Clash of Socio-Economic and Cultural Paradigms*, ed. G. De Schrijver, 153-175. Leuven, Belguim: Leuven University Press, 1998.

________. *Innovations sociales et renaissance de l'Afrique noire*. Paris: Harmattan, 1998.

Magesa, Laurenti:

________. *The Church and Liberation in Africa: Spearhead 44*. Eldoret, Kenya: AMECEA Gaba Publications, 1976.

________. "Instruction on a 'Theology of Liberation:' A Comment," *African Ecclesial Review* 27 (February, 1985): 3-8.

________. "Christ the Liberator and Africa Today." In *Faces of Jesus in Africa*, ed. Robert J. Schreiter, C.PP.S., 151-163. Maryknoll, NY: Orbis Books, 1991.

________. "Am I not a Human Being and a Brother/Sister?" *African Ecclesial Review* 34 (1992): 95-114.

________. "The Church in Eastern Africa: Retrospect and Prospect." In *How Local is the Local Church? Small Christian Communities and Church in Eastern Africa*, ed. Agatha Radoli, SOM, 3-35. Eldoret, Kenya: AMECEA Gaba Publications, 1993.

________. "Christian Discipleship in Africa in the 21st Century." *African Ecclesial Review* 36 (1994): 283-299.

________. *African Religion: The Moral Traditions of Abundant Life.* Maryknoll, NY: Orbis Books, 1997.

________. "Africa's Struggle for Self-Definition During a Time of Globalization." *African Ecclesial Review* 40 (1998): 320-332.

________. "The Political Axis of African Liberation Theology." In *Liberation Theologies on Shifting Grounds: A Clash of Socio-Economic and Cultural Paradigms*, ed. G. De Schrijver, 130-152. Leuven, Belguim: Leuven University Press, 1998.

Mveng, Engelbert, SJ:

________. "De la sous-mission à la succession." In *Civilization noire et Église catholique*, 267-276. Paris: Presence Africaine, 1978.

________. "A Cultural Perspective." In *Doing Theology in a Divided World*, eds. Virginia Fabelle and Sergio Torres, 72-75. Maryknoll, NY: Orbis Books, 1983.

________. "Spiritualité et libération en Afrique." In *Spiritualité et libération en Afrique*, ed. Engelbert Mveng, 13-25. Paris: Editions L'Harmattan, 1985.

________. *L'Afrique dans l'église: Paroles d'un croyant.* Paris: Editions L'Harmattan, 1986.

________. "African Liberation Theology." Translated by Barrie Mackay. In *Theologies of the Third World: Convergences and Differences: Concilium, 199*, eds. Leonardo Boff and Virgil Elizondo, 17-34. Edinburgh: T & T Clark, 1988.

_______. "The African Synod: Prolegomena for an African Council?" Translated by John Bowden. In *Toward the African Synod: Concilium, 1992/1*, ed. Giuseppe Alberigo & Alphone Ngindu Muchete, 112-128. London: SCM Press, 1992.

_______. "Impoverishment and Liberation: A Theological Approach for Africa and the Third World." Translated by Robert R. Barr. In *Paths of African Theology*, ed. Rosino Gibellini, 154-165. Maryknoll, NY: Orbis Books, 1994.

_______ & Lipawing, B. L. *Théologie, libération et cultures africaines: Dialogue sur l'anthropologie négro-africaine*. Yaoundé, Cameroon: Editions CLE, 1996.

_______. "The Historical Background of the African Synod." In *The African Synod: Documents, Reflections, Perspectives*, ed. Africa Faith and Justice Network, 20-31. Maryknoll, NY: Orbis Books, 1996.

Statements of African Episcopal Conferences:

African Delegation to the Synod of Bishops (1983). "Appel à la réconciliation et à la pénitance en Afrique." *La Documentation Catholique* 1864 (1983): 1182-1183.

Association of Episcopal Conferences of Anglophone West Africa (AECAWA). *A Self-Reliant Church*. Kumasi, Ghana: AECAWA, 1998.

Association of Member Episcopal Conferences in Eastern Africa (AMECEA). "La solidarité avec ceux qui souffrent." *La Documentation Catholique* 1928 (1986): 1059-1060.

_______. "The Twelfth AMECEA Plenary Resolutions on Development." *African Ecclesial Review* 37 (Oct./Dec., 1995): 353-359.

Catholic Bishops' Conference of Cameroon. "Les causes de la crise économique." *La Documentation Catholique* 2010 (1990): 706-714.

Catholic Bishops' Conference of Kenya. "A Society Built on Peace and Love." *Catholic International* 1 (October, 1990): 89-92.

_______. "Kenya 1992: Looking Toward the Future With Hope." *Catholic International* 3 (April, 1992): 376-380.

Catholic Bishops' Conference of Malawi. "Living our Faith: Lenten Pastoral Letter of the Catholic Bishops of Malawi." *Catholic International* 3 (May, 1992): 406-412.

Catholic Bishops' Conference of Nigeria. "The People's Responsibility-To Themselves." *Catholic International* 3 (December, 1992): 1039-1041.

Catholic Bishops' Conference of Tanzania. "The Truth Will Make You Free: Solidarity in Truth." *Catholic International* 4 (December, 1993): 576-578.

Catholic Bishops' Conference of Zaire. "Le chrétien et le développment de la nation." *La Documentation Catholique* 1992 (1988): 885-913.

Catholic Bishops' Conference of Zambia. "Economics, Politics, and Justice." *African Ecclesial Review* 32 (1990): 314-321.

________. "You Shall be My Witnesses: A Second Century of Evangelization in Zambia." *Catholic International* 2 (October, 1991): 824-831.

________. "Hear the Cry of the Poor: A Pastoral Letter on the Current Suffering of the People in Zambia." *Catholic International* 4 (October, 1993): 474-478.

Episcopal Conferences of-All Africa. "Report on the Experiences of the Church in the Work of Evangelization in Africa." In *Modern Missionary Documents and Africa*, ed. Raymond Hickey, OSA, 209-245. Dublin: Dominican Publications, 1982.

Inter-Regional Meeting of the Bishops of Southern Africa (IMBISA). "Justice et paix en Afrique australe." *La Documentation Catholique* 1980 (1989): 298-307.

Zambia Catholic Commission for Justice and Peace. "1999 Budget Revisions, Priorities, and Parliamentary Responsibilities." *Catholic International* 10 (June, 1999): 290-296.

Statements of the Symposium of Episcopal Conferences of Africa and Madagascar (SECAM):

________. "Le Symposium des évêques d'Afrique: Déclarations finales du symposium." *La Documentation Catholique* 1548 (1969): 862-863.

________. "Conscience chrétienne et violation des droits de l'homme en Afrique." *La Documentation Catholique* 1722 (1977): 572-573.
________. "Justice et paix en Afrique." *La Documentation Catholique* 1751 (1978): 927-929.
________. "Justice and Evangelization in Africa." In *Seeking Gospel Justice in Africa: Spearhead 69*, 5-28. Eldoret, Kenya: AMECEA Gaba Publications, 1981.
________. "Resolutions on Justice." In *Seeking Gospel Justice in Africa: Spearhead 69*, 29-30. Eldoret, Kenya: AMECEA Gaba Publications, 1981.
________. "Seventh General Assembly of SECAM: Final Communique, Resolutions and Recommendations." *African Ecclesial Review* 26 (December, 1984): 376-382.
________. "L'Eglise et la promotion humaine en Afrique aujourd'hui." *La Documentation Catholique* 1913 (1986): 260-272.
________. "Africa Will Rise." *Catholic International* 8 (August, 1997): 355-359.
________. "Church as Family of God and Hope for Africa." *African Ecclesial Review* 39 (1997): 278-285.

Statements from the Synod for Africa (1994):
Africa Faith and Justice Network, ed. *The African Synod: Documents, Reflections, Perspectives*. Maryknoll, NY: Orbis Books, 1996.
Bishops of Africa, "Forgive Us Our Debts: An Open Letter to Our Brother Bishops in Europe and North America." In *The African Synod: Documents, Reflections, Perspectives*, ed. Africa Faith and Justice Network, 114-116. Maryknoll, NY: Orbis Books, 1996.
Synod of Bishops Special Assembly for Africa. "Lineamenta Questions." *African Ecclesial Review* 32 (1990): 322-329.
________. "Lineamenta." *African Ecclesial Review* 33 (1991): 1-100.
________. "Instrumentum Laboris: Evangelizing Mission of the Church in Africa." *Origins* 22 (1993): 653-684.
________. "Synod of Resurrection for the Family of God: Final Message of the Synod for Africa." *Catholic International* 5 (1994): 360-377.

________. "Propositions." In *The African Synod: Documents, Reflections, Perspectives*, ed. Africa Faith and Justice Network, 87-108. Maryknoll, NY: Orbis Books, 1996.

Secondary Sources

Contributions of African Theologians:

Agré, Bernard. "My Involvement in the Preparatory Work for the African Synod." Translated by John Bowden. In *Toward the African Synod: Concilium, 1992/1*, ed. Giuseppe Alberigo & Alphone Ngindu Muchete, 99-103. London: SCM Press, 1992.

Akpunonu, Peter Damien; Nyom, Barthélémy; and Balembo, Buetubela. "Declaration by the Catholic Institutes of Higher Education." *Catholic International* 3 (1992): 416-417.

Ankrah, Kodwo E. "Church and Politics in Africa." In *African Theology En-Route. Papers from the Pan-African Conference of Third World Theologians (December, 1977)*, eds. Kofi Appiah-Kubi & Sergio Torres, 155-161. Maryknoll, NY: Orbis Books, 1979.

Baitu, Juvenalis. "Christian Ethical Principles and Societal Problems in Sub-Saharan Africa." *African Christian Studies* 15 (September, 1999): 1-18.

________. *Christianity Without Fetishes: An African Critique and Recapture of Christianity.* Translated by Robert R. Barr. Maryknoll, NY: Orbis Books, 1984.

Bujo, Bénézet. *African Theology in its Social Context.* Translated by John O'Donohue. Maryknoll, NY: Orbis Books, 1992.

________. *The Ethical Dimension of Community: The African Model and Dialogue Between North and South.* Nairobi, Kenya: Paulines Publications Africa, 1998.

Bwana, Steven. "The Impact of the New Code in Africa." In *Canon Law- Church Reality: Concilium, 185*, ed. James Provost and Knut Walf, 103-109. Edinburgh: T&T Clark, 1986.

Cheyeka, Austin. "The Distinctive Contribution of the Catholic Church to the Struggle for Justice in Kaunda's Zambia." *African Christian Studies* Vol. 15 number 3 (September, 1999): 19-36.

Chikane, Frank. "EATWOT and Third World Theologies: An Evaluation of the Past and Present." In *Third World Theologies: Commonalities and Divergences*, ed. K.C. Abraham, 147-169. Maryknoll, NY: Orbis Books, 1990.

Eboussi Boulaga, Fabien. "Pour une catholicité africaine." In *Civilization noire et Église catholique: Colloque d'Abidjan, 1977*, 331-372. Paris: Présence Africaine, 1978.

Ecumenical Association of Third World Theologians (EATWOT). "African Report." In *Third World Theologies: Commonalities and Divergences*, ed. K.C. Abraham, 28-56. Maryknoll, NY: Orbis Books, 1990.

________. "The Statement of the Assembly: A Cry for Life." In *Spirituality of the Third World: A Cry For Life*, eds. K.C. Abraham & Bernadette Mbuy-Beya. Maryknoll, NY: Orbis Books, 1992.

Faniran, Joseph Oladejo. "The Council or Synod for Africa: The Overlooked Aspect." *African Ecclesial Review* 36 (1994): 59-67.

Goncalves, Jaime and Aguh, P. Obinna. "Pan African Conference on Justice and Peace," *African Ecclesial Review* 30 (1988): 218-225.

Ilunga Muya, Juvénal. "La réception du Synode des évêques pour l'Afrique." *Nouvelle revue de science missionnaire* 54 (1998): 275-295.

Kalilombe, Patrick. "Self-Reliance of the African Church: A Catholic Perspective." In *African Theology En-Route*, eds. Kofi Appiah-Kubi & Sergio Torres, 36-58. Maryknoll, NY: Orbis Books, 1979.

________. "How Do We Share 'Third World' Christian Insights in Europe?" *African Ecclesial Review* 40 (1998): 12-20.

Kanyandago, Peter. "Ordained and Non-Ordained Ministry In the Local Churches of Eastern Africa." In *How Local is the Local Church? Small Christian Communities and Church in Eastern Africa*, ed. Agatha Radoli, SOM, 139-162. Eldoret, Kenya: AMECEA Gaba Publications, 1993.

Kazingufu, Gilbert, SCA. "Synods in the Life of the Church and in Particular the African Synod." In *What Happened at the African Synod?*, ed. Cecil McGarry, SJ, 12-32. Nairobi, Kenya: Paulines Publications Africa, 1995.

________. "A Call to Africa to Shake Off The Dependent Syndrome." *African Ecclesial Review* 39 (1997): 29-36.

Kimaryo, Rogath, C.S.Sp. "A Call to Africa to Shake Off The Dependent Syndrome." *African Ecclesial Review* 39 (1997): 32-33.

Lwaminda, Peter. "The African Background to the African Synod." *Catholic International* 2 (December, 1991): 1074-1076.

Malula, Joseph, Cardinal. "Pour un développement authentiquement africain." *La Documentation Catholique* 1570 (1970): 823-824.

________. "Allocution du Cardinal Malula." *La Documentaion Catholique* 1852 (1983): 513.

Martey, Emmanuel. *African Theology: Liberation and Inculturation.* Maryknoll, NY: Orbis Books, 1993.

Mazombwe, Medardo, Archbishop. "A Pastoral Perspective for Africa on International Debt." *Origins* 28 (November 12, 1998): 381-384.

Mbiti, John S. *Introduction to African Religion.* Second Edition. Oxford: Heinemann, 1991.

Mbogu, Nicholas I. "The Church in Africa on the Eve of the First African Synod." *African Ecclesial Review* 31 (1991): 298-313.

Mbuy, Tatah H. "The Rwandan Nightmare: A Source of Great Pain for the Synod Fathers." *African Ecclesial Review* 37 (1995): 49-59.

M'mworia, Damaris K. "Theological Basis for the Church Involvement in Social Justice." *African Ecclesial Review* 40 (1998): 271-285.

Mosala, Itumeleng. "Ethics of the Economic Principles: Church and Secular Investments." In *Hammering Swords into Ploughshares*, eds. Buti Tlhagale and Itumeleng Mosala, 119-129. Grand Rapids, MI: Eerdmans, 1986.

Mpundu, Telesphore George. "The Church's Life Style in the Context of Africa's." *African Ecclesial Review* 37 (1995): 270-277.

Munono Muyembe, Bernard. *Eglise, évangélization et promotion humaine: Le discours social des évêques africains.* Fribourg: Editions Universitaires, 1995.

Oduyoye, Mercy Amba. *Daughters of Anowa: African Women and Patriarchy.* Maryknoll, NY: Orbis Books, 1995.

Okolo, Chukwudum. "Diminished Man and Theology: A Third World Perspective." *African Ecclesial Review* 18 (April, 1976): 80-89.

________. "Liberation Theology and the African Church." *Bulletin of African Theology* 4 (July-December, 1982): 173-187.

________. *The Liberating Role of the Church in Africa Today.* Eldoret, Kenya: AMECEA Gaba Publications, 1991.

________. "African Liberation Theology: Concept and Necessity." *Africa: Kairos of a Synod: SEDOS Bulletin* 94 (1994): 102-103.

Okoye, Chukwuma. "The Synod of Bishops/Special Assembly for Africa: Is this Another Roman Programme for Africa?" *African Ecclesial Review* 34 (1992): 208-223.

________. "The Special Assembly for Africa of the Synod of Bishops-The Instrumentum Laboris." *African Ecclesial Review* 35 (1993): 170-191.

Otieno, Aloys Opiyo. "The Role of the Church in Development in the Light of the African Synod." *African Ecclesial Review* 37 (Oct./Dec., 1995): 342-351.

Pan-African Conference of Third World Theologians. "Final Communiqué." In *African Theology En-Route. Papers from the Pan-African Conference of Third World Theologians (December, 1977)*, eds. Kofi Appiah-Kubi & Sergio Torres, 189-195. Maryknoll, NY: Orbis Books, 1979.

Peter, C. B. "Beyond a Theology of Development." *African Ecclesial Review* 35 (1993): 54-67.

Post-Synod Africa Network. "Syn-Hodos: Africans Working and Walking Together." *Catholic International* 5 (1994): 375-377.

Sarpong, Peter K. "Setting Priorities for the Church: A View from Africa." In *American Catholic Identity: Essays in an Age of Change*, ed. Francis J. Butler, 250-266. Kansas City, MO: Sheed and Ward, 1994.

Sesana, Renato Kizito, MCCJ. "An African Synod Without Africa?" *African Ecclesial Review* 35 (1993): 134-143.

Sess, J. N'Guessam, SJ. "Formation of Priests and Religious for a Church that is Family." In *What Happened at the African Synod?* ed. Cecil McGarry, SJ, 96-114. Nairobi, Kenya: Paulines Publications Africa, 1995.

Société Africaine de Culture. "Recommendations." In *Civilization noire et Église catholique: Colloque d'Abidjan, 1977*, 371-374. Paris: Présence Africaine, 1978.

Tzadua, Paulos Cardinal, et. al. "The Road to the Synod for Africa." *Catholic International* 5 (1994): 159-162.

Ukpong, Justin S., C.S.Sp. "Theological Literature from Africa." In *Theologies of the Third World: Convergences and Differences: Concilium, 199*, eds. Leonardo Boff and Virgil Elizondo, 67-75. Edinburgh: T & T Clark, 1988.

________. "A Critical Review of the Lineamenta on the Special African Synod." In *The African Synod: Documents, Reflections, Perspectives*, ed. Africa Faith and Justice Network, 32-42. Maryknoll, NY: Orbis Books, 1996.

Uzukwu, Elochukwu, C.S.Sp. *A Listening Church: Autonomy and Communion in African Churches*. Maryknoll, NY: Orbis Books, 1996.

Waliggo, John Mary. "The North and Africa: A Question of Justice." In *Africa, the Kairos of a Synod: SEDOS Symposium on Africa*, ed. Walter von Holzen, SVD and Seán Fagan, SM, 147-162. Rome: SEDOS, 1994.

Zoungrana, Paul, Cardinal. "Opening Address at the First Assembly of SECAM." *La Documentation Catholique* 1548 (1969): 858-861.

Contributions of Non-African Theologians:

Alberigo, Giuseppe. "A Historic Occasion or Bureaucratization?" Translated by Mortimer Bear. In *Toward the African Synod: Concilium, 1992/1*, ed. Giuseppe Alberigo & Alphone Ngindu Muchete, 147-155. London: SCM Press, 1992.

Ali, Maulana Muhammad. *The New World Order*. St. Lambert, Quebec, Canada: Payette & Simms Inc., 1989.

________. *Islam: The Religion of Humanity*. Columbus, OH: Ahmadiyya Anjuman Isha'at Islam Lahore-USA, 1995.

Alszeghy, Zoltan, SJ and Flick, Maurizio, SJ. "Theology of Development: A Question of Method." In *Theology Meets Progress*, ed. Philip Land, SJ, 105-143. Rome: Gregorian University Press, 1971.

Berthouzoz, Roger, et. al. (eds.). *Economie et développement: Répertoire des documents épiscopaux des cinq continents (1891-1991)*. Fribourg: Editions Universitaires, 1997.

Cheza, Maurice; Derroitte, Henri; & Luneau, René, ed. *Les évêques d'Afrique parlent, 1969-1992: Documents pour le synode africain.* Paris: Centurion, 1992.

Cheza, Maurice, ed. *Le Synode Africain: Histoire et textes.* Paris: Karthala, 1996.

Dorr, Donal. *Option for the Poor: A Hundred Years of Catholic Social Teaching.* Revised Edition. Maryknoll, NY: Orbis Books, 1992.

Dulles, Avery. *Models of Church.* 2nd. Revised Edition. New York: Doubleday, 1987.

Fuchs, Josef, SJ. "Moral Aspects of Human Progress." In *Theology Meets Progress*, ed. Philip Land, SJ, 145-169. Rome: Gregorian University Press, 1971.

Geffré, Claude. *Théologie et choc des cultures.* Paris: Cerf, 1984.

Gibbs, Philip. *The Word in the Third World: Divine Revelation in the Theology of Jean-Marc Éla, Aloysius Pieris, and Gustavo Gutiérrez.* Rome: Pontifical Gregorian University, 1996.

Giblin, Marie. "Taking Africa Seriously: The Challenge of Liberation Theology." *African Ecclesial Review* 30 (1988): 285-298.

Gutiérrez, Gustavo. *A Theology of Liberation.* 15th Anniversary Edition. Translated by Sr. Caridad Inda and John Eagleson. Maryknoll, NY: Orbis Books, 1988.

Hastings, Adrian. *African Catholicism: Essays in Discovery.* London: SCM Press, 1989.

Henriot, Peter, SJ. "Development in Light of the African Synod: An Alternative to the Structural Adjustment Program." *Catholic International* 7 (June/July, 1996): 285-294.

Hillman, Eugene, C.S.Sp. *Polygamy Revisited: African Plural Marriage and the Christian Churches.* Maryknoll, NY: Orbis Books, 1975.

________. *Toward an African Christianity: Inculturation Applied.* Mahwah, NJ: Paulist Press, 1993.

Khalifa, Rashad (translator). *Quran: The Final Testament.* Tucson, AZ: Islamic Productions, 1989.

Lambert, Bernard, OP. "A Personal Report on the Consultation." In *In Search of a Theology of Development: A SODEPAX Report*, 36-50. Lausanne, Switzerland: Imprimerie La Concorde, 1969.

Land, Philip, SJ. "What is Development?" In *In Search of a Theology of Development: A SODEPAX Report*, 180-203. Lausanne, Switzerland: Imprimerie La Concorde, 1969.

Land, Philip, SJ and Abrecht, Paul. "Common Christian Convictions about Development." In *World Development: Challenge to the Churches*, ed. Denys Munby, 137-146. Washington DC: Corpus Books, 1968.

Luneau, René. "The Expectations of the Catholic Church." Translated by John Bowden. In *Toward the African Synod: Concilium, 1992/1*, ed. Giuseppe Alberigo & Alphone Ngindu Muchete, 83-87. London: SCM Press, 1992.

Mahoney, Roger Cardinal. "The Cost of International Debt in Human Terms." *Origins* 27 (November 13, 1997): 387-390.

McGarry, Cecil, SJ. "The Implications of the Synod Discussions for the Church in Africa." *African Ecclesial Review* 37 (1995): 15-33.

________, Ed. *What Happened at the African Synod*? Nairobi, Kenya: Paulines Publications Africa, 1995.

________. "Formation of the Agents of Evangelization for the Realities of Africa Today: Its Urgency and Importance." *African Ecclesial Review* 41 (1999): 194-210.

McGoldrick, Terrence. "Episcopal Conferences Worldwide on Catholic Social Teaching." *Theological Studies* 59 (1998): 22-50.

McKenna, Joseph C. *Finding a Social Voice: The Church and Marxism in Africa.* New York: Fordham University Press, 1997.

Mejia, Rodrigo, SJ. "Presence of the Lay Christians in the Preparation for the Synod of Bishops on Africa." *African Ecclesial Review* 33 (1991): 166-177.

________. "Foreign Missionaries at the Eve of the African Synod." *African Ecclesial Review* 35 (1993): 144-152.

Moltmann, Jürgen. *Theology of Hope: On the Ground and the Implications of a Christian Eschatology.* New York: Harper and Row, 1967.

O'Brien, David J. and Shannon, Thomas A., Eds. *Catholic Social Teaching: The Documentary Heritage.* Maryknoll, NY: Orbis Books, 1995.

Novak, Michael. *Will It Liberate? Questions about Liberation Theology.* New York: Paulist Press, 1986.

Rahner, Karl, SJ. "Theological Justification of the Church's Development Work." In *Concern for the Church: Theological Investigations*, Vol. 20, translated by Edward Quinn, 65-73. New York: Crossroad, 1981.

Ratzinger, Joseph Cardinal and Messori, Vittorio. *The Ratzinger Report*. San Francisco: Ignatius Press, 1985.

Reese, Thomas J., SJ. "The African Synod: You Had to be There." *America* 170 (June 4, 1994): 8-9.

Schonecke, Wolfgang. "Are We Both 'Simple as Doves and Cunning as Serpents?': What Does the Rwandan Tragedy Say to the Church in Africa?" *Catholic International* 5 (December, 1994): 562-567.

Schotte, Jan, P. "Preface" [to the "Instrumentum Laboris"]. *Origins* 22 (1993): 653-655.

Shorter, Aylward. "Two Examples of Development and Continuity in Social Change." In *The African Contribution to World Church*. Kampala, Uganda: Pastoral Institute of Eastern Africa, 1972.

________. *The African Synod: A Personal Response to the Outline Document*. Nairobi, Kenya: St. Paul Publications-Africa, 1991.

________. "The Roman Catholic Church in Africa Today." In *Christianity in Africa in the 1990s*, ed. Christopher Fyfe and Andrew Walls, 22-38. Edinburgh: Centre of African Studies, 1996.

Thompson, J. Milburn. *Justice and Peace: A Christian Primer*. Maryknoll, NY: Orbis Books, 1997.

Witvliet, Theo. *A Place in the Sun: Liberation Theology in the Third World*. Translated by John Bowden. Maryknoll, NY: Orbis Books, 1985.

Papal Statements:

John XXIII, Pope. "Mater et Magistra: Christianity and Social Progress." In *Catholic Social Teaching: The Documentary Heritage*, eds. David J. O'Brien & Thomas A. Shannon, 84-128. Maryknoll, NY: Orbis Books, 1995.

________. "Pacem in Terris: Peace on Earth." In *Catholic Social Teaching: The Documentary Heritage*, eds. David J. O'Brien & Thomas A. Shannon, 131-162. Maryknoll, NY: Orbis Books, 1995.

Paul VI, Pope. "Moto Proprio Datae: Synodus Episcoporum pro universa Ecclesia constituitur." *Acta Apostolicae Sedis* 57 (1965): 775-780.

________. "Populorum Progressio: On the Development of Peoples." In *Catholic Social Thought: The Documentary Heritage*, eds. David J. O'Brien & Thomas A. Shannon, 240-262. Maryknoll, NY: Orbis Books, 1995.

________. "Africae Terrarum: Message of Pope Paul VI to the People of Africa" (October 29, 1967). In *The Gospel of Peace and Justice: Catholic Social Teaching Since Pope John*, ed. Joseph Gremillion, 417-426. Maryknoll, NY: Orbis Books, 1976.

________. "An African Christianity: Address of Pope Paul VI at the closing of the Symposium of African Bishops, July 31, 1969." In *Modern Missionary Documents and Africa*, ed. Raymond Hickey, OSA, 200-205. Dublin: Dominican Publications, 1982.

________. "Octogesima Adveniens: A Call to Action." In *Catholic Social Teaching: The Documentary Heritage*, ed. David O'Brien and Thomas Shannon, 265-286. Maryknoll, NY: Orbis Books, 1995.

________. "Evangelii Nuntiandi: Evangelization in the Modern World." In *Catholic Social Thought: The Documentary Heritage*, eds. David J. O'Brien & Thomas A. Shannon, 303-345. Maryknoll, NY: Orbis Books, 1995.

John Paul II, Pope. "Discours pour l'ouverture de la troisième conférence de l'Episcopat latino-américain." *La Documentation Catholique* 1758 (1979): 164-172.

________. "Redemptor Hominis: Redeemer of Man." In *The Papal Encyclicals: 1958-1981*, ed. Claudia Carlen, IHM, 245-273. Raleigh, NC: McGrath, 1981.

________. "Dives in Misericordia." In *The Papal Encyclicals: 1958-1981*, ed. Claudia Carlen, IHM, 275-298. Raleigh, NC: McGrath, 1981.

________. *Familiaris Consortio: On the Family*. Washington DC: United States Catholic Conference, 1982.

________. "The Synod of Bishops: A Service to Unity of the Church" [address to the General Secretary of the Synod of Bishops]. *L'Osservatore Romano*, Weekly English Edition (May 23, 1983), 9.

________. "Sollicitudo Rei Socialis: On Social Concern." In *Catholic Social Teaching: The Documentary Heritage*, eds. David J. O'Brien & Thomas A. Shannon, 395-436. Maryknoll, NY: Orbis Books, 1995.

________. *Redemptoris Missio: On the Permanent Validity of the Church's Missionary Mandate.* Washington, DC: United States Catholic Conference, 1990.

________. *Ecclesia in Africa: Post-Synodal Apostolic Exhortation.* Washington DC: United States Catholic Conference, 1995.

Other Contributions from the Roman Catholic Church and Church-based Organizations:

Catholic Fund for Overseas Development. "The Human-Development Approach to Debt Relief." *Origins* 27 (April 30, 1998): 760-764.

Code of Canon Law, Latin-English Edition. Washington DC: Canon Law Society of America, 1983.

Congregation for the Doctrine of the Faith. *Instruction on Certain Aspects of the Theology of Liberation.* Washington DC: United States Catholic Conference, 1984.

________. *Instruction on Christian Freedom and Liberation.* Washington DC: United States Catholic Conference, 1986.

International Cooperation for Development and Solidarity and Caritatis Internationalis. "Putting Life Before Debt: A Catholic Guide for Reflection on the International Debt." *Catholic International* 9 (August, 1998): 355-370.

Pontifical Commission for Justice and Peace. "An Ethical Approach to the International Debt Question." *Origins* 16 (February 5, 1987): 601-611.

Second Vatican Council. "Christus Dominus: Decree on the Pastoral Office of Bishops in the Church." In *Vatican Council II: The Conciliar and Post Conciliar Documents*, New Revised Edition. Ed. Austin Flannery, O.P., 564-590. Dublin: Dominican Publications, 1992.

________. "Ad Gentes: Decree on the Church's Missionary Activity." In *Vatican Council II: The Conciliar and Post Conciliar Documents*, New Revised Edition. Ed. Austin Flannery, O.P., 813-856. Dublin: Dominican Publications, 1992.

________. "Gaudium et Spes: Pastoral Constitution on the Church in the Modern World." In *Catholic Social Thought: The Documentary Heritage*, eds. David J. O'Brien & Thomas A. Shannon, 166-237. Maryknoll, NY: Orbis Books, 1995.

Synod of Bishops, 1971. "Justice in the World." In *Catholic Social Thought: The Documentary Heritage*, ed. David J. O'Brien & Thomas A. Shannon, 287-300. Maryknoll, NY: Orbis Books, 1995.

Synod of Bishops, 1974. "Evangelization of the Modern World." In *The Gospel of Peace and Justice: Catholic Social Teaching Since Pope John*, ed. Joseph Gremillion, 593-598. Maryknoll, NY: Orbis Books, 1976.

United States Catholic Conference. "Economic Justice for All." In *Catholic Social Thought: The Documentary Heritage*, eds. David J. O'Brien & Thomas A. Shannon, 572-680. Maryknoll, NY: Orbis Books, 1995.

United States Catholic Conference Administrative Board. *Relieving Third World Debt: A Call for Co-Responsibility, Justice, and Solidarity*. Washington DC: USCC, 1989.

Vatican Secretariat of State. *Annuarium Statisticum Ecclesiae, 1998/Statistical Yearbook of the Church, 1998*. Vatican City: Libreria Editrice Vaticana, 2000.

Contributions from the Secular Social Sciences:

Adjibolosoo, Senyo B-S. K. *The Human Factor in Developing Africa*. Westport, CT: Praeger, 1995.

"African Charter on Human and People's Rights." *Catholic International* 2 (1991), 631-632.

Agbango, George Akeya. "Political Instability and Economic Development in Sub-Saharan Africa." In *Issues and Trends in Contemporary African Politics: Stability, Development and Democratization*, ed. George Akeya Agbango, 13-51. New York: Peter Lang, 1997.

Ake, Claude. *A Political Economy of Africa.* New York: Longman, Inc., 1981.

Ayittey, George B. N. "Obstacles to African Development." In *Issues and Trends in Contemporary African Politics: Stability, Development and Democratization*, ed. George Akeya Agbango, 321-335. New York: Peter Lang, 1997.

________. *Africa In Chaos.* New York: St. Martin's Press, 1998.

________. "Combating Corruption in Africa: Analysis and Context." In *Corruption and Development in Africa: Lessons from Country Case Studies*, ed. Kempe Ronald Hope & Bornwell Chikulo, 104-118. New York: St. Martin's Press, 2000.

Baur, John. *2000 Years of Christianity in Africa: An African Church History.* Nairobi, Kenya: Paulines Publications Africa, 1994.

Callaghy, Thomas M. "Between Scylla and Charybdis: The Foreign Economic Relations of Sub-Saharan African States." In *Africa: Dilemmas of Development and Change*, ed. Peter Lewis, 382-399. Boulder, CO: Westview Press, 1998.

Chikulo, Ben C. "Structural Adjustment and the New Conditionalities: Towards Development in Africa." In *Structural Adjustment, Reconstruction and Development in Africa.* Ed. Kempe Ronald Hope, 24-34. Aldershot: Ashgate Publishing, 1997.

Coolidge, Jacqueline & Rose-Ackerman, Susan. "Kleptocracy and Reform in African Regimes: Theory and Examples." In *Corruption and Development in Africa: Lessons from Country Case Studies*, ed. Kempe Ronald Hope & Bornwell Chikulo, 57-86. New York: St. Martin's Press, 2000.

Cummings, Robert J. "Religious Belief and Economic Behavior in Contemporary Africa South of the Sahara: Linking Religion and Development." In *Religious Belief and Economic Behavior*, ed. Jacob Neusner, 119-168. Atlanta: Scholar's Press, 1999.

Curtin, Phillip; Feierman, Steven; Thompson, Leonard & Vansina, Jan. *African History: From Earliest Times to Independence.*" Second edition. New York: Longman, 1995.

Edoho, Felix Moses. "Overview: Africa in the Age of Globalization and the New World Order." In *Globalization and the New World Order: Promises, Problems, and Prospects for Africa in the Twenty-First Century*, ed. Felix Moses Edoho, 1-25. Westport, CT: Praeger, 1997.

Elliott, Charles. *The Development Debate.* New York: Friendship Press, 1971.

Freund, William. *The Making of Contemporary Africa: The Development of African Society since 1800.* Boulder, CO: Lynn Rienner Publishers, Inc., 1998.

Gakuru, O. N. "The Social Security Systems in Traditional and Modern Societies: The Concept of Social Security." In *Evolving Strategies for Alleviating Poverty in Kenya*, 1-27. Nairobi, Kenya, Catholic University of East Africa, 1999.

Gifford, Paul. *African Christianity: Its Public Role.* London: Hurst & Co., 1998.

Gooneratne, Wilbert and Obudhu, R. A. "Introduction." In *Contemporary Issues in Regional Development Policy: Perspectives from Eastern and Southern Africa*, ed. Wilbert Gooneratne and R. A. Obudhu, 1-14. Aldershot, England: Avebury Ashgate Publishing Ltd., 1997.

Greene, Daniel. "Ghana: Structural Adjustment and (Re)Formation." In *The African State at a Critical Juncture: Between Disintegration and Reconfiguration*, ed. Leonardo A. Villalón & Phillip A. Huxtable, 185-211. London: Lynne Rienner Publishers, 1998.

Hallett, Robin. *Africa Since 1875: A Modern History.* Ann Arbor, MI: University of Michigan Press, 1974.

Harvey, Charles. "Constraints on Sustained Recovery from Economic Disaster in Africa." In *Constraints on the Success of Structural Adjustment Programs in Africa*, ed. Charles Harvey, 130-151. New York: St. Martin's Press, 1996.

Herbst, Jeffrey. "The Structural Adjustment of Politics in Africa." In *Africa: Dilemmas of Development and Change*, ed. Peter Lewis, 431-449. Boulder, CO: Westview Press, 1998.

Hochschild, Adam. *King Leopold's Ghost.* Boston: Houghton Mifflin Company, 1998.

Hope, Kempe Ronald. "Corruption and Development in Africa." In *Corruption and Development in Africa: Lessons from Country Case Studies*, ed. Kempe Ronald Hope & Bornwell Chikulo, 17-39. New York: St. Martin's Press, 2000.

Ihonvbere, Julius. "Democratization in Africa: Challenges and Prospects." In *Issues and Trends in Contemporary African Politics: Stability, Development and Democratization*, ed. George Akeya Agbango, 287-320. New York: Peter Lang, 1997.

________. "Pan-Africanism: Agenda for African Unity in the 1990's?" In *Issues and Trends in Contemporary African Politics: Stability, Development and Democratization*, ed. George Akeya Agbango, 337-366. New York: Peter Lang, 1997.

Kanyinga, Karuti. "Into the Land Question in Kenya: Alienation of Public Land and the Intensity of Landlessness." In *Alienation of Public Land in Kenya*, 10-17. Nairobi, Kenya: Catholic University of East Africa, 2000.

Lancaster, Carol. *Aid to Africa: So Much to Do, So Little Done.* Chicago: University of Chicago Press, 1999.

Law, Robin. *The Slave Coast of West Africa 1550-1750: The Impact of the Atlantic Slave Trade on an African Society*. Oxford: Clarendon Press, 1991.

Lewis, Peter. "Introduction: Development and Change in Africa." In *Africa: Dilemmas of Development and Change*, ed. Peter Lewis, 1-11. Boulder, CO: Westview Press, 1998.

________. "Political Economy: Crisis and Reform [Introduction]." In *Africa: Dilemmas of Development and Change*, ed. Peter Lewis, 359-362. Boulder, CO: Westview Press, 1998.

Longman, Timothy Paul. "Christianity and Democratization in Rwanda: Assessing Church Responses to Political Crisis in the 1990s." In *The Christian Churches and the Democratization of Africa*, ed. Paul Gifford, 188-204. Leiden: Brill, 1995.

Maipose, Gervase. "Aid Abuse and Mismanagement in Africa: Problems of Accountability, Transparency, and Ethical Leadership." In *Corruption and Development in Africa: Lessons from Country Case Studies*, ed. Kempe Ronald Hope & Bornwell Chikulo, 87-103. New York: St. Martin's Press, 2000.

Mamdani, Mahmood. "A Critical Analysis of The IMF Programme in Uganda." In *African Perspectives on Development: Controversies, Dilemmas & Openings*, eds. Ulf Himmelstrand, et. al., 128-136. Nairobi: East African Academic Publishers, 1994.

Mbaku, John Mukum. "A Balance Sheet of Structural Adjustment in Africa: Towards a Sustainable Development Agenda." In *Preparing Africa for the Twenty First Century: Strategies for Peaceful Coexistence and Sustainable Development*, ed. John Mukum Baku, 119-149. Aldershot: Ashgate Publishing, 1999.

Mongula, Benedict. "Development Theory & Changing Trends in Sub-Saharan African Economics 1960-1989." In *African Perspectives on Development: Controversies, Dilemmas & Openings*, eds. Ulf Himmelstrand, et. al., 84-96. Nairobi: East African Academic Publishers, 1994.

Ngunyi, Mutahi. "Risks of a Bandit Economy: New Study Shows that Crime and Corruption Generate More Money than Formal Economy." *Sunday Nation* (Kenya), July 9, 2000, 9.

Nyang'oro, Julius and Shaw, Timothy M. "The African State in the Global Economic Context." In *The African State at a Critical Juncture: Between Disintegration and Reconfiguration*, ed. Leonardo A. Villalón & Phillip A. Huxtable, 27-42. London: Lynne Rienner Publishers, 1998.

Nyerere, Julius. *Freedom and Socialism*. London: Oxford University Press, 1968.

Omolo, Ken. "Peace and Conflict Resolution in Kenya." In *Promoting Economic Development through the Strategy of Self-Reliance*, 5-18. Nairobi, Kenya: Catholic University of East Africa, 1999.

Osuji, Louis O. "Structural Adjustment and Persistence of Economic Crisis in Africa." In *Globalization and the New World Order: Promises, Problems, and Prospects for Africa in the Twenty-First Century*, ed. Felix Moses Edoho, 83-98. Westport, CT: Praeger, 1997.

Ritchie, Ian. "African Theology and Social Change: An Anthropological Approach." Ph.D. Study, McGill University, April, 1993.

Rodney, Walter. *How Europe Underdeveloped Africa*. Washington DC: Howard University Press, 1974.

Sahn, David E. "Economic Crisis and Policy Reform in Africa: An Introduction." In *Adjusting to Policy Failure in African Economies*, ed. David E. Sahn, 1-22. Ithaca, NY: Cornell University Press, 1994.

________. "Economic Crisis and Policy Reform in Africa: Lessons Learned and Implications for Policy." In *Adjusting to Policy Failure in African Economies*, ed. David E. Sahn, 366-386. Ithaca, NY: Cornell University Press, 1994.

________. "Economic Reform and Poverty: An Overview." In *Economic Reform and the Poor in Africa*, ed. David E. Sahn, 3-26. Oxford: Clarendon Press, 1996.

Todaro, Michael. *Economic Development in the Third World.* London: Longman, 1985.

United Nations. "Universal Declaration of Human Rights." In *Freedom's Charter: The Universal Declaration of Human Rights*, No. 76, 55-62. New York: Foreign Policy Association, 1949.

United Nations Development Programme. *Human Development Report, 2000.* New York: Oxford University Press, 2000.

Valy Tuho, Charles. "L'Afrique." In *Ethique, économie et développement: L'enseignement des évêques des cinq continents* (1891-1991), ed Roger Berthouzoz and Roberto Papini, 101-125. Fribourg, Switzerland: Editions Universitaires, 1995.

Van de Wall, Nicolas and Johnson, Timothy A. *Improving Aid to Africa.* Washington DC: Overseas Development Council, 1996.

Vaillant, Janet G. *Black, French and African: The Life of Léopold Sédar Senghor.* Cambridge, MA: Harvard University Press, 1990.

Vansina, Jan. "A Clash of Cultures: African Minds in the Colonial Era." In *African History: From Earliest Times to Independence*, ed. Philip Curtin et. al., 469-489. New York: Longman, 1995.

Villalón, Leonardo A. "The African State at the End of the Twentieth Century: Parameters of the Critical Juncture." In *The African State at a Critical Juncture: Between Disintegration and Reconfiguration*, ed. Leonardo A. Villalón & Phillip A. Huxtable, 3-25. London: Lynne Rienner Publishers, 1998.

World Bank. *Development in Practice: Taking Action to Reduce Poverty in Sub-Saharan Africa.* Washington DC: World Bank Publications, 1997.

________. *African Development Indicators 2000.* Washington DC: World Bank, 2000.

INDEX

www.ingramcontent.com/pod-product-compliance
Ingram Content Group UK Ltd.
Pitfield, Milton Keynes, MK11 3LW, UK
UKHW041102150926
475561UK00001BA/8

9 780761 824473